6 × 7/08 LT 7/08
11 × 1/13 LT 11/11

WITHDRAWN

THE MEN
WHO INVENTED
THE
CONSTITUTION

David O. Stewart

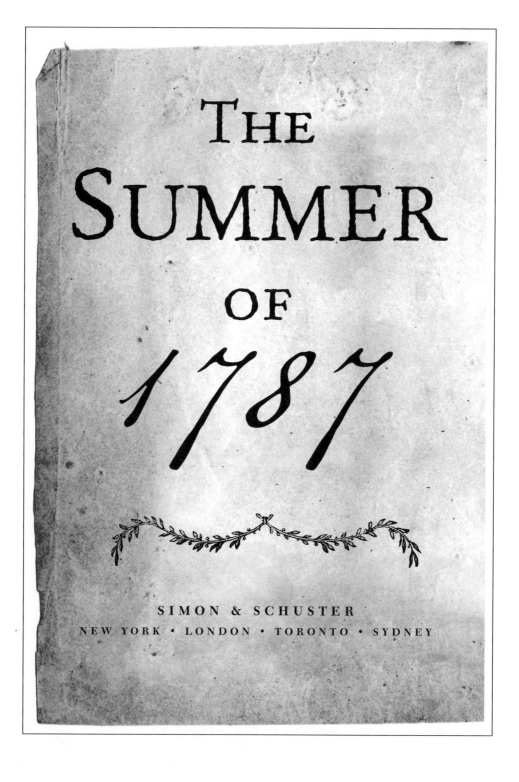

THE SUMMER OF 1787

SIMON & SCHUSTER

NEW YORK · LONDON · TORONTO · SYDNEY

SIMON & SCHUSTER
Rockefeller Center
1230 Avenue of the Americas
New York, NY 10020

Copyright © 2007 by David O. Stewart

For information about special discounts for bulk purchases,
please contact Simon & Schuster Special Sales at
1-800-456-6798 or business@simonandschuster.com

Designed by Dana Sloan

Manufactured in the United States of America

1   3   5   7   9   10   8   6   4   2

Library of Congress Cataloging-in-Publication Data
Stewart, David O.
The summer of 1787 : the men who invented the constitution / David O. Stewart.
          p.   cm.
Includes bibliographical references and index.
1. United States. Constitutional Convention (1787).   2. Constitutional history—
United States.   3. Constitutional conventions—United States—History—18th
century.   4. United States. Constitution—Signers—Biography.   I. Title.
II. Title: Men who wrote the U.S. constitution.
KF4510.S74 2007
342.7302'9—dc22   2006051249
ISBN-13: 978-0-7432-8692-3
ISBN-10:   0-7432-8692-8

Illustration credits will be found on page 351.

FOR NANCY

Contents

Contents

The Delegates

NEW HAMPSHIRE

Nicholas Gilman, 32, merchant

John Langdon, 44, merchant

MASSACHUSETTS

Elbridge Gerry, 43, merchant

Nathaniel Gorham, 49, businessman

Rufus King, 32, lawyer

Caleb Strong, 44, lawyer

CONNECTICUT

Oliver Ellsworth, 42, lawyer

William Samuel Johnson, 60, lawyer

Roger Sherman, 67, lawyer

NEW YORK

Alexander Hamilton, 32, lawyer

John Lansing, 33, lawyer

Robert Yates, 49, lawyer

NEW JERSEY

David Brearley, 42, lawyer

Jonathan Dayton, 26, lawyer

William Churchill Houston, 41, lawyer

William Livingston, 64, lawyer

William Paterson, 44, lawyer

PENNSYLVANIA

George Clymer, 48, businessman

Thomas Fitzsimons, 46, merchant

Benjamin Franklin, 81, inventor

Jared Ingersoll, 38, lawyer

Thomas Mifflin, 43, merchant

Gouverneur Morris, 35, lawyer

Robert Morris, 53, businessman

James Wilson, 46, lawyer

DELAWARE

Richard Bassett, 42, lawyer and planter

Gunning Bedford, 42, lawyer

Jacob Broom, 35, merchant

John Dickinson, 55, lawyer

George Read, 54, lawyer

MARYLAND

Daniel Carroll, 57, planter

Daniel of St. Thomas Jenifer, 64, planter

Luther Martin, 39, lawyer

James McHenry, 34, physician

John Francis Mercer, 28,
  planter

VIRGINIA

John Blair, 55, lawyer

James Madison, 37, planter

George Mason, 62, planter

James McClurg, 41, physician

Edmund Randolph, 34, lawyer

George Washington, 55,
  planter

George Wythe, 61, lawyer

NORTH CAROLINA

William Blount, 38, planter

William R. Davie, 31, lawyer

Alexander Martin, 47, merchant

Richard Dobbs Spaight, 39,
  politician

Hugh Williamson, 52, physician

SOUTH CAROLINA

Pierce Butler, 43, planter

Charles Pinckney, 29, lawyer and
  planter

Charles Cotesworth Pinckney, 43,
  lawyer and planter

John Rutledge, 48, lawyer and
  planter

GEORGIA

Abraham Baldwin, 33, lawyer

William Few, 39, lawyer

William Houstoun, 32, lawyer

William Pierce, 48, merchant

The United States in 1787

New England States ("Eastern")

New Hampshire
*Massachusetts**
Rhode Island
Connecticut

Middle States

New York
New Jersey
*Pennsylvania**
Delaware

Southern/Slave States

Maryland
*Virginia**
North Carolina
South Carolina
Georgia

* Considered the "large" states by the Convention delegates.

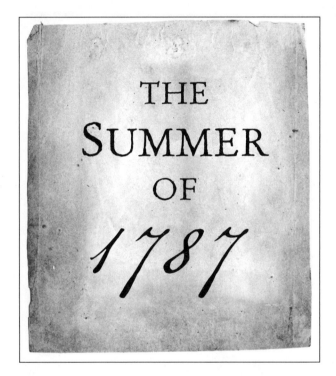

THE
SUMMER
OF
1787

Chapter One

It Started at Mount Vernon

MARCH 1785

S NOW WAS FALLING outside as George Washington mulled over the problem with his neighbor, George Mason. A fire in the west parlor, where the Washingtons entertained guests, pushed back the night chill. Both men favored sweet Madeira wine in the evening, and Mount Vernon's house slaves made sure they had everything they wanted. Dedicated farmers, the men talked easily of the cold weather that would delay spring planting, and of the grafts Mason recently sent for Mount Vernon's cherry trees.

On the other side of the mansion, the wide lawn sloped down to the Potomac, which curved gracefully between Maryland and Virginia on its journey from the western mountains. The river was the problem. The two states were fighting over it, and their argument was a symptom of the deepening crisis of the new United States.

Washington, seven years younger than his guest, had earned an honest fatigue during a day on horseback, supervising work around his plantation. Mason, though, knew only the jangling irritation that follows a day of impatient waiting. They had been friends for almost forty years, spending days and nights in each other's homes. Together they had hunted for deer, talked politics, hosted dancing schools, shared farming strategies, and schemed to develop the Potomac as a center of trade. Both were local leaders, serving as vestrymen for Truro Parish and trustees of the City of Alexandria.

Each in his own way had led the rebellion against Great Britain. In 1774, Washington had presided over the county convention that adopted the Fairfax Resolves, which Mason had drafted in that same parlor at Mount Vernon. Mason's aggressive resolves proclaimed that imposing British laws on Americans without their consent violated "the privileges of a free people, and the natural rights of mankind." Washington went on to personify the American Revolution with his moral and military leadership, while Mason played a more local role through Virginia's General Assembly.

By different paths, they each had reached a stage in life where he had many admirers, not so many friends. Each now described himself as retired.

The firelight exaggerated the contrasts between them. Known to crack walnuts with a single large hand, the strongly built Washington had thrived on outdoor living and battlefield dangers. At fifty-three, he retained the grace and power of a superb horseman and dancer, but it was something from the inside that made him the master of every room he entered. Certainly, he was a Virginia gentleman of courtesy and integrity, but so were others. Equally, he had his flaws, including being "addicted to gambling . . . avid in the pursuit of wealth, . . . a most horrid swearer and blasphemer," and unrelentingly ambitious.

Washington's force came from the antagonistic qualities he blended. His "gift of taciturnity" radiated dignity and calm, yet he simultaneously implied, in the words of one admirer, "passions almost too mighty for man." No one who saw Washington's rage ever forgot it. The combination of steely discipline and powerful drive generated a charisma so compelling that, by one account, every king in Europe "would look like a valet de chambre by his side." The leader of a successful rebellion against the world's greatest empire, he was the first citizen of the American continent, an international figure.

Mason, just sixty, was small and erect, with "clear gray eyes" and "few white hairs." A man of thought, he wrote Virginia's Declaration of

*George Washington (Virginia). Courtesy of The
Pennsylvania Academy of the Fine Arts,
Philadelphia. Bequest of Mrs. Sarah Harrison
(The Joseph Harrison, Jr., Collection)*

Rights in early June of 1776. When Thomas Jefferson assembled the Declaration of Independence later that month, he borrowed large portions from Mason's document, though the older man's effort was largely forgotten.

Subject to painful gout and often reluctant to leave his Gunston Hall estate, Mason was blunt and sarcastic where Washington was guarded and tactful. Once, Mason had been viewed as a mentor to Washington, who was a teenager when they first met, but that time was long past. During the war, Washington had been exasperated when the older man stayed in Virginia rather than pitch in to the national effort. "Where are our men of abilities?" he wrote to Mason. "How do they not come forth to save their country[?] Let this voice my dear sir call upon you." But because of Mason's illnesses, because he was a widower with nine children on whom he doted, because he simply preferred staying close to home, he did not heed that call.

Still, Washington relied on Mason for help with intimate matters. When snarls developed with his stepdaughter's estate or with his stepson's assets, Washington had turned to Mason for help. Only four months before, he had asked Mason to loan his brother, John Washington, "four, five, or six hundred pounds," a substantial sum. If any man could speak with the General as his peer and his friend, it was Mason.

Several days before they sat in front of the fireplace at Mount Vernon, Mason had received a letter from two Marylanders saying they looked forward to meeting him in Alexandria. The letter stated that Mason was one of four Virginia commissioners with whom they were to negotiate the dispute between the two states over trade, as well as fishing and navigation rights on the Potomac. Mason was nonplussed. The letter said the meeting had been scheduled for weeks, but the Virginian knew nothing about it or about his appointment as a commissioner.

Communication was slow in 1785. Capricious delivery arrangements made correspondence difficult. Distances were daunting as travelers floundered along bad roads and waited for unreliable ferries. Still, news of this significance should have reached Mason from Richmond, the state capital. Mason surmised that Virginia (actually, Governor Patrick Henry) had neglected to notify its commissioners of their appointments, and of the Alexandria meeting.

Hoping for the best, Mason managed to scrounge up another Virginia commissioner (Alexander Henderson of nearby Dumfries) and joined the Marylanders at Gadsby's Tavern in Alexandria. After three purgatorial days waiting for the last two Virginians to arrive, Mason was certain they would not.

The situation was maddening. Mason did not even have the resolution that established his authority. He knew that the river dispute grew from the charter for Maryland that King Charles I issued in 1632. That document defined Maryland as extending to the *far* bank of the river, fostering chronic conflict with Virginia over tolls and taxes and fishing. In 1785, similar squabbles were flaring among America's thirteen independent, yet not quite united, states. Connecticut and Pennsylvania fought over land; New York and New Hampshire wrestled for Vermont; New Jersey assailed New York's taxes on shipping. The conflicts limited trade and all forms of economic activity. If the states were to prosper, much less become a nation, they had to stop fighting each other.

Appreciating the importance of the project, Mason turned to Washington, who corresponded widely and was well informed. But the General had only a resolution of the Virginia Assembly that *expanded* Mason's responsibilities to include negotiating with Pennsylvania over access to the Ohio River. The document shed no light on dealings with Maryland over the Potomac.

In running their plantations, Mason and Washington depended on the river for access to markets in Europe and in the other states, but Washington saw it as much more. He envisioned the Potomac as a highway to the lands on the far side of the Appalachians, knitting them together with the existing communities on the East Coast. Pursuing this vision eight months before, he had spent weeks in the wilderness searching for the best overland route between the Potomac and the Ohio River. By January 1785, he had persuaded Maryland and Virginia to charter a company, with him as its head, to develop the river; soon crews would begin hauling rocks out of the upper river to try to create a shipping channel.

After Mason joined the Maryland commissioners at the Alexandria tavern, Washington kept an eye on the perplexing situation, even dining once with the idling commissioners. Now, on March 24, Washington had sent his carriage to bring Mason to Mount Vernon. Sitting together on that snowy night, they knew the time for waiting was over. Either Mason would negotiate with half a delegation, and in ignorance of his instructions, or the Marylanders would go home. They had to decide what to do.

They resolved that Mason should push on. To men who had helped start a revolution, Mason's lack of instructions was no reason to pass up the opportunity to achieve something important. As Mason told it later, the Marylanders had "brought with them the most amicable dispositions, and expressed the greatest desire of forming such a fair and liberal compact."

The General's influence was pivotal: but for his "activity and urgency," the conference might have been abandoned. Almost as important as Washington's encouragement was the political protection he provided. Who would challenge Mason's actions if they had been blessed by Washington?

The General invited the entire conference to Mount Vernon, where the commissioners could proceed in the comfort of his hospitality (as host, Washington was reported to "sen[d] the bottle about pretty freely after dinner"). Though five unscheduled guests would tax any household, the Washingtons were better prepared than most. Mount Vernon had nine extra bedrooms, and in 1785 accommodated overnight guests on 235 days.

Neither Mason nor Washington worried that they might be violating the Articles of Confederation, the document by which the thirteen states had made themselves a nation in 1781, only four years before. The Articles barred any two states from entering into an agreement without the consent of Congress, but disregard for that toothless charter was rampant. Under the Articles, the government consisted only of Congress, with neither an executive branch nor courts. Worse, Congress at this time (often referred to as the Confederation Congress) frequently lacked a quorum to take official action and rarely had money to pay for any action it might take.

View of Potomac River from back porch of Mount Vernon

After years of battling Congress for his soldiers' pay and supplies, Washington considered it "a half-starved, limping Government that appears to be always moving upon crutches, and tottering at every step." The feeble Confederation Congress was no reason not to negotiate with Maryland.

The next three days brought more harsh weather, including snow, but the General rode out every day to supervise the planting of pine trees. Inside the mansion, the feelings among the commissioners were warm. Washington's encouraging spirit infused their meetings, while the mansion offered panoramic views of the river over which they bargained.

Their agreement, reached on the fourth day, declared the Potomac a "common highway" for citizens of both states. The states would share taxes on foreign cargoes, fishing rights, and the cost of lighthouses. Virginia promised not to impose tolls on Chesapeake Bay, though Mason discovered later that he had no authority to negotiate over the Chesapeake. Indeed, he and his fellow commissioner had no authority to proceed at all, since the Virginia Assembly had required the presence of at least three commissioners. In "this blundering business," Mason later wrote to Virginia's Assembly, he hoped that "forms will be dispensed with," as the compact was a good one.

Mason's report to the Assembly included a key provision. He recommended that the conference with Maryland become an annual event to review other issues, such as the many forms of money then in circulation, import and export taxes levied by states, and the regulation of bills of exchange. Maryland expanded on Mason's proposal when it ratified the compact, inviting Delaware and Pennsylvania to join annual negotiations.

In the Virginia Assembly, the compact was referred to a committee chaired by James Madison, one of the two Virginia commissioners who never made it to Alexandria. Madison would see in it a unique opportunity for the nation.

A generation younger than the neighboring Georges, Madison at thirty-four was already a seasoned politician, having served at Virginia's Constitutional Convention in 1776 and also in the Confederation Congress after adoption of the Articles in 1781. Short and barely one hundred pounds, the reserved Madison cut a modest figure in the drawing room. He would not marry until his forty-third year. But on matters of public concern, Madison's intelligence and industry won respect and influence beyond his years.

Madison first worked with General Washington in 1784, sponsoring the legislation to develop the upper Potomac. Ironically, Madison also sponsored the resolution that convened the Mount Vernon Conference, though he, like Mason, was never told when it would convene. Madison had intended the conference to address only riverine disputes. Now, more than a year later, the picture was changing, and Madison's perspective was lengthening. He was convinced now that the government established by the Articles had to be replaced.

The Madisons were planters on a scale with Washington and Mason, though not quite so prosperous. More than a hundred slaves worked Montpelier, the estate managed by Madison's father in the western hills. But where the Potomac neighbors were passionate farmers, Madison's passions ran to libraries and legislatures, where he could imagine and test political philosophies. He completed his studies at the College of New Jersey (later renamed Princeton) in record time, driving himself to a form of breakdown. For the rest of his life, his health anxieties would border on hypochondria, though he ultimately reached his eighty-fifth year.

By late 1785, Madison recognized that individual states would never regulate commerce fairly. States with active ports could not resist taxing goods from nearby states, while their neighbors retaliated in any manner they could. When three New England states tried to win concessions from the British by restricting their trade, Connecticut undermined them by aggressively promoting its own trade with Britain.

Only a national government could regulate commerce fairly, but the Confederation Congress lacked the power to do so under the Articles. Amending the Articles required unanimous agreement of the thirteen state legislatures, but unanimity never seemed possible. In the spring of 1786, twelve states voted to give Congress the power to tax imports, only to see New York torpedo the measure. "Every liberal good man," one patriot wrote, "is wishing New York in Hell."

One idea in circulation was to call a convention of the states to write a new charter of government. The legislatures in New York and Massachusetts had adopted resolutions proposing such a convention, though the proposals had gone nowhere.

Visiting Mount Vernon in October of 1785, Madison wondered whether Mason's report on the Mount Vernon Conference might pave the way to such a convention. Washington encouraged the notion. As he impatiently wrote to Madison, "We are either a united people, or we are not. If the former, let us, in all matters of general concern act as a nation. . . . If we are not, let us no longer act a farce by pretending to it."

Madison soon reported to Washington that Virginia might call for the states to meet to consider "the requisite augmentation of the power of Congress over trade." Such a step, he added, "seems naturally to grow out of" the Mount Vernon Conference. By January 21, 1786, it was done. The Virginia Assembly called on the other states to send delegates to Annapolis on the first Monday in September to consider "a uniform system in their commercial regulations" and appointed Madison as one of Virginia's five delegates.

Arriving eight months later at George Mann's Tavern in Maryland's capital, Madison found but two other delegates. He confided his fears to a younger brother: Nothing "can bear a worse aspect than our federal affairs. . . . No money comes into the public treasury, trade is on a wretched footing, and the states are running mad after paper money." A few days later, Alexander Hamilton of New York, long an advocate of replacing the Articles, joined him. But only twelve delegates from five states reached Annapolis. None came from New England (called the "Eastern states" at that time) or from the Deep South (the Carolinas and Georgia), or even from Maryland, the host.

Talking at Mann's Tavern, where rooms were a shilling a night, the twelve Annapolis delegates considered going home without even convening. Then they thought better of it. They were stout patriots, half of whom would sign the Constitution a year later. They were certainly too few to go forward, but they would not give up the game. With the same boldness that Mason and Washington had displayed the year before, they decided to play the convention card once more, this time double-or-nothing.

They needed a pretext for this move, and found it in New Jersey's direction to its delegates to address commercial issues *"and other important matters."* The nation's problems were far from merely commercial. Other countries took advantage of America's weakness. The British occupied forts in the West and refused to trade with Americans. Spain had closed the Mississippi River to Americans. In the Mediterranean, the Barbary States seized American ships and enslaved their crews. This was no time for half-measures. Why not a convention to address *all* of the national government's defects?

Hamilton drafted a fiery call for a new convention, which Madison and others toned down. The final version soberly noted "the embarrassments which characterize the present state of our national affairs," then urged the states to send delegates to a convention in Philadelphia "May next," to "devise such further provisions that appear to them necessary to render the constitution of the Federal Government adequate to the exigencies of the Union." Having convened a week late, the delegates adjourned on their second day.

Traveling home, the Annapolis delegates knew much had to be done for the Philadelphia Convention to succeed. Powerful supporters had to be enlisted, none more important than the retired general on the Potomac. Washington's strong-armed intervention had started the process by saving the "bumbling business" at Mount Vernon, and his support again would be crucial. The larger question was whether conditions were bad enough for the states to put aside their parochial interests and create a strong national government. Terrible events brewing in central Massachusetts would persuade many Americans that conditions were at least that bad.

The effort to create a new government, which started in earnest when two old friends sat before a Mount Vernon fire and chose to act with no authority, would prove arduous. Change, especially fundamental change, always is painful, and always inflicts casualties. In this case, one casualty would be their friendship.

Chapter Two

Blood on the Snow

WINTER 1787

THE COLD was bitter. Horse-drawn carts crossed the wide Connecticut River over a thick layer of ice. Two thousand American rebels were marching through almost four feet of snow toward Springfield, Massachusetts. The farms they passed were small and struggling, but the residents freely offered food and drink. The rebels themselves were mostly farmers, not part of any formal military structure, though many had been soldiers before. Some carried old muskets. Some had only swords and clubs.

The newspapers were calling it "Shays' Rebellion," for Daniel Shays, one of the leaders. Thrust to the fore because of his military experience, Shays was a reluctant commander, proud that so far his troops had avoided combat in this ragtag rebellion. Prominent Americans like George Washington and George Mason knew nothing of Daniel Shays, but they were learning.

The men's spirits were high. They were fighting for their rights. Bundled against the winter, some wore sprigs of evergreen in their caps, symbols of their rebellion. Their grievances were many. They groaned under "ancient debts, made still more burdensome from an increase of interest"; they were taxed too heavily and there was little hard currency for paying taxes; the expensive court system seemed always to favor creditors, foreclosing on the property of farmers and tradesmen. They were not all poor, but the times were hard. As many as two-thirds of them had been hauled into debtors' courts, facing humiliation and even jail. For years, the government in distant Boston had turned a deaf ear to their complaints.

The rebels moved in three columns, miles apart from each other. As they trudged through the "severest winter . . . in many years," their goal was the arsenal in Springfield. It held cannon, thousands of new muskets with bayonets, and 1,300 barrels of powder. The rebels had cut off the roads to the arsenal on three sides while they seized grain and meat from local merchants. Once they had the arsenal's weapons, they would be a force to be reckoned with. In a chilling ultimatum, they promised that unless the building's defenders surrendered, the rebels would "give nor take no quarter," pledging to slaughter any prisoners captured in battle. Most of the 1,200 troops opposing them were their neighbors.

The rebellion had begun six months before, during the summer of 1786, when crowds of angry farmers prevented court from convening in Northampton. Their reasoning was linear: no court hearings meant no judgments for creditors, and no foreclosures.

In September—while the Annapolis delegates gathered—other crowds blocked courts in Worcester, in Taunton, in Great Barrington, even in Concord, already storied as the birthplace of the Revolution. Angry debtors had closed courts in New Hampshire and Connecticut, too, but only in Massachusetts had the militia refused to oppose the unrest, sometimes even joining it.

In October, Congress met in New York City, 140 miles away, to authorize the recruitment of federal troops to restore order in Massachusetts. To avoid spreading alarm about the rebellion, the congressional resolution stated that the troops would put down threats from the Shawnee, the Potawatami, and the Chippewa. No one was fooled. Unlike the farmers of Massachusetts, those tribes were not on the warpath.

It mattered little whether anyone was fooled by Congress's ruse. The thirteen states refused to pay for federal troops, so only a few were recruited, then sent home. Once Congress's failure was clear, the rich men of Boston passed the hat to underwrite a state force of 4,000. With other state troops, William Shepard, a Revolutionary War veteran, defended the Springfield arsenal. Shepard, who himself had been hauled into court for his debts, had little sympathy for the rebels. "I have lost eight years hard service," he wrote, "to suffer frost and defend the lives and property of a set of d——d rascals who are daily threatening to cut my throat."

Daniel Shays led one of the three rebel columns on that snowy day in late January 1787. Surprisingly little is known about the man, including what he looked like. He enlisted as a private when the Revolutionary War began, fighting at Bunker Hill and Saratoga as he rose to sergeant and then captain. A commander of state troops remembered him as "a brave and good soldier." The Marquis de Lafayette gave him a gold sword, but Shays sold it, probably to pay expenses of his farm in Pelham in the central part of the state, where he moved after the war.

Though Shays' farm was more than 100 acres, he was no more prosperous than his neighbors. In 1786, he owed money to at least ten different creditors. Shays was a member of his town's Committee of Safety. He and his wife, Abigail, joined the Second Parish Church when it was incorporated in 1786. When the rebellion began, Shays declined the first command offered to him, then relented and joined his neighbors. Just a month before leading the rebels to the Springfield arsenal, he protested that "it was always against my inclination to engage in this business," but when his friends persisted, "I could not withstand their importunity."

The attack on the arsenal went badly. Although both sides included veteran soldiers, the state forces had artillery and better weapons. The rebels were poorly coordinated. Only two of their columns—about 1,500 men—advanced on the arsenal from the west. They marched over flat, open ground. The state troops formed a line in front of the arsenal and soldiers' barracks, cannon interspersed among them. General Shepard sent messengers to ask what the rebels wanted and to warn that he would fire on them. The rebels would not be deterred by palaver. Their officers ordered, "March on, march on."

The first cannon shots sailed over the heads of the rebels, who "dropped prostrate, but instantly [rose] in place again soon as the balls

Battle at Springfield Arsenal

had passed." They kept coming. Shepard finally gave the order. The artillery roared again, crashing in "at waistband height." The rebels ran, outraged cries of "Murder!" in their throats. Four attackers died and many more were wounded, flesh and blood yielding to grapeshot. A ball ripped both arms off a cannoneer with the state troops who misjudged the weapon's fuse; he, too, died of his wounds. Shays tried to stop the headlong flight, but his men paid him no heed. "There was not a single musket fired on either side."

State troops pursued the rebel force for the next week. Bent on surprising the rebels, on the night of February 3 the state forces marched through a blizzard to Petersham, slogging through drifts "half leg high." According to one soldier, the wind and snow came "in whirls and eddies and penetrated the all of my clothes and filled my eyes, ears, neck, and everything else."

Exhausted and frozen, the state troops heaved into Petersham at 9 A.M. on a Sunday. The rebels were stunned. Outnumbered and unprepared, Shays and his men granted the state troops "a peaceable entrance" to the town. The rebels abandoned their provisions, some still warming over breakfast fires, along with firearms and swords. They "throng[ed] into a back road towards Athol." The state troops took their places before the fireplaces of the town.

Most of the rebels went home, though the leaders lit out for Vermont, which was led by a renegade government that defied claims of New York and New Hampshire to control the area. The rebellion died with their flight, though sporadic violence continued through June.

The victors had little appetite for vengeance. They hanged two captured leaders and imprisoned a score more, but most of the rebels evaded punishment. From Vermont, Shays petitioned for a pardon and received it in 1789. He made his way to Sparta, New York, where he farmed and later drew his military pension until his death in 1825.

Despite the rebels' failure, their political impact was immense. Ten years after the Declaration of Independence, and not even four years after a victorious peace with the British, Americans were slaughtering each other on the field of battle. Neighbors warring with neighbors— incontestable proof of political failure.

The rebels raged at a state government dominated by merchants who insisted on high taxes to repay the state's war debts, then awarded seats in the State Senate on the basis of the wealth of each community. That rage, great enough to send husbands and fathers and sons and brothers into the frigid Massachusetts winter, loosed a flurry of self-examination and doubt.

Henry Knox of New England wrote to Washington, his former war commander, that the rebellion "wrought prodigious changes in the minds of men . . . respecting the powers of government—everybody says they must be strengthened." Knox's reports troubled Washington, eclipsing thoughts of retiring from public life, of devoting himself to farming and developing the Potomac as an inland waterway.

From the first reports of rebellion, the hero-general suffered an acute distress. "I am mortified beyond expression," he wrote in October 1786, "when I view the clouds that have spread over the brightest morn that ever dawned upon any country." A week later, he insisted that decisive action was needed: "Without some alteration in our political creed, the superstructure we have been seven years raising at the expense of so much blood and treasure, must fall. We are fast verging to anarchy and confusion!"

Even before the Shays rising, the nation stitched together during the Revolution was beginning to dissolve. The national government had neither a consistent currency, nor a military force, nor the power to regulate trade, nor the power to levy taxes.

Shays and his neighbors provided a critical push in the effort to create a new American government. Winning independence from Britain, it turned out, was but the first step to becoming a nation. As John Adams had predicted, establishing a truly national government would be "the most intricate, the most important, the most dangerous and delicate business."

Americans needed to think long and hard about what sort of government would preserve their independence and their precious liberties. They needed a government that could hold the states together, develop the huge western territories, and lead Americans to their rightful place in the world. Four months after Americans marched into the mouths of cannon manned by other Americans, the Philadelphia Convention would meet to create that new government. In an act of inspired improvisation, it would produce the world's longest-running experiment in self-rule, twenty-two decades and counting.

Yet the results of that gathering were far from certain. Straining to balance the conflicting needs and worldviews of the thirteen states, the Convention delegates would struggle with basic questions of human slavery, personal liberties, and how to structure a working democracy. The people of America would hold their breath for four months while the Convention met, secretly, to decide their fate. Had they been able to view the confusion and conflict among the delegates, they might have lost hope altogether.

Chapter Three

"A House on Fire"

SPRING 1787

EVEN BEFORE Daniel Shays led his men into the muzzles of cannon, four states had appointed delegations for the Philadelphia Convention. The bloodshed in the icy fields of Massachusetts built powerful momentum behind the Convention. Who could deny the peril when thousands marched in rebellion through New England blizzards? By late February, Congress endorsed the effort. In March, Madison reported to Thomas Jefferson in France that all but three states had picked delegates for Philadelphia.

Washington agonized over whether to accept appointment as a Virginia delegate. On March 28, he sent Governor Edmund Randolph a slightly coy agreement to serve at the Convention. Complaining of "a rheumatic complaint in my shoulder" that was so bad that he could not "raise my hand to my head or turn myself in bed," Washington agreed to attend if his health permitted and no one was appointed in his place, "the word of which would be highly pleasing to me."

However inevitable Washington's decision may appear today, it probably was a difficult one for him. Over the winter, he had endured the death of his brother and his own illness. Having been absent from Mount Vernon for eight years during the Revolution, another extended absence had little appeal. And for Washington the stakes were uncommonly high. As the preeminent man in America, his every public action was noticed and interpreted. If he seemed too eager to reconstitute the government, some would see a power grab. Indeed, his prestige was so great that it could hardly be increased by a successful convention; yet it surely would be tarnished if the Convention went badly.

What was so terribly wrong with the Articles of Confederation? By 1787, they had been in effect for only six years, during which time the Americans beat the British and turned their energies to peacetime pursuits. Did the rash acts of Massachusetts hotheads have to condemn the Articles, especially in view of that state's reputation for ill temper? Jefferson, 3,000 miles away in Paris, viewed the Shays rising with a bemused shrug, observing that it was the *only* American rebellion for the last eleven years: "God forbid we should ever be 20 years without such a rebellion," he wrote. "The tree of liberty must be refreshed from time to time with the blood of patriots and tyrants; it is its natural manure."

But Washington's alarmed response was far more typical, as expressed in his question to Madison: "What stronger evidence can be given of the want of energy in our government than these disorders?" After the Shays rising, the government's weakness was visible to every American. It was weak because that was what the thirteen states wanted.

With their own histories and traditions, the states mistrusted each other. New Englanders and southerners found each other's speech foreign. During the war with Britain, troops from the rest of the country "tended to draw together in a common unfriendliness toward the New Englanders," resenting their "leveling democracy" and "moral narrowness."

The economic interests of the regions diverged widely. New England depended on shipping and fishing. The Middle States (New York, New Jersey, Delaware, and Pennsylvania) grew grain and had infant industries. In the South, slave-based agriculture needed export markets for tobacco from Maryland and Virginia, for rice and indigo from South Carolina. Each state tailored its tax system to its own economy; southern states favored free trade, while the eastern states used import duties to protect industry.

Political divisions followed regional lines. A southerner wrote resentfully in January 1787 that the "Yankees" opposed a North Carolinian as president of the Confederation Congress. Stressing "the great extent of territory to be under one free government," one Convention delegate found that in the various regions the "manners and modes of thinking of the inhabitants differ nearly as much as in different nations of Europe."

Indeed, some Americans proposed to dissolve the Confederation. Southern newspapers openly discussed dividing the country into four nations—Eastern, Middle, Southern, and Trans-Allegheny. Congressional delegates from Massachusetts and Pennsylvania expected the nation would be divided.

In August 1786, James Monroe (the future president) wrote from Congress in New York, "Certain it is that committees are held in this town of Eastern men and others of [New York] upon the subject of a dismemberment of the States East [of] the Hudson from the Union and the erection of them into a separate govt." Monroe added, "[T]he measure is talked of in Massachusetts familiarly and is supposed to have originated there." A North Carolinian also feared that the Confederation was no more than a "rope of sand" that could not prevent dissolution of the union. Six months later, Madison anticipated public support for "a partition of the Union into three more practicable and energetic Governments."

For Washington and Madison, the problem with the Articles was the states. They had too much power, while Congress had far too little. Washington lamented that "[t]hirteen sovereignties pulling against each other, and all tugging at the federal head, will soon bring ruin on the whole." Henry Knox fulminated on the subject to one Convention delegate:

> The state systems are the accursed thing that will prevent our being a nation. . . . [T]he vile state governments are sources of pollution, which will contaminate the American name for ages— machines that must produce ill, but cannot produce good; smite them in the name of God and the people.

In a letter written halfway through the Philadelphia Convention, Washington sputtered that the states were "the primary cause of all our disorders." Because of the states' "tenacity" in clinging to power, he added, "weak at home and disregarded abroad is our present condition, and contemptible enough it is."

The government's impotence inflicted on every American twin plagues of bad money and confusing money. During the war, Congress issued millions in unsecured bills of credit, which promptly slid to such little value that the phrase "not worth a Continental" entered the idiom. By July of 1779, a Continental dollar was worth five cents or less. In 1780, a sheep could be purchased for $150 in paper money, or $2 in hard currency.

Since Congress's money was worthless, the British pound was the prevailing currency, a residue of colonial times. When Madison in 1786 excoriated the states for issuing their own paper money, he expressed their currencies in pounds sterling. But what was the value of a pound sterling? In Virginia, it held 1,289 grains of silver, but in Pennsylvania only 1,031.

To establish an American currency in 1785, the Confederation Congress adopted the dollar—initially a Spanish currency—but what was *its* value? The New England states and Virginia pegged a dollar at 6 shillings, while the mid-Atlantic states valued it at 7 shillings and 6 pence; New York and North Carolina set the value at 8 shillings, but South Carolina and Georgia chose a value of 4 shillings and 6 pence. Transactions also might be conducted in Spanish doubloons, Prussian carolines, or Portuguese moidores or johannes.

This kaleidoscope of currency allowed the states to curry favor with their citizens by issuing their own paper money and pretending it had the same value as gold or silver specie. Madison blamed Pennsylvania and North Carolina for taking "the lead in this folly." South Carolina, New Jersey, and New York followed.

With its government controlled by the most democratic forces on the continent, Rhode Island went the furthest. The state issued £100,000 of paper notes that by law *had* to be accepted on the same terms as gold. Madison wrote of the little state in horror: "Supplies were withheld from the market, the shops were shut, popular meetings ensued, and the state remains in a sort of convulsion." The Virginian despaired that this "fictitious money" produced "warfare and retaliation among the states." Monetary anarchy was not too strong a term. With different currencies of doubtful value yet not enough hard currency, every citizen was a currency trader, and every transaction presented a risk of being cheated.

When it came to political power, Congress also could not conceal its debility. The British, not deigning to send a full-rank ambassador, refused to trade with Americans, including in the West Indies, a devastating blow to American merchants.

Some states persisted in charting their own foreign policies. Georgia, a frontier community with only 50,000 souls, was waging war against the Creek Indians, with neither notable success nor any involvement of Congress. Martial law prevailed in the state, and Spain (which held Florida) was suspected of arming the Creeks. Virginia separately ratified the peace treaty with Britain, while Maryland negotiated directly with the British government to recover stock it held in the Bank of England.

More serious, Spain allowed no American trade through its port in New Orleans, crippling the trade of western settlers who had to ship their goods down the Mississippi River. For a year, the Confederation Congress tried to reach agreement with Spain on this essential issue, but abandoned the talks when the Spaniards insisted on closing the river to Americans for another twenty-five years.

The treaties the United States had signed were not respected by either side. British troops still manned forts around the Great Lakes even though the Treaty of Paris required their withdrawal; American states ignored their obligation under the same treaty to pay loyalists for property confiscated during the Revolution. Despite a treaty guaranteeing equal treatment for Dutch wines and brandy, Virginia granted preference to French products. Though Virginia's policy might be justified on esthetic grounds, it was no way to thank the Dutch for loans that kept the American government afloat.

The Confederation Congress fared no better in maintaining internal peace, beginning with its failure to raise troops to meet the Shays rebels. There were other examples. From Massachusetts to South Carolina, nine states claimed to have their own navies. Western settlers proclaimed the new state of Franklin and elected a governor. Vermont functioned as a sort of free state, offering haven to Shays and his colleagues amid rumors that it might join Canada as part of the British Empire.

Connecticut in 1776 had claimed Pennsylvania's Wyoming Valley, calling it Westmoreland County, establishing courts there and receiving its representatives to the Connecticut legislature. The state lost the land claim before a national commission in 1782, but fighting erupted two years later when Pennsylvania moved to assert power over the valley. In recompense, Connecticut was granted the Western Reserve in what is now northern Ohio.

And what of trade, the issue that drove the Virginia-Maryland compact? States that were blessed with thriving ports—Massachusetts, New York, Pennsylvania, South Carolina—happily taxed any shipment on the way to or from bordering states. Forced to subsidize those states with good ports, the neighbors could only gnash their teeth. Madison later wrote that New Jersey, "placed between Philadelphia and New York, was likened to a cask tapped at both ends; and North Carolina, between Virginia and South Carolina, to a patient bleeding at both arms."

To retaliate, New Jersey formed its own customs service, taxed the lighthouse for New York Harbor on Sandy Hook, and refused to provide funds to a Confederation Congress that did not help it. No state could contest Britain's trade policies, while Congress could not protect American merchants from the Barbary pirates. Rufus King, a young Massachusetts congressman who would make his mark at the Philadelphia Convention, wrote despairingly to John Adams that because of jealousies among the states, "[o]ur commerce is almost ruined."

Lack of revenue was the ultimate indignity for the Confederation. Congress could impose no taxes; it could only make "requisitions" for funds from the thirteen states. Its requisitions met with very mixed results.

In August 1786, after debating what to do about the ten states that had not paid their requisitions, Congress issued an "address" urging payment, then dispatched members to state assemblies to plead for funds. Although the Treasury "afforded a most melancholy aspect," the pleas went for naught. South Carolina paid nothing for three years. New Jersey and Connecticut consistently failed to meet their obligations. Georgia never paid.

In truth, the lack of government revenue resulted in part from the crippling lack of currency. The states raised revenues through property taxes and poll taxes on individuals. Without enough hard money in circulation, citizens like the Shays rebels could not pay, forcing state governments either to punish nonpayment or to forgo revenue. Many decided to let tax collections slide and ignore Congress's need for funds; Massachusetts chose the other course and incited a rebellion.

Congress seemed to grow weaker with each month. "[N]o respect is paid to the federal authority," Madison wrote. "Not a single state complies with the requisitions, several pass over them in silence, and some positively reject them." Government without revenue can scarcely go by the name. The Confederation Congress owed tens of millions of dollars on the bonds and bills it sold to fund the war against Britain. The debts festered, destroying the nation's ability to borrow again.

A potent symbol of Congress's frailty was its homelessness. It fled Philadelphia in June of 1783 when mutinous troops demanded their pay and the Pennsylvania militia was slow to provide protection. Princeton, little more than a hamlet, was Congress's next home. After a spell in Annapolis, the fugitive legislature lodged for a time in Trenton, finally coming to rest in New York City. Vagabondage is not the hallmark of a great government.

The Articles, which had taken sixteen months to prepare, were drafted to make sure that Congress was weak and the states remained strong. In throwing off the British yoke, Americans in October 1777 refused to create another government that was "superior" to the new states. Still, ratification of the Articles was not completed until early 1781, mostly because Maryland refused to act until Virginia relinquished its claim to own most of the western territories.

The Articles proclaimed an agreement "between the states of New Hampshire, Massachusetts Bay, Rhode Island," and so on, which entered "a firm league of friendship with each other." Each state retained "its sovereignty, freedom, and independence," along with any power not "expressly delegated to the United States." In a provision resented by large states and cherished by small ones, each cast a single vote in Congress.

Thus, the Articles were a compact between the *states* of America, not a charter of government by the *people* of America. As Governor Edmund Randolph of Virginia described it, the Confederation Congress was "a mere diplomatic body, and always obsequious to the views of the states."

Consistent with the primacy of the states, the Articles established neither executive officers nor courts. Congress managed all public business through its clumsy, one-vote-per-state rule. Few governments in history—and none of any duration—have so disdained the executive and judicial functions. Indeed, in 1787 no American state followed that peculiar one-branch structure: every state constitution provided for an executive and a court system. Only the national government lacked those essential offices.

The powers that Congress actually possessed—declaring war, entering into treaties, coining and borrowing money—could be exercised only with the votes of nine states. Because absenteeism was rife, only infrequently were that many states present in Congress. As a final guarantee of state supremacy, the Articles could be amended only if all thirteen state legislatures agreed, a requirement that doomed attempts to empower Congress to impose taxes or enforce treaty provisions.

The weakness of the Confederation Congress, combined with the practical impossibility of amending the Articles, meant that many delegates in Philadelphia agreed with Madison and Washington that America needed a new government with "energy." One New England delegate lamented the Confederation's "deranged condition," while another warned that without action, "[t]he present phantom of a government must soon expire."

At Madison's prodding, Virginia was first to answer the call to the Philadelphia Convention. The reluctant Washington stood at the top of its delegate list, followed by Madison, George Mason, and Governor Edmund Randolph. In all, twelve states appointed seventy-four delegates to the Convention. Rhode Island's populist leaders, understanding that the Convention was intended to eliminate their right to issue paper money, refused to participate. Washington did not lament Rhode Island's absence, though he bewailed that state's "scandalous conduct, which seems to have marked all her public councils of late."

Only fifty-five of the appointed delegates actually made it to Philadelphia, and no more than thirty attended the full four months of the deliberations. Notable omissions from the delegate list were John Adams and Thomas Jefferson, who were serving as ministers to Britain and France, respectively. Just as important, several opponents of a stronger national government did not attend. The absence of states' rights advocates like Samuel Adams of Massachusetts and Patrick Henry of Virginia (who said he "smelt a rat" in the call to the Convention) would make consensus easier to reach.

Most of the delegates had served the new nation before. Eight signed the Declaration of Independence, fifteen helped draft their state constitutions, and twenty-five were members of the Continental Congress during the Revolution. Almost three-fourths of them had served in the Confederation Congress since 1781, so they knew firsthand the frustrations of governing under the Articles. The delegates' distinction led Jefferson to exclaim in a letter to Adams, "It really is an assembly of demigods."

On the eve of the Convention, Washington and Madison each drew on images of collapse and destruction. "The present system neither has nor deserves advocates," Madison wrote, "and if some very strong props are not applied will quickly tumble to the ground." The General was even more emphatic. The national government had to be strengthened, and soon. Otherwise, he warned, "like a house on fire, whilst the most regular form of extinguishing it is contended for, the building [will be] reduced to ashes."

They agreed on the solution. Power must be taken from the states and given to a national government. To achieve that solution, the delegates would have to navigate through state jealousies, competing economic interests, and the clashing egos of individual delegates. The delegates also would have to reconcile the revolutionary ideal of liberty with the reality of slavery, which was the economic foundation of almost half the nation. And, without incorporating any structural flaws in the design, they had to do it all before the existing government fell down or burned up.

Chapter Four

Demigods and Coxcombs Assemble

MAY 1787

JAMES MADISON reached Philadelphia on May 3, ten whole days before any other delegate (except for the ones who lived there), and
eleven days before the Convention was scheduled to begin. His
early arrival reflected both his eagerness and his lifelong habit of exact-
ing preparation. Always gentle with his health when he could be, the
Virginian gave himself ample time to recover from the grinding stage-
coach ride from New York, where he had been representing Virginia in
the Confederation Congress.

Although Philadelphia was the nation's largest city, home to about
40,000 people, lodging was at a premium. In addition to the Federal
Convention (as it was called), the city was hosting a gathering of Presby-
terian ministers from around the country. Also in town was the Society
of the Cincinnati, an organization of Continental Army officers that
some feared as a political force. The *Pennsylvania Herald* took pride in
the confluence:

James Madison (Virginia), by Charles Willson Peale

Here, at the same moment, the collective wisdom of the continent deliberates upon the extensive politics of the confederated empire, an Episcopal convention clears and distributes the streams of religion throughout the American world, and those veterans whose valor and perseverance accomplished a mighty revolution are once more assembled. . . .

Madison settled in at Mrs. House's boardinghouse at Fifth and Market, where Virginians on public business often stayed. It was familiar ground. Madison had lodged with Mrs. House in 1783 during his first term in the Confederation Congress, and the quiet, serious Virginian was little trouble. As one contemporary described him, "His ordinary manner was simple, modest, bland, and unostentatious, retiring from the throng and cautiously refraining from doing or saying anything to make himself conspicuous." Another attributed to him "an air of reflection which is not very distant from gravity and self-sufficiency," but also found "little of that warmth of heart."

In the ten days until the next delegate arrived, Madison could review the two essays he had written in anticipation of the great convention. The first was an examination of republics and confederacies throughout history, including Belgium, Switzerland, and Germany, along with classical examples—the Lycian, Amphictyonic, and Achean republics. His second essay, called "Madison's Vices" in ironic tribute to its author's undoubted virtue, was an incisive catalog of the infirmities of the Articles. The vices numbered eleven, and the remedy for all of them was a strong central government. The Virginian was keenly aware of the risk that strong governments may take oppressive measures, as the British Parliament had. His goal was a government that not only was strong, but also would respect the rights of its citizens.

For Madison, the accommodation of competing forces was the central job of government. "All civilized societies are divided into different interests and factions," he wrote, including "debtors or creditors," "rich or poor," "members of different religious sects," "followers of different political leaders," "inhabitants of different districts," or "husbandmen, merchants or manufacturers." Government must be "sufficiently neutral between the different interests and factions, to control one part of the society from invading the rights of another."

During those ten days on his own, Madison did more than plan for the coming conclave. Correspondence from home forced his attention to his responsibilities as a slave owner. Had other servants or slaves assisted the escape of Anthony, a runaway brought back to the plantation? Madison had to judge the case from afar. He also called on Dr. Benjamin Franklin, his fellow delegate and recently installed as president of Pennsylvania. Feeling his eighty-one years, Franklin went out little but was happy to receive guests in his garden, particularly under a favorite mulberry tree. Knowing of the slight Virginian's role in pushing for the Convention and of his relationship with Washington, Franklin extended to the younger man the respect warranted by both.

General Washington arrived second, having taken five days to cover the 140 miles from Mount Vernon in his own carriage, driven by his slaves. The contrast with Madison's quiet entry into Philadelphia was stark.

At midday on May 13, the General was at Mrs. Withy's Inn in

Chester, south of the city, dining with former army colleagues. The party pressed on to a greeting by the Philadelphia Light Horse, nattily turned out in white britches, high boots, and black and silver hats. The troopers escorted the hero over a floating bridge that spanned the Schuylkill River. An artillery company fired a thirteen-gun salute (once for each state), church bells pealed, and cheering crowds lined the streets despite what the *Pennsylvania Herald* called "the badness of the weather." It was another demonstration, if one was needed, that it was within the General's power to be an American Caesar.

Like Madison, Washington had taken rooms with Mrs. House. Alighting at her establishment, he was met by the financier Robert Morris and his wife, who prevented the General from unloading his luggage. Washington had declined the Morrises' written offer of lodging during the Convention, but they would not accept his refusal in person. They bundled the General to their home, acclaimed the finest in the city, a short walk away. Washington did not tarry there, but immediately set off to pay his own respects to Dr. Franklin. Along that four-block jaunt, he shook hands with Philadelphians, who cheered and gaped at the tall man with such an impressive bearing.

Though the Morrises' intervention meant that Madison and Washington would not share the same roof, the studious younger man must have felt a particular satisfaction in the General's arrival. Applying the General's stature to Madison's strategy, they had formed an effective partnership in bringing the Convention to pass. Madison was relying on that partnership to continue through the summer. Their challenges would increase as Philadelphia filled with delegates who had different visions of the nation to be formed, and different interests to protect.

On the next morning, May 14, Washington and Madison walked the short distance to the Pennsylvania State House (today called Independence Hall) for the scheduled opening of the Convention. They strode through a light drizzle with three more Virginians who had just arrived—George Wythe, John Blair, and James McClurg.

Wythe, sixty-one, was America's first law professor. At the College of William and Mary he trained a generation of leaders that included Thomas Jefferson, John Marshall, and James Monroe. A signer of the Declaration of Independence and former Speaker of the Virginia House of Delegates, Wythe was his state's leading judge from 1778 until his death in 1806. Blair, fifty-five, served alongside Wythe on Virginia's chancery court and had participated in his state's constitutional convention. McClurg, forty-one, a physician and professor at William and Mary, was a member of Virginia's executive council.

Thanks to a cold winter and a wet spring, the Virginians shared the streets with Philadelphia's aggravating black flies, which would linger through the humid summer. At the State House, they found only one other delegation, the Pennsylvanians led by Dr. Franklin. Raw weather had delayed many delegates, but the Pennsylvanians brought flair enough for the occasion.

The Pennsylvania Assembly elected its delegates in late 1786, almost two months before Congress endorsed the Convention. As the second largest state (after Virginia), Pennsylvania was essential to any effort to remake the government. The state's cosmopolitan outlook derived from its diverse population, which included German immigrants, Quakers, and free blacks. Where the Virginians had forebears rooted in their state's soil for a century and more, the eight Pennsylvanians were more mobile and more urban. Three were immigrants: Thomas Fitzsimons from Ireland, Robert Morris from England, and James Wilson from Scotland. Three hailed from other states: Connecticut (Jared Ingersoll), New York (Gouverneur Morris, who still lived there), and Massachusetts (Franklin).

All eight Pennsylvanians worked at city-based pursuits like trade and law. Only a week before, six of them had been at Dr. Franklin's for a session of the Society for Political Inquiries. The presentation was on American trade and manufacturing, matters of less than the first moment to Virginia planters, but central to the national future.

At the Convention, the most prominent Pennsylvania delegates were the ones chosen last. When the state Assembly voted, James Wilson and Gouverneur Morris trailed less-distinguished colleagues by a wide margin, while Franklin was omitted altogether because he was thought too ill to serve. He was later unanimously added to the delega-

State House, Philadelphia (W. Birch & Son, 1800)

tion when his health proved adequate to the task. Each of those three brought noteworthy qualities.

None could match Dr. Franklin for political theater, beginning with his universally recognized title of "Doctor." The title dated from his honorary degree from St. Andrews in Scotland, granted for his scientific achievements (as were his honorary degrees from Oxford, Harvard, Yale, and William and Mary—not bad for a man who left school at the age of ten).

When attending diplomatic soirées in Paris, his theatrical instincts had draped him in American homespun and crowned him with fur caps. Now he challenged American rusticity by traveling in a glass-windowed sedan chair from France, borne by four husky prisoners from the nearby Walnut Street jail. As Dr. Franklin progressed through Philadelphia's republican streets, his regal trappings drove home the message that honor in America grew from talent, not birth. Yet the swaying procession also must have brought a smile to those it passed, and to the doctor himself.

At eighty-one, Franklin most nearly contended with Washington for celebrity among Americans. His gifts and achievements defied summary. From humble beginnings, he found success as a businessman, inventor, publisher, scientist, writer, and statesman. His curiosity and creativity produced the lightning rod, the Franklin stove, and the first urinary catheter developed in America. His gentle wit would charm generations after his death, obscuring the pronounced aloofness of his family and personal relationships. Those meeting him in 1787 noted the contrast between his titanic reputation and his mundane appearance—in the words of one, he was a "short, fat, trunched old man."

Most important for the Convention were Franklin's decades of political experience. More than thirty years before, in 1754, he had drafted the Albany Plan of Union for the thirteen British colonies (which was never adopted). He served in the Stamp Act Congress of 1765 and in the Revolutionary Congresses of 1774, 1775, and 1776, during which he edited the Declaration of Independence. He negotiated the crucial alliance with France during the Revolution, and then the peace treaty with Britain. Despite protestations of age and infirmity, which would cause him to skip sessions through the summer, Franklin's talent for compromise would help the Convention over its roughest patches.

Over the summer, Franklin at times had something to say but did not feel strong enough to give a speech. He relied on James Wilson to read his remarks on those occasions, untroubled that they were delivered in Wilson's distinctive Scottish burr. Being the doctor's confidant and spokesman no doubt enhanced Wilson's stature, though his standing as a lawyer and statesman was already considerable. Sharing with Washington and Madison the view that the national government must be stronger, he would play a far larger role in the coming Convention than anyone expected.

Born into a farm family in Fifeshire, Scotland, Wilson won a classical education through a scholarship to St. Andrews University. Pious parents marked him for the clergy, but the ambitious son threw over their plans and sailed to America at the age of twenty-four. His gifts earned him a coveted place in the Philadelphia law offices of John Dickinson (who would attend the Convention as a delegate from Delaware).

Wilson dove into the life of his adopted country and never looked back, despite nagging from family members he left behind. (Two years before the Convention, his mother wrote, "I am ashamed of your unconcerned and unnatural like behavior to us.")

Wilson won election to the Continental Congress in 1775. He was learned and hardworking, and his law practice flourished. He won Pennsylvania's land dispute with Connecticut and represented the king of France in America. He helped organize the Bank of North America in 1781, then defended the bank against populist attacks. As a member of the Confederation Congress in the 1780s, he unsuccessfully tried to strengthen its power to tax and command state militias. With Washington and some other delegates, he shared a weakness—more like a fever in Wilson's case—for speculation in frontier lands. For Wilson, the fever would prove fatal.

Tall, well dressed, and solidly built, his auburn hair fashionably powdered, Wilson radiated a lowering intensity while inspiring little affection. Speaking often in favor of a stronger central government, he led (in the words of one delegate) "not by the charm of his eloquence, but by the force of his reasoning." His accent and formal deportment brought him the mocking nickname "James de Caledonia." One lawyer described Wilson's voice as "powerful, though not melodious; his cadences judiciously though somewhat artificially regulated," while "his manner was rather imposing than persuasive."

An early biographer recorded that his features "were far from disagreeable; and they sometimes bore the appearance of sternness, owing to his extreme nearness of sight." He peered through thick spectacles, one contemporary noted, "like a surveyor through a compass." Another said the Scot's "lofty carriage" was adopted to prevent his eyewear from sliding off his nose.

No one questioned Wilson's toughness. In 1778, he tenaciously defended two Quakers against charges of complicity with the British. The lingering effects of that controversy, along with his opposition to price controls, made him a target of militiamen disgruntled over the sacrifices they made while others profiteered. Rather than flee from a militia parade in 1779, Wilson and some allies barricaded themselves in his house. From what became known as "Fort Wilson," they engaged in a musket battle—indeed, some think the gentlemen inside the house started the shooting—that cost the lives of four soldiers and two of Fort Wilson's defenders.

Where Wilson was determined and disciplined, Gouverneur Morris (no relation to Robert Morris) was all flamboyance and talent. Called "Tall Boy" by some, Morris at thirty-five rivaled Washington in height and bearing, and was valued by hostesses as a bachelor and a charming raconteur. A female admirer reported that during a three-day wedding party, Morris "kept us in a continual smile (I dare not say laughter for all the world but you may admit it in the back room)." Happy to share his opinions on any subject, Morris suffered fools not at all. A Frenchman in 1782 found Morris "to possess the most spirit and nerve amongst those I met at Philadelphia," but predicted "that his superiority, which he has taken no pains to conceal, will prevent his ever occupying an important place."

Morris's magnetic presence was made more dramatic by the oaken peg leg below his left knee. Seven years earlier, he had lost the lower part of the leg in a carriage accident just a few blocks from the State House. Owing to his rakish reputation, many assumed the injury occurred in flight from a jealous husband. Contemporaries suggested that the loss in no way reduced his appeal to women.

Morris's ebullience permeates the tale (possibly apocryphal) of his assurance to Hamilton that the great Washington was not so austere as often thought. Hamilton, the story goes, proposed that Morris prove his point by delivering a matey slap to the General's back at an impending social occasion. Morris duly administered the casual greeting, which moved the General's customary reserve from cool to arctic, to Hamilton's delight and Morris's instant dismay.

Born to great wealth (his family's estate is remembered as the Morrisania area of the Bronx), Morris would speak more often during the Convention than anyone else. One delegate observed that Morris "throws around him such a glare that he charms, captivates, and leads away the senses of all who hear him," yet he also could be "fickle and inconstant." He emerged as a passionate goad, a brilliant floater of trial balloons, some incisive and some ill considered. When debate blazed over slavery, the aristocratic Morris would distinguish himself beyond any other delegate.

For that first day's encounter at the State House, after polite conversation about journeys and sedan chairs, there was little to do but retire and hope for better attendance on the morrow. A quorum of seven state delegations would not be present for another eleven days.

The Virginia delegation reached full strength quickly. Governor Randolph, heir to a leading family, arrived the next day, May 15, and joined Madison and McClurg at Mrs. House's. Though younger than Madison, Randolph already had served as a delegate to his state's constitutional convention, as a member of the Continental Congress during the Revolution, and as Virginia's attorney general. Two days later, George Mason completed the state's complement when he and his son settled at the nearby Indian Queen, which also was owned by the enterprising Mrs. House.

The Virginians personified the plantation aristocracy of the South

Edmund Randolph (Virginia)

and its professional class. They knew each other well, beginning with Mason and Washington, lifelong neighbors and friends. Wythe and Blair were judicial colleagues. Three had attended the College of William and Mary in Williamsburg, where Wythe and McClurg were on the faculty, while four lived in and around that town of only a few thousand. Madison's Montpelier estate was relatively distant in the state's western hills, but it closely resembled in organization both Mount Vernon and Gunston Hall, while various Randolphs owned plantations throughout Virginia. All seven of them owned slaves.

The Virginians put to good use the delay in the Convention's opening. Every morning they convened for several hours at Mrs. House's, then met again at the State House at 3 P.M. to greet arriving delegates. Mason wrote to another son that the morning sessions were intended "to form a proper correspondence of sentiments" among the Virginians. Madison later gave the more forthright explanation that "it occurred to [the Virginia delegates] that from the early and prominent part taken by that State in bringing about the Convention some initiative step might be expected from them." The Virginians' deliberations benefited from afternoon conversations at the State House with delegates from other states. Though there is no record of those early discussions, it was a perfect opportunity to share hopes and ideas while staking out positions on points of special importance.

Those informal exchanges cheered George Mason. He wrote to a son that "the principal states" agreed that there should be a "total alteration of the present federal system." In a prescient addition, he noted that the general concurrence did not include "the little states." Mason also foresaw "much difficulty" in establishing a strong national government and "at the same time reserving to the state legislatures a sufficient portion of power." He was surprised to find that the New Englanders, despite their reputation for democratic views, were almost "anti-republican," which he attributed to "the unexpected evils they have experienced" with Daniel Shays and his men.

The Virginia-only sessions at Mrs. House's marked the true beginning of the Convention. With the benefit of Madison's preparation, as well as the General's eloquent presence, the Virginians assembled the skeleton of a national charter. Preparing to lead when the Convention started, the seven Virginians little suspected that only three of them would sign the final Constitution.

As with any group deliberation involving dozens of people, the dynamics of the Convention were complex. Delegates played the roles dictated by personality and relationships, by their beliefs, and by the politics and economies of the states they represented. Some, like Madison and Wilson and Gouverneur Morris, pushed to the front of the stage and speechified on a daily basis; others, like Franklin, were more selective in their remarks, but exercised important influence offstage; and some, like Blair of Virginia and Jared Ingersoll of Pennsylvania, sat mute for four months, leaving scarcely a trace that they had been there.

For ingenuity in making oneself heard, no one matched John Adams, then on diplomatic duty in far-off London. Beginning on May 18 and every Friday thereafter, the entire front page of the *Pennsylvania Mercury* was devoted to excerpts from Adams's recently published "Defense of the Constitutions of Government of the United States of America." Adams's prose was still appearing weekly when the Convention finished on September 17, though its impact on the delegates is doubtful. "Men of learning find nothing new in it," Madison sniffed, adding, "men of taste many things to criticize."

Though important contributions came from many delegates, including Connecticut's late-arriving men of compromise, the Convention's central actors were concentrated among the Virginians and Pennsylvanians, and with the third delegation to achieve a quorum in Philadelphia—South Carolina.

John Rutledge of Charleston reached Philadelphia on May 17 and stayed briefly at the Market Street home of James Wilson, with whom he had served in the Confederation Congress. Young Charles Pinckney moved into Mrs. House's lodgings on the same day. The two remaining delegation members arrived a week later on the same ship—General Charles Cotesworth Pinckney with his wife and Major Pierce Butler with his wife and four daughters.

The South Carolina contingent was an ingrown affair. The Pinckneys were first cousins, but that was just the beginning of the interconnections. The sister of General Pinckney's wife had married Rutledge's brother, while Major Butler's wife was cousin to the two sisters who had wed General Pinckney and the Rutledge brother. All four men owned plantations in the state's Low Country, using slave workers to grow rice and indigo. All but Butler were lawyers, with both Rutledge and General Pinckney having read law in London. Despite their claustrophobic web of relationships, the Carolinians came to Philadelphia with an appetite for work, and they would exercise an outsized influence.

Rutledge was their leader. The forty-eight-year-old lawyer had been near the center of American affairs since the Stamp Act Congress of 1765. A feared trial lawyer—"possibly the most successful lawyer in the American colonies"—he could be overbearing. Pleasant enough when he wanted to be, Rutledge did not play the courtly southerner. Some complained that he cut them off abruptly, to the point of rudeness. Despite his success in the courtroom, many rated him no more than middling on his feet, "too rapid in his public speaking to be denominated an agreeable orator."

When he met Rutledge in 1774, John Adams saw in the fast-talking southerner "no keenness in his eye, no depth in his countenance. Nothing of the profound, sagacious, brilliant or sparkling in his first appearance." Rather, Adams described Rutledge in terms worthy of Shakespeare's Iago, as maintaining "an air of reserve, design, and cunning." (Sadly, Rutledge left no record of his first impression of Adams.) Rutledge's hard edge was evident when he insisted that the South Carolina Assembly give the state's delegates free rein to take any necessary action at the Continental Congress in 1774. What, the objection arose, if those delegates did the wrong thing in the dispute with Britain? "Hang them," was Rutledge's reply.

Even Adams's wary assessment implicitly acknowledged the force of Rutledge's personality. Tall, with long, powdered hair and a dignified manner, he favored "strong and argumentative" speech that "hurried you forward to the point it aimed at, with powerful impetuosity." As South Carolina's governor during its wartime occupation by the British, he was called "the Dictator." During later years as a judge, "court, jury and audience quailed before him."

Rutledge's remarks at the Convention tended to be brief and unadorned, but they were shrewdly timed. He often presented motions, or seconded motions, on central matters. A steady and persuasive force, he worked best in drawing-room conferences, committee rooms, and taverns. A member of five committees through the summer, Rutledge chaired the most important one, the Committee of Detail, which produced the first—and in places, startling—draft of the Constitution.

The cousins Pinckney, doomed to be confused with each other through history, were eleven years apart in age. Both led American troops but ended the Revolution in British prison camps. The elder cousin, General Charles Cotesworth Pinckney, was admired for his polish as a gentleman and maintained cordial relations with northern colleagues. A Massachusetts delegate called him "the cleverest being alive," adding, "I love him better every time I meet him." Twice the unsuccessful Federalist candidate for president, General Pinckney's contributions to the Constitution largely involved defending slavery.

His energetic relative, known simply as Charles Pinckney, was deeply engaged in the Constitution-writing process. Sometimes sharp-elbowed, as reflected in the occasional nickname of "Blackguard Charlie," Charles misstated his age so he could claim to have been the youngest delegate (a distinction held by Jonathan Dayton of New Jersey at twenty-six, three years younger than Charles). Charles then had the ill luck to have his lie uncovered.

While in the Confederation Congress in 1786, Charles chaired a "grand committee" that prepared amendments to the Articles of Confederation. He also, however, was an early supporter of a national convention to create a new charter of government. In a March 1786 speech, he said that such a Convention was the "only true and radical remedy for our public defects."

Young Charles arrived in Philadelphia with a draft constitution, something not even Madison had attempted. Charles showed his draft to any delegate who would stand still long enough to see it, and later insisted it was the model for the Constitution. This last claim triggered pointed rejoinders from the elderly Madison and even the accusation that Charles was "a sponger and a plagiarist." Charles's *post hoc* glory-seeking has obscured his real contributions during the Convention.

The final South Carolinian, universally referred to as Major Butler, had come to America as a British army officer in the 1760s. Marriage to a local heiress persuaded him to join those he had been sent to pacify. Like General Pinckney, Butler's contributions in Philadelphia focused on slavery questions, though he also made an impression with the ardor of his speech. More than any other, his comments are noted as "contending" or "objecting," sometimes "warmly," sometimes "decidedly," sometimes "strenuous" and even "vehement."

As the delegates straggled into Philadelphia, many met familiar faces. Some knew each other from war service; twenty-nine wore a uniform during the Revolution. Many had served overlapping terms in the Continental Congress, and since 1781 in the Confederation Congress. Nine, like Madison, simultaneously held seats in that Congress during the summer of 1787. Most shared a few occupations. Thirty-five were lawyers, thirteen were involved in trade, and twelve owned or managed plantations worked by slaves. About two dozen owned considerable (and sometimes precarious) amounts of public debt.

The city that greeted them was a worldly one. Ships filled Philadelphia's port on the Delaware River, discharging exotic cargoes and crew members. Like any city of its time, it was no Arcadian paradise. "The streets and alleys reeked of garbage, manure, and night soil," and water wells "must have been dangerously polluted." A few years before the Convention, a Philadelphian complained that on the streets "dead dogs, cats, fowls, and the offals of the market are among the cleanest articles to be found. Dead animals—horses and cows—are left to putrefy on vacant lots." Pigs running free consumed some of the street refuse. No wonder that General Washington started a practice of Sunday rides in the countryside. On Wednesday, May 23, he sneaked off for a midweek ride with Madison, John Rutledge, and some others, though many times he rode alone.

Philadelphia had a lurid reputation for disease. Yellow fever had struck in 1747 and 1762, and a devastating epidemic would spread in 1793. At least two delegates—one from Connecticut and one from Maryland—refused to attend the Convention because they feared the city's contagion. "Having never had the small pox," the Connecticut appointee wrote, referring to himself in the third person, "a disorder to which he would be greatly exposed in the City, . . . he cannot suppose it would be prudent for him to hazard his life." By August, Elbridge Gerry of Massachusetts called the city "very sickly" for children, "a great number of whom had died."

Some visitors found the city visually dull, built on a rectangular grid of streets laid out by William Penn when the colony was founded. A German carped, "[T]here is nothing but streets all alike, the houses of brick, of the same height mostly, and built by a plan that seldom varies." Still, visitors admired the frequency of public pumps for water service. To fight crime, the roads were lit with whale-oil lamps and patrolling constables called out the hour and the state of the weather.

Crime and its consequences were often before the delegates, as the Walnut Street prison stood behind the State House. The inmates called to passing delegates "with Billingsgate language," extending "long reedpoles, with a little cap of cloth at the end" to solicit donations. A citizen who failed to deposit alms would trigger "the most foul and horrid imprecations." In March of 1787, eighteen inmates escaped through and over the prison's walls, prompting municipal consternation. On May 12, the day before General Washington arrived, Philadelphia hanged one Robert Eliot for a burglary he committed before the laws were made "less sanguinary." Even sanguinary punishments proved an incomplete deterrent to crime. In late June, a newspaper reported that a "nest of footpads" was attacking citizens near Broad Street.

More pleasant were the city's bells. Christ Church in Second Street had a full octave of chimes, and "[a]t Philadelphia there is always something to be chimed, so that it seems as if it was an Imperial or Popish city."

Twice a week, the evening bells would announce the next morning's market (held on Wednesdays and Saturdays). Visitors marveled at the market, which extended for two roofed blocks in the middle of town. "Everything is adjusted in perfect order, and as neat and clean as a dining-hall." A Frenchman wrote home, "Even meat, which looks so disgusting in all other markets, has an attractive appearance." The offerings included raccoon, opossum, fish-otter, bear-bacon, and bear's foot. The orderliness of the people also drew favorable comment, with one guest writing, "One would think it is a market of brothers."

The inns and taverns were the social hubs of the city, particularly for long-term visitors like the delegates. In 1774, Philadelphia had a tavern for every 140 residents. The better inns were full in the summer of 1787, forcing some delegates to share rooms. A Delaware delegate described Mrs. House's establishment as "very crowded, and the room I am presently in [is] so small as not to admit of a second bed." Some roommates were decidedly unwelcome. A British traveler in the 1790s recorded that his room at the City Tavern (one of Philadelphia's premier hostelries) included his "old tormenters, the bugs."

Still, genuine comforts could be had at the Indian King, the George, and the Bunch of Grapes. The Indian Queen boasted sixteen rooms for lodgers, plus four garret rooms. A visitor there in 1787 described being greeted by a liveried servant in coat, waistcoat, and ruffled shirt. The servant produced two London magazines, called for a barber, brought a bowl for washing off road dust, and served tea.

Most obviously, the inns offered drink. Although the enthusiastic drinking habits of Maryland delegate Luther Martin would draw special notice, the delegates were no different from other Americans in their affection for porter beer, Madeira wine, rum punch, and hard cider. The consumption patterns of the day were impressive. When the Philadelphia City Troop honored Washington with a dinner at the end of the Convention, the fifty-five attendees consumed seven "large bowls" of rum punch, over a hundred bottles of wine (divided between Madeira and claret), and almost fifty bottles of beer and cider.

After sweaty summer days in the Convention, the delegates naturally congregated at taverns to slake their thirsts. William Samuel Johnson of Connecticut incurred large charges as a host at the City Tavern. Much politicking occurred at such occasions—Washington's diary reflects at least a dozen of them—though no record remains of their substance.

A bond grew among those delegates who shared an inn for lodging or dinner. A Delaware delegate wrote that one group established a regular "table" at the City Tavern for every night except Saturday. For July 2, Pennsylvania's chief justice received a dinner invitation from "the gentlemen of the Convention at the Indian Queen," who included George Mason (and his son, John), one Pinckney, two Massachusetts delegates, and two from North Carolina.

The out-of-towners faced a long summer away from family and duties. Of the thirty-eight delegates who were both married and not from Philadelphia, fewer than ten were accompanied by their wives. The separation strained delegates and spouses. The daughter of William Samuel Johnson wrote that her father's absence led her mother "to melancholy reflections which destroy her happiness and health." Torn by other obligations, almost half the delegates arrived after the Convention began, or left before it ended, or slipped off in the middle.

Yet thirty of them stuck it out for the entire summer, attending virtually every session from May 25 to September 17. More than half of those came from the three delegations that led the Convention: all four South Carolinians, seven of the eight Pennsylvanians, and five of the seven Virginians. Even in the eighteenth century, leadership began with showing up.

By May 25 a quorum, at last, was at hand. Seven state delegations were present. With a majority of the states represented, along with individual delegates from two other states, the Convention was called to order. Anticipation ran high both inside and outside the chamber. "Upon the event of this great council," wrote the *Pennsylvania Journal and Weekly Advertiser,* "depends every thing that can be essential to the dignity and stability of the national character." Henry Knox wrote from New England that the Convention was the "only means to avoid the most flagitious evils," while George Mason noted with pride that the Revolution had been "nothing compared to the great business now before us." Mason's eagerness pulses through a letter to his eldest son:

> [T]he influence which the [government] now proposed may have upon the happiness or misery of millions yet unborn, is an object of such magnitude, as absorbs, and in a manner suspends the operations of the human understanding.

The Convention's prospects induced a sort of euphoria, which can be detected in Jefferson's reference to the delegates as demigods. More than forty years later, the euphoria persisted in Tocqueville's description of the Convention as containing "the choicest talents and the noblest hearts which had ever appeared in the New World." The nation's greatest leaders had gathered to wrestle its fundamental problems to the ground, and in the process to create a model of self-government for all humanity. Though it was begun to solve crises and troubles, the Constitution-writing process also was an act of profound optimism and self-confidence.

Still, the delegates gathering in Philadelphia were humans, with all the strengths and fallibility of the breed. George Mason, for one, was far from starry-eyed over the men who wrote the Constitution. After the Convention adjourned, the Virginian's view of his colleagues was distinctly astringent:

> You may have been taught [said Mason] to respect the characters of the members of the late Convention. You may have supposed that they were an assemblage of great men. There is nothing less true. From the Eastern states [New England] there were knaves and fools and from the states southward of Virginia they were a parcel of coxcombs and from the middle states office hunters not a few.

Whether demigods or coxcombs, or something in between, the nation's future rested squarely on their shoulders.

Chapter Five

Virginia Leads

MAY 25–JUNE 1

TWENTY-NINE DELEGATES—barely half of those who would participate over the summer—splashed through a steady rain to the official opening of the Federal Convention on Friday morning, May 25. On that first day, Virginia's primacy was unmistakable, beginning when the Convention chose its presiding officer. Robert Morris of Pennsylvania proposed his houseguest, the incomparable Washington. The delegates agreed unanimously. The General responded with modesty, "lament[ing] his want of better qualifications, and claim[ing] the indulgence of the House towards the involuntary errors which his inexperience might occasion."

The man and the role matched perfectly. Washington's forte was presence, essential for the presiding officer. Better yet, the position exempted him from the thrust-and-parry of floor debate, an activity he always avoided.

It was important, Madison wrote, that a Pennsylvanian made the nomination, since only Dr. Franklin of that state might have competed for the honor. By seconding the motion and proposing that the choice be unanimous, John Rutledge of South Carolina added southern support and presaged his own leadership role through the coming summer.

Independence Hall Interior, First Floor. Assembly Room. View from northwest corner looking toward the presiding officer by Robin Miller, 2001.

The diminutive Madison, hair brushed forward to conceal his receding hairline, followed the General to the front of the room, taking a place of less prominence but of comparable significance. Clad in the sober black he favored, Madison chose "a seat in front of the presiding member, with the other members on my right and left hands." From that vantage point facing the delegates, which only he and Washington had, he would take notes for the next four months. While researching earlier republics, Madison had been frustrated to find no records of "the principles, the reasons, and the anticipations, which prevailed" in their formation. He was resolved to make that record for the American Constitution.

Never missing a day of the Convention, never leaving the chamber for more than "a casual fraction of an hour," Madison worked on his notes every evening throughout the sultry summer. For several decades after the Convention, he "corrected" his notes when other records became available, a process that never fails to cause a flutter of discomfort for historians, particularly since Madison got the last word. When he died in 1835, almost fifty years after the Convention, he had outlived all the other delegates. No one was left to challenge his version of events when it was published five years later.

Despite anxiety about their completeness or accuracy, Madison's notes are the invaluable source for reconstructing the conflicts and compromises that produced the Constitution. Fully aware that Madison was creating this unofficial official record, the other delegates evidently trusted his discretion and fair-mindedness to do so faithfully. Still, four of them (including the experienced Franklin) took the precaution of giving Madison the texts of their speeches, sending their remarks to posterity unmediated by the Virginian.

Save for an occasional aside, Madison's notes dutifully record many views with which he strongly disagreed. Though he plainly intended to preserve an evenhanded account of the deliberations, his judgments on what to record and what to leave out necessarily reflected his personal attitudes. Robert Yates of New York, who opposed a strong national government, made his own notes until he abandoned the Convention after only six weeks. In Yates's version the states' rights delegates speak more eloquently, while those favoring the central government sound more extreme. More disturbing, after Yates's death his notes may have been revised for political purposes. Though the Yates notes provide a further window on the debates, as do the occasional jottings made by other delegates, Madison's effort stands as a bravura achievement in drudgery, and the best record of that pivotal summer.

The Convention's setting equaled the solemnity of the occasion. A high-ceilinged chamber, the East Room in the State House measured forty feet by forty feet. By modern standards it was not a great hall, but it embodied the nation's short history. In that room the Second Continental Congress had signed the Declaration of Independence.

The room held thirteen tables covered with green baize, arranged in a loose semicircle. Each table accommodated several Windsor chairs, more sturdy than comfortable. The chairs were angled toward the high-backed seat of the presiding officer, which was on a raised platform. The members sat according to state delegation, very likely in geographic order, with the northern states on one side, the middle states clustered in the center, and the southern delegations on the other side. Geography also dictated voting order, with the states voting from north to south, as was the practice in Congress.

No more than eleven states were represented at any one time. Rhode Island never did send delegates. The two New Hampshire delegates arrived two months late, at the end of July. By then, Yates and another conservative New Yorker were long gone, leaving Alexander Hamilton as a lone New York delegate without a delegation, a status which prompted him to forsake Philadelphia for much of July and August.

The seating was intimate, close enough for the delegates to inspect each other's faces and gestures. It did not take a strong voice to be heard through the chamber. Though what they said in that room was a closely guarded secret, their meetings could hardly have been more conspicuous, occupying the largest room in the most prominent building in the nation's most populous city. Passersby could see the delegates through the large windows that lined either side of the East Room.

Had they looked in from the street, citizens would have seen proceedings that were both sober and serious. Upon arriving in late July, a New Hampshireman was impressed by the decorum in the East Room:

> Figure to yourself the Great Washington, with a dignity peculiar to himself, taking the chair. The notables are seated in a moment and after a short silence the business of the day is opened with great solemnity and good order. The importance of the business, the dignified character of many who compose the Convention, the eloquence of some and the regularity of the whole gives a ton[e] to the proceedings which is extremely pleasing.

In the last event of that first day, another Virginian gained prominence when George Wythe was appointed to chair a committee (consisting of Hamilton and Charles Pinckney) to prepare the Convention's rules. Wythe reported recommendations on the following Monday, May 28. With nine weekend arrivals filling out the state tables, the delegates unanimously adopted the rules, which granted great power to the presiding officer.

Most important, the rules followed Congress's practice of granting one vote to every state delegation. Each delegation's vote was cast as directed by a majority of those members who were present. Maryland and Connecticut allowed a single delegate to cast its vote. New York required all three of its delegates to be present, while the others insisted that at least two, three, or four (for Pennsylvania) be present in order for the state to vote. The Pennsylvanians urged that per-state voting be abandoned, but the Virginians "discountenanced and stifled" the suggestion, fearing it would "beget fatal altercations between the large and small states." Those altercations were only delayed, not prevented.

Per-state voting magnified the influence of the smaller states. That impact increased when a state's delegates divided evenly on a motion, preventing that state from casting its vote and reducing the number of states which did vote on the motion. With New York and New Hampshire absent for long stretches, and Rhode Island refusing to attend, northern (nonslave) interests were chronically underrepresented.

On May 28, these consequences were in the future. Two important rules were proposed from the floor. Major Butler urged a rule "against licentious publications of [the Convention's] proceedings," while a North Carolinian proposed that the delegates "might not be precluded by a vote upon any question, from revising the subject matter of it." After caucusing overnight, Wythe's committee added versions of both.

The rule against publication was a code of silence: a complete news blackout. As recorded by Madison, "nothing spoken in the House [would] be printed, or otherwise published or communicated without leave" from the Convention. To enforce the rule, the East Room's windows remained closed through the steamy summer and sentries were posted outside, at Virginia's expense, lest the delegates' exchanges be overheard and misunderstood.

Adherence to the rule was strict. Few press stories mentioned the Convention that summer, and those that did were often inaccurate. The *Pennsylvania Packet* reported on May 31 that one delegate from each state would serve on a committee that would "receive communications from the other members and arrange, digest and report a system for the subsequent discussion of the whole body." The report was completely wrong.

Some of the press errors may have resulted from eighteenth-century "spin." During an especially acrimonious stretch, the same newspaper chirped happily, "So great is the [Convention's] unanimity, we hear, . . . that it has been proposed to call the room in which they assemble—Unanimity Hall." Such a perfectly incorrect report smacks of placement by some delegate (Franklin is a leading suspect) who wished to sustain the morale of those inside and outside the Convention's walls.

In deference to the rule of secrecy, Washington stopped noting Convention activities in his daily diary. Mason applauded the rule as a "necessary precaution" in view of "the material difference between the appearance of a subject in its first and undigested shape, and after it shall have been properly matured and arranged." The secrecy certainly permitted the delegates to speak with greater candor than they would have otherwise.

The second added rule specified that delegates could demand reconsideration of every decision the Convention made. Through the coming months delegates would employ this procedure with exasperating frequency. Difficult questions were never resolved in a single discussion and vote. They came up again and again, even after they apparently had been decided. Variations would be offered on earlier proposals, new and old arguments mustered. Often the previous outcome would hold, but every now and then alliances shifted and the constitutional structure changed. This practice gave the Convention a looping, repetitive quality, but—combined with the rule of secrecy—allowed the delegates to revise their views upon wider consultation and deeper reflection, a luxury both precious and not often afforded to public officials, even in the slower pace of the eighteenth century.

With the rules in place, a fourth Virginian stepped into the spotlight. A large, burly figure, Edmund Randolph rose to present Virginia's proposals for a new constitution, the fruit of those morning sessions at Mrs. House's. Though lacking Washington's stature or Madison's learning, Governor Randolph was the head of the state delegation and an able speaker. The Convention would provide wide scope for Randolph to demonstrate his talents; by the end of the summer, it revealed his Achilles heel: an indecision that could be paralyzing.

Randolph presented the outline, known ever after as the Virginia

Plan, but its author was understood—then and now—to have been Madison. The delegates expected an initial proposal from Virginia, and one that would draw on the thirteen state constitutions written since 1776 (many by men then seated in the East Room). Though the delegates expected the plan to sketch out a stronger government, many were surprised by how completely it tossed the Confederation aside.

The Virginia governor began by canvassing the Union's woes. Noting the rebellion in Massachusetts, he warned of "anarchy from the laxity of government." Randolph denounced the "imbecility of the Confederation" and warned that America's greatest danger was too much democracy. None of the state constitutions, he observed, "have provided sufficient checks against the democracy."

Randolph presented the plan in the form of fifteen draft resolutions that the delegates could debate and vote on. The fifteen resolutions outlined basic principles, which then would have to be transformed into a true Constitution. Modeled on the state governments, the Virginia Plan proposed a legislature of two houses, with the critical additions of an executive and a judiciary. The national government would be superior to the states, with the power to veto state laws. Assemblies chosen directly by the people would ratify the Constitution.

The government framed by the fifteen resolutions did not have the careful system of "checks and balances" which emerged by the end of the Convention. The Virginia Plan called for all power to flow from a single legislative body. The people would elect the "first branch" of the legislature, which would control the entire government. That "first branch" (the future House of Representatives) would choose the "second branch" of the legislature (the future Senate). Together, those two houses would select the president and appoint all the judges. Though Madison would fervently support the final Constitution, it was a far cry from his own Virginia Plan.

The Virginia Plan's resolutions also failed to address significant points. They made no effort to spell out the powers of the national government (such as levying taxes), and did not recognize state sovereignty.

When Randolph sat down, the plan was referred to "a Committee of the whole House," a parliamentary fiction that had been agreed to in advance. While sitting as the Committee of the Whole, the same delegates could assemble in the East Room and discuss the Virginia Plan, but they could take no final actions. The Committee of the Whole could only make recommendations to the Convention, at which point exactly the same delegates would reconstitute themselves as the Convention to consider the recommendations they had made to themselves. The circular device, which prevailed for the next two weeks, was designed to encourage open discussion.

Charles Pinckney of South Carolina rose to describe his plan for a charter of government. The note takers in the room put down their quill pens as Pinckney began, so there is no record of his remarks. Moreover, the version of his plan later published by Pinckney is suspect, at best. Though the South Carolinian's proposal also was referred to the Committee of the Whole, no further word of it would be breathed until early August, when the Committee of Detail (chaired by Rutledge of South Carolina) would make use of it.

Forty-one delegates turned to the Virginia Plan on May 30. Their transformation into the Committee of the Whole was reinforced by the installation of Nathaniel Gorham of Massachusetts in the presiding chair. Though Washington took a seat at the Virginia table, temporarily descending to the same plane as mere delegates, the General maintained his customary posture above the fray, offering no remarks from the floor.

The selection of Gorham, a genial merchant who had recently served as president of the Confederation Congress, recognized the importance of Massachusetts and offered a geographic counterweight to the conspicuous Virginians. Gorham, though, was a pale substitute for Washington. Just six months before, he had been so unhinged by the Shays rising that he wrote to Prince Henry of Prussia, brother of Frederick the Great, asking if the prince "could be induced to accept regal powers on the failure of our free institutions." The German rejected Gorham's overture, observing that Americans seemed unenthusiastic about kings—a point that Gorham had overlooked.

The delegates were slow to engage on the issues that morning. When the Virginia Plan's first three resolutions were read, the room was deadly still. Seconds ticked by. Then a minute. Then more. After the time had lengthened uncomfortably, George Wythe said archly that he "presume[d] from the silence of the house" that the delegates were ready to vote. Tentatively, the delegates began to find their voices.

An early topic was the odd fact that the Virginia Plan started with a lie. Its first resolution stated that the Articles of Confederation should be "corrected and enlarged." But the Virginia Plan neither corrected nor enlarged them; it replaced them entirely.

No delegate was misled, certainly not Gouverneur Morris of Pennsylvania, who called the first resolution "unnecessary . . . as the subsequent resolutions would not agree with it." Randolph hurriedly suggested that the delegates move on to the next three resolutions, but the South Carolinians broke in. Charles Pinckney asked pointedly if Randolph "meant to abolish the state governments altogether." His elder cousin, joined by Elbridge Gerry of Massachusetts, questioned whether the state legislatures had given the delegates authority to do anything other than amend the Articles.

When the delegates turned to Randolph's resolution on the legislative branch, the same issue emerged in new garb. That resolution proposed to eliminate the one-state/one-vote system, but the Delaware legislature had barred its delegates from agreeing to any such change. The Delaware men pleaded for an adjournment to determine whether they could even be present during such discussions. When they resumed their seats on the next day, they made no comment about their conundrum, though they must have concluded that they could at least discuss the Virginia Plan.

That fundamental question remained, even if it was temporarily shuffled from view. Was the Convention merely amending the Articles? Or was it creating a new, stronger government? The answer was tangled up with the delegates' puzzlement over how to blend the states with the strong central government that the Virginia Plan would create. Would the states be abolished? How best to reconcile two sovereigns exercising power over the same territory at the same time? The questions would not be answered until early August, when John Rutledge and James Wilson worked out a creative balance in response to this novel challenge.

Two days later, on June 1, the delegates were tongue-tied again. Madison recorded "a considerable pause" in the debate, which prompted Rutledge of South Carolina to comment with disapproval "on the shyness of the gentlemen." A Delaware delegate complained of the "general silence." Even the press got wind of the problem (for once, getting it right). The *Pennsylvania Herald* reported on June 2 that "[s]uch circumspection and secrecy mark the proceedings of the federal convention that the members find it difficult to acquire the habit of communication even among themselves." As the summer wore on and the East Room grew familiar, the delegates' diffidence turned into a volubility that John Rutledge would lament even more.

Working through the resolutions of the Virginia Plan, the delegates steadily neared two provisions that would trigger their stormiest conflicts. First, the Virginians proposed to replace the one-state/one-vote system of the Articles with voting by individual representatives in Congress. The more populous states (Virginia, Pennsylvania, and Massachusetts) had long resented per-state voting, feeling like helpless Gullivers trussed up by self-important Lilliputians. Small states desperately feared the end of one-state/one-vote.

The Virginia Plan would also reduce the power of the states themselves by having the people elect the House of Representatives and allowing that body to choose the Senate. The state assemblies were bound to resent losing the power to select representatives to Congress. The proposal to shift power to the larger states, and away from all states, would nearly blow the Convention apart.

Second, though the Virginia Plan made no mention of slavery, one feature would ignite a conflagration over that most volatile issue. The conflict would concern a central question for any representative government: who is to be represented? The Virginia Plan offered two alternatives. One approach would assign representatives "proportioned to the quotas of contribution" of that state—that is, the number of representatives could be based on the wealth of each state as reflected in the taxes it paid. That calculation would include the value of a state's slaves, who counted as property for tax purposes. Accordingly, quotas of contribution would give representation based on southern slaves. But many questioned how to calculate "quotas of contribution" in an era without widespread taxation or reliable statistical information. Generally, that alternative was dismissed as impractical.

Randolph's more feasible alternative would assign representatives on the basis of "the number of free inhabitants" in a state. That simple phrase, proposed by seven Virginia slaveholders, would exclude slaves from the allocation of representatives. As delegates from Maryland through Georgia instantly perceived, counting only free inhabitants would be highly detrimental to their states, where 40 percent of the population was manifestly not free.

The problem of representation would bring slavery into the center of the East Room, trailed by a host of thorny questions. How, exactly, should slaves be counted? Were they people or were they property? What stake did they have in the government? What stake did the government have in them? How on earth could the principles of representative democracy be reconciled with slavery?

For a few days yet, these explosive questions would lie dormant. Other issues would occupy the Convention's early days. Two fuses, though, had been lit, and combustible materials lay close at hand.

Chapter Six

Wilson's Bargain

MAY 31–JUNE 10

MONDAY, JUNE 11, was the first really hot day of summer. The thick heat pressed down as James Wilson left his Market Street home for the Convention's morning session. On some days, America still seemed like an exciting new world for Wilson. Though this swelter was a world apart from the brisk airs he had known in Scotland, Wilson could not dwell on the heat as he walked the two blocks to the State House.

Nodding absently at neighbors and acquaintances, ignoring the animals that roamed the streets, Wilson thought through his plan one more time. He had worked it out during the Convention's Sunday recess the day before. It was a bold plan that would catch many delegates by surprise. The prize could not be greater. Wilson's goal was to establish the new government as a democratic one.

At stake was nothing less than who would have power in America. The new Congress would write the nation's laws. Whoever controlled it would control the nation. Wilson fervently believed that the new government must be founded on the people. Using the construction metaphor that many delegates favored, Wilson told the Convention on the last day of May that he wanted to "rais[e] the federal pyramid to a

James Wilson (Pennsylvania)

considerable altitude," which meant it had to have "as broad a basis as possible."

Wilson wanted every American to be equally represented in the Congress. To achieve that goal, he would have to overcome the brief but unbroken tradition that gave each state the same voting power in Congress, a tradition that exaggerated the influence of the smaller states. Though only a fraction the size of states like Virginia and Pennsylvania, small states like Delaware wielded an identical vote in Congress. Jealous of that power, the small states fiercely opposed any change in that tradition.

For James Wilson, the traditional voting pattern made no sense. It violated democratic principles by giving extra weight to the votes of small states while reducing the influence of his own state, Pennsylvania. To overcome the small states, Wilson had just made an unlikely alliance—later, some would call it an unholy one—between democracy and slavery.

If things broke the right way on June 11, Wilson's plan would change the course of the Convention.

After two weeks in session, the delegates' routine was familiar. The day began, as described by a French visitor, "like every other day in America, [with] a great breakfast." The Convention met from ten until three. For a short period in August, the hard-driving John Rutledge shamed his colleagues into working an extra hour in the afternoon, but after only a few days a revolt restored the previous schedule. After their second meal of the day ("dinner"), the delegates could sample what diversions Philadelphia might offer for the evening, or they could scheme and prepare for the next day's session. Bedtime followed a late supper.

The delegates dwelt in close quarters, deliberating for thirty hours every week, eating and sleeping at the same inns, often attending the same performances and parties. During that summer, delegates "walked together, they talked together, and they went to one another's rooms." Indeed, "the very closeness of association had its disadvantages; members sometimes got on one another's nerves."

The excitement of writing a constitution faded quickly. Speakers ran long, repeated themselves, strayed into irrelevancies. By June 8, Pierce Butler of South Carolina was doodling through debate, sketching nine separate caricatures of delegates in profile and idly executing penmanship drills.

Though the delegates addressed many subjects in those early days, the largest problem was how to allocate representatives in Congress: would each state elect exactly the same number of legislators, or would representatives be allocated based on population? The question would dog the delegates for another five weeks. No other issue would so dominate the Convention.

The three large states (Massachusetts, Virginia, and Pennsylvania) were squared off against the others, all of whom deemed themselves small by comparison. Under the Articles, the large states had put up with per-state voting for Congress, but that had been in the midst of a desperate war with the British. In any event, the concession had not

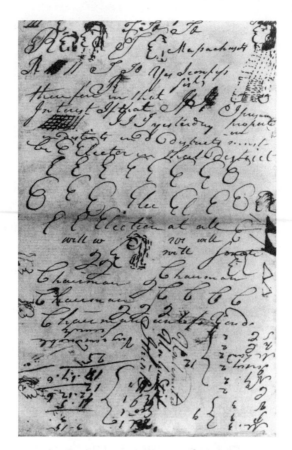

Doodles by Pierce Butler (South Carolina),
from Pierce Butler Papers at Library of Congress,
June 8, 1787

been such a great one since that Congress was so weak. This new government would have substantial powers. The large states were determined to secure their fair share of those powers.

On the first day of real debate, May 30, the Delaware delegates
complained that the Virginia Plan would jettison the one-state/one-vote
system, a step their legislature had specifically barred them from accepting. One Delaware man suggested that if that change were
adopted, "it might become their duty to retire from the Convention." It
was the first threat to abandon the Convention, only five days into the
deliberations. It was the first of many.

Rather than force the battle on May 30, the Delaware men held their fire. Instead, they built alliances and plotted strategy.

The small-state delegates faced a difficult task. Pennsylvania and Virginia were wealthier and more populous, and their demand for proportional representation grew naturally from the principles of the Revolution. Also, they had sent to Philadelphia their great leaders. The small states had neither a Madison nor a Wilson, much less a Franklin or a Washington.

The leading men from the small states, John Dickinson of Delaware and Roger Sherman of Connecticut, tended to be of a quieter sort. Having led the colonists in the political struggles with Britain before the Revolution, Dickinson saw his public career stall when he refused to sign the Declaration of Independence. At fifty-five, he was ill for much of the Convention. Sherman, the second-oldest delegate at sixty-seven, was a canny political veteran whose influence would be felt through the summer. Having arrived late in Philadelphia, he did not immediately plunge into the debates, preferring to watch the conflict unfold.

Lesser-known figures had to step forward to carry the banner for the small states. What they lacked in reputation or talent, they made up with tenacity.

The Virginia Plan mixed the issues of democracy and slavery by proposing that representation in Congress be based on the number of "free inhabitants." On the last day of May, the delegates addressed a proposal to replace "free inhabitants" with an ambiguous call for election of the lower house of Congress "by the people."

Two New Englanders opposed the motion, betraying the impact of the Shays rising only months before. Wealthy merchant Elbridge Gerry of Massachusetts, a member of the "codfish aristocracy" north of Boston, warned against "the excess of democracy." Though of humble origins himself, Sherman of Connecticut urged that the people "should have as little to do as may be about the government," since "they want information and are constantly liable to be misled."

George Mason fired back, demanding that the delegates "attend to the rights of every class of the people." Mason insisted, with customary bluntness, that he "had often wondered at the indifference of the superior classes of society to this dictate of humanity." Days later he argued that "even the diseases of the people should be represented—if not, how are they to be cured?"

Election of the House of Representatives "by the people" carried by a vote of 6–2, with two state delegations evenly divided and one absent. The only nays came from the South Carolina aristocrats and the states' rights enthusiasts of New Jersey.

The delegates next argued over how to select the second legislative branch (the future Senate), which would become the prize in the long battle over representation. Modeled on the British House of Lords and the upper house of the Maryland legislature, this second house was intended to stabilize the government against swings in public passions. Noting that the Convention was a response to the "turbulence and follies of democracy," Randolph explained that "a good Senate" would check that "tendency."

The Virginia Plan allowed the House of Representatives to select the Senate. Others, however, thought state legislatures should choose the Senators, which would preserve the states' powers. Wilson argued for the people to elect them directly. When no agreement could be reached, the delegates passed over the question, leaving what Madison grumpily called "a chasm . . . in this part of the plan." The delegates would return to that chasm numerous times, and would wrestle precariously on its rim.

The Convention spent several days working through other parts of the Virginia Plan, including an extended reflection on how the executive branch could have energy and force, but not too much. On June 6, while a cool rain fell outside, the delegates circled back to the Senate, to Madison's chasm.

General Pinckney proposed that state legislatures elect both houses of Congress. Madison joined the opposition to this move, endorsing popular representation. To drive his point home, the Virginia slave owner selected an arresting example of governmental failure: "We have seen the mere distinction of color, made in the most enlightened period of time, a ground of the most oppressive dominion ever exercised by man over man."

General Pinckney's motion failed, but he won half his goal the next day, June 7, when John Dickinson moved that the state legislatures choose the members of the Senate. The motion carried unanimously.

Dickinson introduced a powerful image when he "compared the proposed national system to the solar system, in which the states were the planets and ought to be left to move freely in their proper orbits." On the next day, Madison tried to adopt that image in defense of his pet proposal to let Congress veto state laws. The Virginian warned that without such a veto, the states "will continually fly out of their proper orbits and destroy the order and harmony of the political system."

Madison's message was greeted with suspicion. A Delaware delegate thought that Madison's "order and harmony" translated into the oppression of small states. He asked, "Will not these large states crush the small ones whenever they stand in the way of their ambitions or interested views?"

When the delegates returned on the following day, June 9, the simmering conflict exploded. Led by New Jersey delegates, the small states started the fight. They insisted that each state must have exactly the same voting strength in Congress, just as they did under the Articles, and as they did at the Convention. They were "astonished" and "alarmed" that the Virginia Plan would base a state's voting strength on its population. It was unthinkable. Each sovereign state was the equal of every other state. The conflict reflected fundamentally different visions of the nation. Was it to be an amalgam of autonomous states, or a single nation? The delegates had to choose.

On June 9, William Paterson, the attorney general of New Jersey, led the small-state attack. More aggressive than thoughtful, he proposed acidly that the only fair way to follow the Virginia Plan's approach would be to carve the nation into thirteen states of exactly equal size. Clinging to state sovereignty, he insisted that giving greater voting power to large states was like granting additional votes to "rich individual citizen[s]" at the expense of the indigent. The Jerseyman declared truculently that his state "will never confederate on the plan before the Convention."

Never short on truculence, and ever prepared to point out lacunae in the logic of others, James Wilson met ultimatum with ultimatum, gauntlet thrown with gauntlet thrown. For Wilson, the question was a simple one of democratic principles: "[A]s all authority was derived from the people, equal numbers of people ought to have an equal number of representatives." He asked pointedly, "Are not the citizens of Pennsylvania equal to those of New Jersey? Does it require 150 of the former to balance 50 of the latter?" Wilson's words drove home, like a fist thumped rhythmically into the palm of his hand:

> Shall New Jersey have the same right or influence in the councils of the nation with Pennsylvania? I say no. It is unjust. I will never confederate on this plan.

That the Articles had adopted per-state voting, he snorted, was "improper."

The explosion had come on a Saturday afternoon, just before the Convention's day off. After Wilson's harsh speech, Paterson suggested that, "as so much depended on it," the delegates postpone until Monday the vote on legislative representation.

As the delegates dispersed, Wilson knew he had to do some fast politicking. Two elements of the representation question had been resolved: the people would choose the lower house; state legislatures would choose the upper house. Still undecided was how to allocate representatives in both. Wilson framed the issue as one of democratic theory. No republican could give 50 citizens of New Jersey the same voice as 150 Pennsylvanians.

Most delegates, however, lacked Wilson's penchant for theory. They were politicians. The one-state/one-vote system might offend Pennsylvanians and Virginians, but delegates from the smaller states admired it greatly. Theory would not win this argument. Wilson needed votes, and he would have to do some horse-trading to get them.

The Convention's rules gave the small states the advantage in this showdown. If all eight of them stood firm (New Hampshire and Rhode Island had no delegations at the Convention at the time), proportional representation would be buried by an 8–3 margin, even though the three big states (Massachusetts, Pennsylvania, and Virginia) held almost half of the nation's population. Over the next forty-plus hours, Wilson had to find three more votes.

Wilson's choices were limited. Maryland, Delaware, and New Jersey were devotees of one-state/one-vote, and also were neighbors of Pennsylvania; for both reasons they mistrusted the intentions of anyone from that large state. New York had lined up with the small states. Connecticut might be more flexible, but even if Wilson could woo it to his side, he still would be two votes short.

For the three votes he needed, Wilson had to look to the Deep South—to Georgia and the Carolinas. He had two advantages with those states. First, he had a solid relationship with the leading southern delegate, John Rutledge. Wilson could approach the South Carolinian with familiarity and candor. The second advantage was more important: the southern delegates wanted something.

For the southerners, no goal was greater than the protection of slavery. Without such protection, southern states might not join the new government. At the very least, southern delegates would face ostracism and denunciation if they brought home a Constitution that did not protect slavery. Careers would be ruined.

But the southerners' objective collided with the principles of freedom and liberty that America proclaimed so loudly. To protect slavery, the southerners would need intellectual and tactical agility.

Wilson had reason to suspect that the southerners would be open to proportional representation. When contesting the Mississippi River negotiations with Spain, southerners had feared the numerical superiority of the northern states in Congress—eight northern states to five southern ones. Moreover, many southerners believed their warmer climate and open lands would draw population faster than the rest of the nation. Proportional representation would reward faster-growing states. The price for southern support was simple: slavery.

As reflected in the debates on Monday, June 11, Wilson cut a deal with the South Carolinians. He and John Rutledge yoked the democratic principle of equal representation to the southerners' need to protect slavery. To secure representation in Congress based on population, Wilson embraced the fiction that southern slaves should be partly represented. Though Wilson made the deal in order to establish democracy, future abolitionists would denounce his Faustian bargain as a central feature of the Constitution's "covenant with death."

• • •

No delegate came to Philadelphia intending to grapple with the social and moral issues of slavery. After all, at least a third of them owned slaves.

The subject was not mentioned in the Annapolis delegates' call for a convention, nor in the resolution adopted by the Confederation Congress. Washington and Madison never referred to it in their pre-Convention correspondence. Twelve states adopted resolutions sending delegations and outlining their duties; none mentioned slavery.

But slavery crept into the Convention as soon as the Virginia Plan proposed to apportion legislators on the basis of "the number of free inhabitants." Madison had shown his usual delicacy when he moved to strike that phrase from the resolution. The words, he warned, "might occasion debates which would divert [us] from the general question."

In debate, Madison himself was rarely diverted. His presentations were low-key but focused. He could underwhelm those accustomed to more swagger in public speaking. One observer called his language "very pure, perspicuous, and to the point," but found the Virginian "a little too much of a book politician." Another wrote that "the warmest excitement of debate was visible in [Madison] only by a more or less rapid and forward seesaw motion of his body." His modest style may account for the number of occasions when he spoke at length, and made good sense, yet made little impression on the other delegates. Also, reason did not often subdue political interest.

Still, Madison's instincts about the volatility of the slavery question were dead-on. Before the summer was over, that question would draw the delegates into angry confrontations and show its potential to fracture the Convention, and the Union.

In America in 1787, slavery was ubiquitous. The census of 1790 counted 681,000 slaves, or one-sixth of the total population. Nearly half of the slaves lived in Virginia, where they constituted one-third of that most populous state. Even Pennsylvania had 3,700 slaves.

All eleven delegates from Virginia and South Carolina owned slaves, though the size of their holdings ranged widely. The two professors (Wythe and McClurg) owned a handful each, while hundreds of slaves toiled for Washington, for Madison, for Mason, for Rutledge, for each of the Pinckneys, and for Major Butler. Large plantations assumed slave labor. Slaves cultivated fields, operated mills and smithies, performed carpentry and skilled labor.

In Philadelphia, the South Carolinians never faltered in their defense of slavery. The Virginians, though, were different. While eating food raised and prepared by slave hands, wearing clothes laundered by slaves and purchased with the profits of slave labor, they found the subject profoundly disquieting. Their intimacy with the practice sharpened their awareness of how completely it contradicted the principles they espoused.

When Madison served in the Confederation Congress in Philadelphia in 1783, his slave Billey ran off, inspired by revolutionary rhetoric. After Billey was captured and returned, Madison candidly recognized the reason for flight when he declined to punish the man:

> I . . . cannot think of punishing him . . . merely for coveting that liberty for which we have paid the price of so much blood, and have proclaimed so often to be the right & worthy pursuit of every human being.

Sympathy with Billey's yearnings did not cloud Madison's business sense. He noted both that Billey's "mind is too thoroughly tainted to be a fit companion for fellow slave[s] in Virginia," and that Pennsylvania laws "do not admit of his being sold for more than 7 years, [so] I do not expect to get near the worth of him." Making the best deal he could under the circumstances, Madison sold Billey to a Philadelphian for another seven years of bondage.

Though he never escaped the schizophrenia of being a slave-owning champion of democracy, Madison did not sugarcoat that contradiction. His "Vices" memorandum—written before the Convention and not shared with others—declares with unanswerable simplicity, "Where slavery exists the republican theory becomes still more fallacious." Early in his career Madison wrote Randolph that he wanted "to depend as little as possible on the labor of slaves," a goal he never achieved and which he seems to have abandoned later.

The other Virginians professed comparable discomfort over the wrong of slavery. A year before the Convention, Washington wrote to Robert Morris (his future host) that "there is not a man living who wishes more sincerely than I do, to see a plan adopted for the abolition of [slavery]." George Wythe freed his slaves a year after the Convention. Two years after the Convention, Randolph wrote to Madison that he might move his family to Philadelphia, where "I should emancipate my slaves and thus end my days, without undergoing any anxiety about the injustice of holding them." None matched George Mason's cold assessment of the vicious effects of slavery:

> Every gentleman here is born a petty tyrant. Practiced in acts of despotism & cruelty, we become callous to the dictates of humanity. . . . Taught to regard a part of our own species in the most abject and contemptible degree below us, we lose that idea of the dignity of man which the hand of nature had implanted in us. . . . Habituated from our infancy to trample upon the rights of human nature, every generous, every liberal sentiment . . . is enfeebled in our minds.

The Virginians embodied the moral self-contradiction of the nation. The early patriots understood slavery's refutation of their principles. As the colonies lurched toward rebellion in 1774, Washington wrote a fellow Virginian that Americans must not "submit to every imposition that can be heaped on us till custom and use shall make us tame and abject slaves as the blacks we rule over with such arbitrary sway."

Jefferson's initial draft of the Declaration of Independence blamed King George III for maintaining the slave trade, a "cruel war against humanity itself." Others struck that clause while retaining the proclamation that all men are created equal, suppressing any discomfort with the inconsistency between proclaiming the one phrase and omitting the other. Wythe, Mason, and Jefferson served on a Virginia Assembly committee from 1776 to 1779 that considered gradual emancipation but then thought better of it.

In 1787 only Massachusetts banned slavery, and that state's prohibition came from a court ruling, not from a legislative act. Four other states (New Hampshire, Connecticut, Rhode Island, and Pennsylvania) had "gradual emancipation" laws that freed children of slave parents. New York adopted gradual emancipation in 1799, and New Jersey followed in 1804. Under those statutes, slaves were held in northern states into the 1840s. In 1802, Virginia enacted a manumission law allowing masters to set slaves free, but not many took the opportunity to do so.

Though the Pennsylvania delegates were intimate with the practice, they were not ensnared in it. In part because of the North's lesser dependence on slavery, the northern response to the Revolution was one of fitful progress toward abolition.

A slave owner at times in his long life, Dr. Franklin had turned against the practice. Shortly before the Convention began, he agreed to head the Pennsylvania Society for Promoting the Abolition of Slavery. Delegates were still straggling into town on May 23 when a local newspaper published the society's charter, listing Franklin as president. Southerners surely were unsettled by Dr. Franklin's prominent antislavery position.

Wilson, the transplanted Scot, owned a kitchen slave until his second marriage in 1793 to a Quaker woman, then freed the man. Gouverneur Morris's family had used slaves to farm its huge New York estates and to run its New Jersey manufacturing business. Morris himself, however, owned none. Having pressed for an abolition clause in the New York Constitution of 1777, he would be the major antagonist of slavery at the Convention, his speeches growing more fervent as the summer wore on.

In the South, though, slavery was deeply embedded in every economic and social structure. It had withstood both revolutionary ideology and the direct shocks administered by British soldiers and by the slaves themselves.

From the first days of the Revolution, the British welcomed escaped slaves into their lines. In November 1775, Lord Dunmore, Virginia's royal governor, promised freedom to slaves who joined the British side. He formed an "Ethiopian Regiment" with over 300 escaped slaves, many of whom wore sashes proclaiming "Liberty to Negroes." Washington's steward at Mount Vernon acknowledged that every slave on the estate "would leave us, if they believed they could make their escape." As he predicted, seventeen of them followed British troops who raided the area in 1781. Washington reclaimed two of the slaves after the battle of Yorktown and tracked down several others in Philadelphia.

Many slaves took advantage of revolutionary turbulence to help themselves to freedom. Some fled into empty lands and formed their own communities. Others drifted to cities or up North, passing as free blacks. By the end of the war, as many as 10,000 were gone from Virginia and Maryland plantations, and in the Deep South many more fled or died in the turmoil. The slave population in Georgia fell from 15,000 to 5,000, while South Carolina may have lost one-fourth of its slaves, or more than 25,000. Although these numbers were not great enough to uproot slavery, they unsettled both the owners and the owned.

After the war, southern slave owners reasserted control over their chattels. Washington spoke for his peers when he directed his overseers to have his slaves

> at their work as soon as it is light—work till it is dark—and be diligent while they are at it. The presumption being that, every laborer (male or female) does as much in the 24 hours as their strength, without endangering their health, or constitution, will allow of.

Writing in 1789 as president of the new republic, Washington was equally unflinching: "If the Negroes will not do their duty by fair means, they must be compelled to do it."

After 1783 the Deep South states resumed the importation of slaves from Africa to replace those lost. John Rutledge, General Pinckney, Major Butler, all had to replenish their slaveholdings. Those losses hardened their resolve at the Convention.

Philadelphia was home to the nation's largest community of free blacks, many drawn by the antislavery views of the city's Quakers. The 1790 census placed in that city over 2,000 "other free persons" (other than white, that is), plus four colored families recorded as themselves owning slaves. Many free blacks worshiped at St. George's, a Methodist congregation a few blocks from the State House. On May 17, 1787, while the Virginians awaited a quorum, eight free blacks met in the home of Richard Allen to adopt Articles of Association for the Free African Society. Allen left that nondenominational group seven years later to found the first African Methodist Episcopal Church.

In the Convention's first days, perhaps the most noteworthy event for the slavery issue was one that did not take place. On June 2, the Pennsylvania Abolition Society adopted an Address asking the delegates to end the slave trade. The Address warned: "In vain will be [Americans'] pretensions to a love of liberty . . . while they share in the profits of a commerce that can only be conducted upon rivers of human tears and blood."

The society submitted the Address to its president, Dr. Franklin, but he never presented it to the Convention. The Society was informed later that he "thought it advisable to let [the matter] lie over for the present."

The New York Manumission Society traveled a similar road later in the summer. In mid-August, the New Yorkers resolved to petition the Convention for abolition, only to reverse themselves the following day upon "being informed that it was probable that the Convention would not take up the business." That second meeting was attended by Alexander Hamilton, Convention delegate and lifelong opponent of slavery, who presumably advised against pursuing the petition.

Led by such prudent champions, the antislavery cause could have only limited prospects at the Convention. Certainly, James Wilson betrayed no pangs of conscience over his bargain with slavery.

Chapter Seven

Three-Fifths of a Human Being

JUNE 11

I T WAS PROBABLY James Wilson or John Rutledge who first proposed that the large states join forces with the Deep South. Each of them had the subtlety and experience to develop the strategy. The idea could even have come from Dr. Franklin, perhaps the subtlest politician in the East Room. On June 11, all three men helped execute the day-long gambit that cemented the alliance between large states and slave states that would prevail for many weeks.

At this and other key points during the summer, the delegates' activities mostly recede from view. Much essential work transpired outside the State House, during evenings and weekends, beyond the reach of Madison's ears and pen. What agreements were struck and stratagems hatched at corner tables at the City Tavern? Next to the fireplace at the Indian Queen? In James Wilson's parlor or over Ben Franklin's dinner table? Only rarely has evidence survived of those crucial exchanges.

As debate began on that stifling Monday, June 11, Wilson bided his

**Interpretation of Assembly Room, Independence Hall,
Independence National Historical Park, National Park Service,
Philadelphia, Pa. (restored 1965–75)**

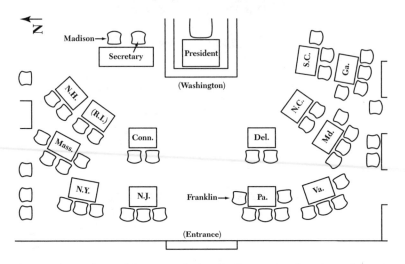

*Seating chart of state delegations during the Convention, based on schematic
provided by Independence National Historical Park. Rhode Island never sent
delegates to the Convention.*

time. Sherman of Connecticut endorsed allocating seats in the House of
Representatives based on the "numbers of free inhabitants," but insisted that each state should have a single vote in the Senate. Though
ultimately the states would have equal Senate votes, on June 11 Sherman received scant notice. Rutledge rose to speak for the slave interests. Without apology, he brought out the usual southern chestnut,
representation based on quotas of contribution (or the tax payments
made by each state). The "justice" of that approach, he assured the Convention, "could not be contested." Major Butler agreed.

Wilson ventured his opening move, the first half-step toward his
true goal of representation based on population. He offered a resolution
that the first branch not be apportioned as it was under the Articles (one
vote per state), "but according to some equitable ratio of representation." The ambiguous phrase aimed to bridge differences. The delegates, however, were not ready to vote. Debate lurched onward. Wilson
waited.

Two northern delegates—Rufus King of Massachusetts and Dickinson of Delaware—criticized the quotas-of-contribution alternative. Two weeks before, King had pointed out how impractical "quotas of contribution" would be: What, he asked, if the national government did not impose direct taxes such as property or head taxes (which, over the ensuing century, it almost never did)? Without direct taxes, a state's "contribution" to the national government could not be calculated and representatives could not be assigned! King also warned that any such taxes would vary "continually" as policies shifted, further disrupting the assignment of representatives.

With the representation question "about to be put," Wilson played a second, much stronger card: the redoubtable Dr. Franklin. Franklin "had thrown his ideas on the matter on a paper," which Wilson read aloud. Franklin's words echoed the resolution Wilson had offered, arguing that "the number of representatives should bear some proportion to the number of the represented." After reviewing the arithmetic of voting by the thirteen states, as well as the merger of the Scottish and English parliaments at the beginning of the century, Franklin's remarks closed by noting that in 1774 the Continental Congress had adopted per-state voting only because it lacked a way to count the population of each state.

So endorsed, Wilson's resolution was adopted; three small states voted no, while the Maryland delegation deadlocked (as became its habit). The Deep South states—all "small" ones in the calculus of the day—joined the large states and Connecticut in agreeing that the people should have "equitable" representation.

Having established the foundation for their deal, Wilson and Rutledge made their next move, using the same sequence of presentation. A South Carolinian would stake out a proslavery position; then Wilson would step in with a compromise that commanded southern support.

Rutledge took the floor, proposing once more to revive the moribund "quotas of contribution." The man was nothing if not persistent. Once more, Major Butler seconded. Wilson took the next step in the parliamentary gavotte, moving to postpone Rutledge's motion and offering an alternative. Tellingly, General Pinckney, sitting at Rutledge's right hand, seconded Wilson's motion.

And what alternative did Wilson propose and General Pinckney second? The infamous three-fifths clause. Wilson's new resolution required the allocation of seats in the House of Representatives on the basis of an

> [e]quitable ratio of representation in proportion to the whole number of white & other free Citizens & inhabitants . . . and three-fifths of all other persons not comprehended in the foregoing description, except Indians not paying taxes. . . .

In a final flourish, Wilson asserted that the Confederation Congress and eleven states had supported this "rule" for "apportioning quotas of revenue on the States."

Only Gerry of Massachusetts tried to disrupt the dance. The wealthy delegate from Marblehead could leave a lingering impression, if not always a favorable one. Described as "of middling stature and spare frame," Gerry's stammer made his speech "halting," while he had "a singular habit of contracting and expanding his eye." One delegate called him a "hesitating and laborious speaker," who "speaks on, without respect to elegance or flower of diction." Exercising a rich man's disregard for his own limitations, Gerry addressed the Convention more than 150 times that summer. However idiosyncratic his delivery, his comments could be tart and insightful.

A corresponding member of the Pennsylvania Abolition Society, Gerry protested that in the South, "Blacks are property, and are used . . . as horses and cattle" were in the North. So, he continued with stammering contempt, "[W]hy should their representation be increased to the southward on account of the number of slaves, [rather] than [on the basis of] horses or oxen to the north?"

No one answered the question, not solely because it was an uncomfortable one. The deal had been made; it was time to close. The vote was 9–2 in favor of the three-fifths rule. The small states had been routed. Only New Jersey and Delaware stood apart from the dance.

Wilson had spoken truly when he said that the weird calculus of the three-fifths ratio was familiar to the delegates, as it had been for him and John Rutledge. While Wilson sat in the Confederation Congress in

March 1783, a committee including four future Convention delegates (Rutledge, Madison, Gorham, and Hamilton) proposed the ratio as a solution for deriving the "requisitions" for revenues that the Confederation Congress impotently delivered to each state.

Under the 1783 proposal, requisitions would be based on a state's free population plus three-fifths of all "others." The committee toyed with counting slaves at one-half their number, but settled on three-fifths, which Congress approved. The ratio never took effect in 1783 because the states did not affirm it unanimously, as the Articles required.

Notably, the 1783 proposal used the ratio to apportion tax burdens, not as the standard for structuring a representative government. The two exercises surely bore material differences. Indeed, in one of those stinging ironies that bristled around the slavery issue, southerners in 1783 objected that the ratio overstated the value of slaves and thus would raise their taxes too high, while northerners protested that it understated the value of slaves and would fail to tax the South enough. When Wilson applied the ratio to legislative representation, the leaders of each region suddenly saw the force of the other's argument. Now northerners thought the ratio overstated the value of slaves; southerners begged to differ.

At its core, the disagreement turned on whether black slaves were human beings or property. In all its perversity, the three-fifths ratio captured their identity as both, though they had no voting rights and played no role in the nation's political life.

The politicians in the East Room calculated instantly the value of the three-fifths rule. If congressmen were allocated on the basis of population, an owner of 100 slaves (such as Washington or Madison) would count as 61 people—himself plus three-fifths of his slaves. This effect would be extended to presidential elections when the delegates created the electoral college to choose the president. The additional southern representation in Congress, and added sway in voting for the president, would be significant. With almost 700,000 slaves in the southern states from Maryland to Georgia, and an allocation of one congressman for every 30,000 persons, the three-fifths ratio gave the South at least a dozen additional congressmen, and a like number of additional electoral votes. To defeat the small states and achieve representation based on population, Wilson paid a high price: powerful reinforcement of the slave interest.

The large-state/slave-state alliance briefly enjoyed success beyond even Wilson's goals. As soon as the vote was tallied in favor of proportional representation in the House of Representatives, Sherman moved to give each state but one vote in the Senate, as he had urged early in the day. "The smaller states would never agree to the plan," he cautioned, "on any other principle."

Perhaps Sherman thought the large-state/slave-state alliance did not extend to the Senate, or perhaps he was panicked by the emergence of the Wilson-Rutledge pact. His motion was a major misstep, underestimating the momentum of the large-state/slave-state deal. The Carolinas and Georgia stood fast with the three big states; Sherman's motion failed by a 5–6 margin.

Wilson, supported by Hamilton, swiftly moved to take advantage of the moment. He proposed that the Senate have the same "ratio of representation" as the lower house. The motion carried 6–5, supported by the same six large and Deep South states. Now both houses of Congress would be based on free population plus three-fifths of all slaves. Wilson and his proslave allies had run the table, though by the narrowest of margins. Indeed, Wilson's victories on June 11 would become a chronic sore point as the delegates returned to the representation question again and again.

Though Wilson led the charge for the three-fifths ratio on June 11, the trail leads back to South Carolina and Charles Pinckney's neglected plan for the Constitution. In an odd bit of backfilling, Pinckney expunged the three-fifths ratio from the renditions of his plan that he issued publicly in late 1787 and in 1819. Nevertheless, versions of his actual plan were found in Wilson's papers; it proposed to allocate seats in the lower house of the legislature based on the "inhabitants[,] ⅗ of Blacks included."

Throughout the maneuvering of June 11, a question occurs: where were the Virginians? They had boldly led the Convention only two weeks before, one after another seizing the spotlight. Washington ascended to the presiding chair, Madison seized the pen, Wythe wrote the rules, and Randolph took the floor. Mason's trenchant comments were already well regarded. Yet during this critical sequence they sat largely silent.

Did any expression cross Washington's stony features as Wilson unveiled the three-fifths compromise? Why did Madison—Wilson's ally in the fight for popular representation—remain mute at this critical juncture? Had he been consulted on the strategy and blessed it? Was he distracted by his note-taking, closeted in his room over the weekend while the deals were reached? Or did his ambivalence over slavery anchor him to his chair when the deal played out that would help slave interests control the federal government for the next seventy-five years? Where was Randolph, the nominal head of delegation who presented the Virginia Plan? What of Mason, who despised the slave trade and took pride in speaking his mind to any audience on any occasion?

Whatever the reasons for the Virginians' reticence, it reflected an emerging reality of the Convention. Although Virginians initiated the process of writing a Constitution, they would not control it. The project would be remade by many other hands. James Wilson and John Rutledge, along with Sherman of Connecticut and Gouverneur Morris and a half-dozen others, would exert powerful influence over the next three months of deliberations.

Another emerging reality in mid-June was the heat.

By June 18 a Massachusetts delegate complained of being "quite overcome" by it, and not only New Englanders were suffering. Major Butler's wife left town because she "could not support the excessive heat of that climate," while Paterson of New Jersey described Philadelphia as "the warmest place I have been in." Indeed, the Convention's legend has always featured bewigged patriots mopping their brows in equatorial swelter while thrashing out a charter of liberty.

Although the delegates themselves were the source of that legend, records suggest that Philadelphia's summer of 1787 was not all that bad, at least no worse than most on America's often-humid East Coast. The sketchy diary of William Samuel Johnson, a Connecticut delegate, records "hot" or "very hot" on thirty-three of the eighty days for which he noted the weather; the frequency of the entry does not startle; it was, after all, summertime. Daily weather records maintained by Philadelphians also do not suggest an unusually hot season. A twentieth-century study concluded that "in general terms Philadelphia enjoyed a cool summer in 1787."

No one felt that way in the East Room of the State House. The Convention's secrecy rules worsened the problem, keeping the East Room's windows and doors firmly closed against eavesdroppers. Delegates gazed longingly through those windows, imagining cool zephyrs that would not be felt until the blessed arrival of quitting time. Eighteenth-century America had no practice of "casual dress," so the delegates were encased in coats, vests, and waistcoats, often made of suffocating wool. Those lucky enough to have linen suits (mostly southerners) fared slightly better.

The experience of the heat was enhanced by the urban character of Philadelphia. Homes made of stone or brick retained the day's warmth. One French visitor had found "the heat renders walking the streets intolerably inconvenient; the houses and footpaths being generally of brick, are not even cooled until some hours after sunset." A German visitor in June 1784 insisted that during a three-day period "not less than 30 sudden deaths were announced in the Philadelphia newspapers, martyrs to the heat by the coroners' returns." He agreed that "narrow streets, houses, and footways of brick . . . makes for a high degree of dead heat in the city."

Many worried especially about the deleterious impact of drinking the city's frosty well water after a day of scalding temperatures. A second Frenchman reported "it is no uncommon thing to see a laborer after quenching his thirst at a pump, drop down dead upon the spot." In early July of 1787, the Humane Society of Philadelphia published advice for countering the "fatal effects of drinking cold water, or cold liquids of any kind, in warm weather"; happily for the afflicted, the recommended treatments involved laudanum and rum.

The heat did not deter the delegates from seeking respite in Philadelphia's social life. Through the summer, General Washington attended receptions, readings, and plays. He heard concerts at the City Tavern staged by a European-trained musician recently arrived in the city. He dined with the Friendly Sons of St. Patrick and with the Society of the Cincinnati. He met with the Agricultural Society. On a Tuesday in mid-July, he and some other delegates enjoyed an afternoon at Gray's Ferry on the banks of the Schuylkill River.

Every Sunday morning, the General rode into the green country-side, free for a few hours of the Convention and the city, relishing the fresh air. He enjoyed stopping at farms to examine local practices in raising grapes or managing bees.

For Washington and the other delegates, though, most relaxation revolved around the homes of Philadelphia's elite. On ten evenings that summer Washington visited Mayor Samuel Powel's house; he spent seven at the home of Reese Meredith, an old friend. By midsummer the General was dining on Sundays with the Springsbury Club, a group of families associated with the Penns, descendants of the colony's founder. Washington records so many occasions on which he "drank tea" with Philadelphia hosts that one hopes the term was a euphemism for a stur-dier beverage.

A favored destination for the delegates was the home of William and Anne Bingham, a wealthy and handsome young couple. Washing-ton wrote of dining with them "in great splendor." Mrs. Bingham, who would be a leading hostess during Washington's presidency, was ad-mired for her beauty, her fashion, and her high spirits. Gilbert Stuart's portrait of her depicts a classic profile and a daring neckline. She is gen-erally acknowledged to have been Stuart's model for the figure of lib-erty on the "Draped Bust" coins minted in 1795.

A Kentucky visitor described a party in early June attended by forty people at Robert Morris's home. Guests played cards while Francis Hopkinson (who signed the Declaration of Independence) played a harpsichord of his own design. Several ladies also played and sang. In a menu touch that might account for Morris's corpulence, "before supper a profusion of iced creams was served."

Not all delegates were charmed by Philadelphia society. After only a week, George Mason wrote that he was growing "heartily tired of the etiquette and nonsense so fashionable in this city," complaining that it would "take me some months to make myself master of them." Then again, Mason could be quite the grouch. Oliver Ellsworth of Connecticut was equally cranky about the social niceties: "I mix with company without enjoying it and am perfectly tired with flattery and forms. To be very fashionable we must be very trifling. . . ."

Philadelphia society received negative reviews from other visitors. A few years later, Abigail Adams would describe the city's women as "rouged up to the ears" and fond of fashions so revealing that they "literally look like nursing mothers." A European found the ladies' bonnets "almost as varied as those seen in Paris," but scoffed that the women "pay a great deal of attention to their dresses and hairdos and are too obviously [a]ffected to be pleasing." A French visitor in 1791 was amused by the snobbery of these colonials. Philadelphians, he wrote, "whatever their origins may be," paint coats of arms on their carriage doors. Another Frenchman agreed that Philadelphia women coveted carriages "to a degree that approaches delirium."

Upon entering a Philadelphia dining room, Frenchmen tended to recoil like anthropologists stumbling upon a cannibals' feast. One marquis found it "truly barbarous" that "the first time you drink, and at the beginning of each dinner," the guest was to "call out successively to each individual, to let him know you drink his health." This "ridiculous comedy" could leave the guest "ready to die with thirst, whilst he is obliged to inquire the names, or catch the eyes" of twenty-five or thirty guests.

Through the evening anyone might ask, "Sir, will you permit me to drink a glass of wine with you?" Presented with such an inquiry, "you must agree, then pour out the glass, face each other, and drink it off." Another Frenchman found this practice "promoted a heavy consumption of alcohol," while a Briton called it "worthy of Creeks and Cherokees." If a guest could not toss off his glass, the other guests would hector him or lock the dining-room doors until he did.

The consequences were not for the squeamish. After a main course with roast meats and warm side dishes, followed by pastries, fruits, and nuts, the ladies would retire to some civilized refuge. At that point "the male guests invariably made a rush to the corner of the room to search for night tables and vases in which to relieve themselves in order to make room for more liquor."

Neither social niceties nor the gathering heat of summer would delay the conflicts in the Convention. As the delegates left the State House on June 11, the South Carolinians were the clear winners. When New Jersey and Pennsylvania issued reciprocal threats to bolt the union over representation, the southerners recognized their opportunity and pursued it deftly. With Rutledge going through the motions of pushing for quotas of contribution, General Pinckney executed the true strategy by seconding Wilson's motion for the three-fifths clause. A South Carolinian moved or seconded every motion in the sequence.

But for all of their adroitness on June 11, the southerners had not yet written the three-fifths rule into the Constitution. They had won only one battle, and only in the Committee of the Whole. The question would be debated again when the delegates reconvened as the Convention. New political factors would arise. Rutledge would deploy new strategies to protect the three-fifths rule, or even to improve the protections for slavery and southern interests. Some of Wilson's closest allies would come to rue the bargain he had struck.

Chapter Eight

Festina Lente

JUNE 12–19

EARLY ON, George Mason noted the Convention's grinding process of reevaluation and reconsideration, which moved "so slowly that it is impossible to judge when the business will be finished." "*Festina lente*," he joked, "may very well be called our motto." Translated loosely as "hurry slowly," the motto fit the debates over representation. With agonized deliberation, yet trying for speed, the delegates slogged through the representation issue until they fell into the sharpest confrontation of the summer.

Mason himself was proving something of a revelation to the delegates in the East Room. He arrived in Philadelphia with little reputation beyond Virginia; "the 140 miles he covered to get to the Convention was as far as he ever strayed from Gunston Hall." He had not held high office, not even in his own state. His pen had led Virginians to revolution through the Fairfax Resolves and Virginia's Declaration of Rights, and he served with honor in the state assembly. Yet Mason never was a member of Congress, nor did he serve in the Continental Army. When the Convention began, the sixty-two-year-old planter was unknown to most delegates.

Mason dove into the Convention's business. Having read widely and thought seriously about matters of government, he had much to offer. He took to his feet on each day during the first week. His years gave weight to his views, which were reinforced by his direct manner and plain lack of political ambition. When Edmund Randolph first met Mason, he noted the older man's "indifference for distinction . . . his hatred for pomp."

John Jay (not a delegate himself) knew all of the nation's leaders, yet met Mason for the first time that summer. Instantly impressed, Jay found the Virginian "a man of talents and a worthy companion. There are few with whom on so short an acquaintance I have been so much pleased." A Georgian at the Convention offered unqualified praise:

> Mr. Mason is a gentleman of remarkable strong powers and possesses a clear and copious understanding. He is able and convincing in debate, steady and firm in his principles.

The coming weeks would call for every ounce of Mason's wisdom.

On June 13, two days after adopting the three-fifths ratio, the Committee of the Whole issued its report. As amended, Randolph's resolutions had grown to nineteen. For the small-state delegates, they were a nightmare.

Ominously, the resolutions announced a "national" government. The term reeked of centralized power. Gone was the per-state voting that had *always* applied when the thirteen states gathered. Seats in both houses of Congress would be allocated on the basis of the number of free inhabitants plus three-fifths of all others (the slaves). Legislative powers were virtually undefined; Congress could act when the states were "incompetent," an ambiguity that unnerved those who mistrusted central government. The Committee of the Whole had even adopted Madison's scheme to let Congress override state laws. Staring at these appalling resolutions, delegates from New Jersey and Delaware resolved to redouble their efforts.

From today's perspective the showdown between small states and large states can seem as quaint as a minuet or a duel at dawn. Why would states as different as Massachusetts, Pennsylvania, and Virginia combine to the detriment of the smaller ones? As Madison and Wilson explained during the debates—first patiently, then with exasperation—the large states were not natural allies with reasons to oppress the others. Indeed, their interests varied widely.

The Massachusetts economy depended on fishing, Madison argued, Pennsylvania's on flour, and Virginia's on tobacco. The three states had never combined in the Confederation Congress. "Was a combination to be apprehended," Madison asked, "on the mere circumstance of equality of size?"

The small-state delegates were not persuaded. They bore bruises from high-handed actions by larger neighbors. Delaware and New Jersey suffered from Pennsylvania's tax and trade policies, while every state resented Virginia's grandiose claims to own the lands west of the Appalachians. It is human nature to mistrust those larger or more powerful, and the small-state delegates thought experience justified their mistrust.

Moreover, the large states were undeniably united in attacking the one-state/one-vote standard. Madison could declaim all day about the diverse interests of the large states, but they stood together now. What were they up to? What other schemes would unfold once the Big Three had effective control over Congress? What should the small-state delegates believe—Madison's ceaseless droning, or their own experience?

The issue also became entangled with whether and how the states themselves would survive. In 1787 that question was vexing. At a theoretical level, and a practical one, how could two sovereigns share power over the same place? Britain had imposed a strong central government on America, which fought a war to get rid of it.

Government responsibilities would have to be divided between the sovereigns, but what would happen when duties overlapped or conflicted? Could a central government have "energy" and "strength" yet allow a meaningful role for states?

William Paterson of New Jersey marshaled the small-state forces. Perhaps fittingly, he was recorded to be "of a very low stature." Best remembered as the namesake for a New Jersey city founded in 1791 as a

William Paterson (New Jersey)

model industrial community, Paterson was brought from Ireland as a toddler and grew up around the family store in Princeton. He attended the College of New Jersey shortly before Madison did. The Revolution swept Paterson from small-town law practice to be state attorney general, but his outlook remained parochial. Twice he declined a seat in the Confederation Congress in favor of his state duties and private law practice.

Madison confided in his notes that the small states broke into two groups. Connecticut and New York wanted to preserve the Articles in all of their inadequacy, he wrote, while New Jersey and Delaware would settle for equal votes in the legislature of any new government.

After the report of the Committee of the Whole, Paterson and his allies had only a few days to cobble together an alternative plan of government. On Friday, June 15, they presented what became known as the New Jersey Plan, though debate was put off for another day.

Like the Virginia Plan, New Jersey's alternative purported to enlarge and correct the Articles of Confederation; unlike the Virginia Plan, it actually did so. Some elements were common to both. The New

Jersey Plan gave Congress the power to regulate trade, though it would still have to make requisitions on the states for funds; those requisitions would be based on the number of free citizens plus three-fifths of all others. Congress would elect an executive for a single term and could remove him upon application by a majority of state governors. A national judiciary would apply the law of the United States, which would be supreme.

The central differences concerned the legislature and the process for amending the Constitution. The New Jersey alternative would continue a one-house Congress, with each state casting one vote, and with unanimity required for certain actions and the votes of nine states for others. Thus, the small states insisted not only on equal votes but also on scrapping the proposed Senate, which some delegates considered an important innovation. As Madison saw it, the Senate would be a small body of distinguished citizens who would act "with more coolness, with more system, and with more wisdom than the popular branch" of Congress.

When it came to amending the Constitution, George Mason distilled the relaxed attitude of the Virginia Plan. Because the Constitution "will certainly be defective," he said, "amendment[s] therefore will be necessary, and it will be better to provide for them in an easy, regular and constitutional way than to trust to chance and violence." In contrast, the New Jersey alternative continued the Articles' approach; amendments would have to be unanimously approved by the state legislatures.

The competing plans were debated on Saturday, June 16. Though the weather had cooled, the rhetoric remained heated. The oratorical contest was no even match.

John Lansing of New York led off for the small states. Then thirty-three years old and the mayor of Albany, Lansing had served as Speaker of the New York Assembly. A contemporary attributed to him "a hesitation in his speech," and legal knowledge that was "not extensive, nor [was] his education a good one." A stutterer of modest learning was not likely to impress the hard-eyed worthies in the East Room.

Lansing, followed by Paterson, kept the argument narrow. Both insisted that the delegates lacked authority to replace the Articles and that the people would reject any attempt to do so. Their presentations were restrained, even bloodless. The Jerseyman's concluding point demonstrated a curious instinct for the capillary, not the jugular: under the Virginia Plan, he argued, Congress would be too large and thus too expensive to maintain.

In rejoinder, Wilson dissected the New Jersey alternative *con brio*. The Pennsylvania delegate slashed through thirteen distinctions between the two plans, calling equal state votes "a poison contaminating every branch of government." He drew parallels to the Netherlands, to Rome under Caesar Augustus, and to the kings of ancient Sparta. Wilson dismissed the notion that the Convention could do no more than amend the Articles. Notes taken by Yates of New York almost tremble with the force of Wilson's conviction (and of Yates's dismay):

> As for himself, [Wilson] considers his powers to extend to every thing or nothing; and therefore that he has a right and is at liberty to agree to either plan or none. The people expect relief from their present embarrassed situation, and look up for it to this national convention; and it follows that they expect a national government.

After the Sunday recess, the heat returned on Monday morning, June 18. It was to be a big day. The delegates were ready to choose between the plans. The basic structure of the new government would be settled.

The balloting, however, never started. With a sure sense of the moment, Alexander Hamilton seized the Convention floor for the entire day. Unfortunately for him, he made poor use of it.

Though Hamilton was only thirty-two years old, his brilliance was widely granted. Slim and handsome, always dressed with meticulous style, he was an admired (if lengthy) speaker, spouting perfectly formed paragraphs and exuding a vital charisma. Hamilton's oratory was the stuff of opera—as was his life story.

Born to unmarried parents on an obscure island in the West Indies, Hamilton was effectively orphaned in his early teens. His childhood was one of anguish, loss, and poverty. John Adams captured its crude essence, if not the precise facts, when he called Hamilton "the bastard brat of a Scotch pedlar." Arriving in New York at the age of seventeen without family connections or wealth, Hamilton rose like a rocket. During the Revolution he was the indispensable aide to the indispensable Washington, finally winning a field command and glory at Yorktown. He married the daughter of a great New York landowner, Philip Schuyler, who became his political sponsor.

In matters of government, Hamilton was a prodigy. His precocious gifts in debate and public administration might even be compared with the musical prowess of an Austrian contemporary, Wolfgang Amadeus Mozart. Writing his first newspaper essay when he was twenty, Hamilton made his pen a mighty weapon, producing diatribes, monumental reports, and incisive analyses. He wrote in five months more than fifty of the essays in the landmark *Federalist* series, and was arguably the most prolific advocate on political issues this nation has seen. Jefferson invoked biblical diction when he noted ruefully, "Without numbers, he is an host unto himself."

As the first secretary of the treasury, Hamilton's muscular policies

Alexander Hamilton (New York)

restored the nation's tattered credit in a few short years. No less an observer than Talleyrand ranked him with Napoleon and Charles James
Fox of Britain as "the three greatest men of our epoch and, if I were
forced to decide between the three, I would give without hesitation the
first place to Hamilton."

Hamilton's fall would be as spectacular as his rise, combining a sor-
did public adultery, a mortifying loss of political influence, and the
death of his twenty-year-old son in a tragic duel. The final act was his
own death at age forty-eight in an equally senseless duel with that cyn-
ical archvillain, Vice President Aaron Burr. Pure opera.

But in Philadelphia in 1787, Hamilton embodied unlimited potential. He commanded the close attention of the delegates when he rose
on June 18. So far, he had been uncharacteristically quiet. Outvoted by
Yates and Lansing within the New York delegation, the dashing young
man chafed at his insignificance in the East Room. Worse, he detested
both plans before the Convention.

Hamilton wanted a powerful American government that would
never again leave its soldiers starving through bitter winters, or look on
helplessly while rebellious farmers closed the courts. Hamilton saw an
opportunity to offer a third choice other than the Virginia and New Jersey plans. With a bold enough stroke, his choice might catch fire and be
acclaimed. Glory goes to the daring, and Hamilton never lacked for
daring!

Though his timing was impeccable, Hamilton missed the mark on
substance. He would be haunted for years by accusations about what he
said in his daylong peroration, one of the "flagrant errors in his career."
Lulled by the promise that the Convention's deliberations were secret,
aiming to inspire a new vision of American government, Hamilton committed the unforgivable gaffe of the political naïf. He said what he
thought.

What he thought was that democracy was a poor basis for a government. "The voice of the people has been said to be the voice of God," he
told his colleagues, but "it is not true in fact. The people are turbulent
and changing; they seldom judge or determine right." Better to give
power to "the rich and well born," not to "the mass of the people." This
much of Hamilton's remarks, though baldly stated, was not wildly at

odds with the views of more than a few delegates. But he had more on his mind.

The states, for Hamilton, were a useless excrescence. The cost of a national government would be acceptable "if it eventuates in an extinction of state government," though states might be useful if "reduced to corporations, and with very limited powers." Even if a few of his listeners might agree with this sentiment in a private conversation, the act of proclaiming it to the Convention propelled Hamilton beyond the realm of the reckless and into the land of the foolhardy. No American politician in 1787 could seriously propose eliminating the states.

Hamilton still was not through. In the passages that would most torment him in the future, he came perilously close to demanding an American king. "[N]o good executive could be established on Republican principles," he assured the delegates. "The English model was the only good one." British government "was the best in the world," and "he doubted whether any thing short of it would do in America."

To demonstrate that this was no idle chatter, Hamilton proposed that the chief executive serve for his entire life. Anticipating the objection that this would create a "monarch"—after all, Americans had bled and died for eight years to rid themselves of George III—he blithely observed that "Monarch is an indefinite term" and that *any* executive would function like a monarch, even if only for a term of years. Senators, too, Hamilton said, should serve for life.

In closing, Hamilton memorably belittled the choice between the Virginia and New Jersey alternatives. The two, he said, were both "pork still, with a little change of the sauce."

Hamilton certainly had offered a distinctive cuisine, but the delegates were not tantalized. Despite his charm and fluency, at some point in his speech—perhaps in its fourth hour, or maybe in the fifth—the delegates must have marveled at the epic scope of his miscalculation.

Madison rose the next morning to perform his own disembowelment of the New Jersey alternative. He never mentioned Hamilton's proposal, nor did any other speaker that day. A Connecticut delegate interred Hamilton's efforts two days later. Though Hamilton "has been praised by everybody, he has been supported by none."

Some have professed to find in this episode a dexterous Hamiltonian strategy. By staking out an extreme position favoring a powerful central government, the theory goes, Hamilton made the Virginia Plan seem moderate, and thus achieved his true goal when the New Jersey Plan was rejected. The theory does not match the facts. On June 18, no matter what Hamilton said, the Virginia Plan was well on the way to approval by the large-state/slave-state alliance that Wilson and Rutledge had brokered.

Moreover, Hamilton started backtracking on the following day, saying that he meant for the states only to be extinguished "as states," though they could continue as "subordinate jurisdictions." Had Hamilton intended only to offer a stalking horse for the Virginia Plan, he had little need to bother with the explanation.

In contrast, Madison's address on June 19 drew on the Virginian's long preparation for the Convention, assembling insights from his correspondence and memoranda over the preceding year. Its learning was ferocious, its logic irresistible. He enumerated the violations of the Articles by different states, which the New Jersey Plan could not bring to an end. Madison pointed out that "the great difficulty lies in the affair of representation [in the legislature]; and if this could be adjusted, all others would be surmountable." But, as was his pattern through the summer, Madison offered no compromise. On June 19, thanks to Wilson and Rutledge, he had no need of compromise. His side had the votes.

The balloting was not close. The large-state/slave-state alliance held firm, with Connecticut joining to make a 7–3 margin. (Maryland again divided equally and cast no vote.) The Virginia Plan was triumphant.

Connecticut's incongruous position was the thorn buried within the flower of that triumph. Neither a large state nor a slave state, why had it joined that alliance? What deep strategy was it following?

The Connecticut delegation was a respected one, led by Roger Sherman, who had signed both the Declaration of Independence and the Articles of Confederation. Sherman married confounding qualities, combining a fierce shrewdness with an ungainliness that observers struggled to describe.

He was tall, with blue eyes and thick brown hair that was crudely cut and never powdered. John Adams wrote that "Sherman's air is the

*Roger Sherman (Connecticut) by Thomas Hicks, after
Ralph Earl, c. 1866*

reverse of grace [and] there cannot be a more striking contrast to beautiful action than the motion of his hands." One delegate described Sherman as "the oddest shaped character" and "unaccountably strange." Yet another received this warning from a friend: "[Sherman] is as cunning as the Devil, and if you attack him, you ought to know him well; he is not easily managed, but if he suspects you are trying to take him in, you may as well catch an eel by the tail."

There were few ways to make a living that Sherman had not tried. He started as a cobbler, becoming in turn a surveyor, a farmer, a land trader, a writer of almanacs, a lawyer, a storekeeper, and treasurer of Yale College. Though never rich, Sherman spent his last twenty years in public service, as a justice of the peace and mayor in New Haven, also as a judge and a member of Congress.

From all his vocations Sherman developed a sound political judgment and a gravitas that shone through his peculiar mien. One delegate wrote that "no man has a better heart or a clearer head," while Thomas Jefferson offered the tribute that Sherman "never said a foolish thing in his life." On June 11 he lost the balloting on equal state votes in the Senate because he ignored his own political rule: "When you are in a minority, talk; when you are in a majority, vote." He had called for a vote he could not win. He would not make that mistake again.

As the summer wore on, Sherman and his Connecticut brethren chipped away at the Virginia Plan, ultimately undermining the large-state/slave-state alliance. The consequences for the government would be dramatic.

With the alliance forged by Wilson and Rutledge still ascendant, the delegates dissolved as the Committee of the Whole and reconstituted themselves as the Convention. General Washington resumed the presiding chair. The next task was to put flesh on the bare bones of the plan's nineteen resolutions.

On the day that the Virginia Plan was adopted, a North Carolinian wrote, "We move slowly in our business; it is indeed a work of great delicacy and difficulty, impeded at every step by jealousies and jarring interests."

The slow pace strained the budgets of many delegates. Though the wealthy Mason exulted that "the living is cheap" in Philadelphia, delegates from New Jersey and North Carolina wrote to state officials for additional stipends. By July, the Virginians were drawing extra funds, and a Massachusetts delegate urgently sought help from home to pay his bills. William Samuel Johnson of Connecticut moved from the City Tavern to more frugal lodgings. John Rutledge, complaining that "[w]hen I left Charleston, I had no idea of staying here half as long as I have," asked relatives back home to cover some bills that were falling due. Two weeks before the Convention finished in September, a North Carolinian confided that he would have to borrow money to get home, which he found "extremely distressing."

Yet no delegate left Philadelphia because of money shortages. By mid-June, after almost a month in session, the men of the Convention appreciated how important the work was, especially as it grew more delicate and difficult.

Despite the rejection of the New Jersey alternative, much remained unresolved. The small-state delegates were not prepared to give up equal state votes. The Convention had still to imagine a national executive who would not become a monarch, and how to select him. They also had to accommodate the western expansion of the nation.

And slavery, as well, was not through with them.

Chapter Nine

To the Brink

JUNE 21–JULY 10

BY LATE JUNE, James Madison was worried. After five weeks in session, the Convention was still stalled over how to structure the new Congress. The delegates argued over it on June 20 and on June 21, on June 25 and again on June 26. No question, no matter how simple, seemed ever to be resolved; each would come before the Convention a second time, or a third, even a fourth. Should the Congress have one house or two? Should representatives be chosen on the basis of districts? How should senators be chosen? How long should terms of office be?

On June 27, the restless Rutledge tried to shoulder the delegates ahead. He moved that they consider the "most fundamental points" of how to select members of Congress. Rutledge's shove was immediately countered by Luther Martin of Baltimore, one of the flamboyant figures of the summer. The attorney general of Maryland, Martin was a trial lawyer given to bombast on a numbing scale. Though the passage of centuries has petrified many Framers into marble figures, eons could not do that to Luther Martin. In describing his successful defense of Aaron Burr on treason charges, Henry Adams portrayed

the rollicking witty, audacious Attorney-General of Maryland . . .
drunken, generous, slovenly, grand; . . . shouting with a school-
boy's fun at the idea of tearing [the] indictment to pieces and
teaching the Virginia democrats some law,—the notorious reprobate genius, Luther Martin.

Martin's contemporaries were transfixed by the man's "utter disregard of good taste and refinement in his dress and language." As remembered by Roger Taney, who served three decades as chief justice of
the Supreme Court, Martin was "as coarse and unseemly at a dinner-
table, in his manner of eating, as he was in everything."

After watching Martin argue a case in 1808, another future
Supreme Court justice struggled to explain the man's eminence. He
found Martin to be of "about middle size" whose "dress is slovenly," yet
consisting of a "singular compound of strange qualities."

He labors hard to acquire [wealth], and yet cannot preserve [it].
Experience, however severe, never corrects a single habit. I have
heard anecdotes of improvidence and thoughtlessness which
astonish me . . . You should hear of Luther Martin's fame from
those who have known him long and intimately, but you should not
see him.

On that late June day in 1787, Luther Martin rose to denounce the
Virginia Plan. He kept at the job for more than three hours, decrying the
looming "system of slavery" for the ten small states. Yates of New York,
who *agreed* with Martin, found the Marylander's remarks so "diffuse,
and in many instances desultory, [that] it was not possible . . . to meth-
odize his ideas into a systematic or argumentative arrangement."

By midafternoon, Martin professed himself "too exhausted . . . to
finish" but promised to resume the next morning. To his colleagues' chagrin, he was as good as his word. In a harsh printed exchange after the
Convention, Oliver Ellsworth of Connecticut suggested that Martin
would have spoken for "two months, but for those marks of fatigue and
disgust you saw strongly expressed on whichever side of the house you
turned your mortified eyes."

In more concise remarks, other small-state delegates echoed Martin's sentiments on the "most fundamental" question that John Rutledge had posed. They bewailed their looming enslavement to the large states and spurned the reassurances offered by delegates from those states. The same rhetorical ground was plowed and replowed.

Finally, Dr. Franklin urged the delegates humbly to recognize the role of the Almighty by beginning each session with a prayer. Exhibiting the political tone-deafness that afflicted him through this phase of the Convention, Hamilton opposed prayer. Its commencement, he cautioned, might lead the public to form "unpleasant animadversions" about their progress. In any event, another chimed in, there were no funds to pay for a minister to lead them in prayer, so none was brought in.

Only three weeks before, the alliance forged by Wilson and Rutledge had defeated the New Jersey Plan, yet the small-state delegates were still fighting, insisting that each state have an equal vote in the Senate. They honored Roger Sherman's maxim now; they were in the minority, so they kept on talking.

As Madison reflected on the stalemate, he made an intuitive leap that disregarded the words being spoken. He concluded that slavery was causing the stalemate, though no delegate had mentioned it for more than two weeks.

Madison started to explain his insight on June 29. The largest danger to the new government, he said, was "the great southern and northern interests of the continent, being opposed to each other." Showing an ingenuous belief that facts could persuade, he instructed the delegates: "Look to the votes in congress, and most of them stand divided by the geography of the country, not according to the size of the states."

The Virginian returned to this theme the next day. Oliver Ellsworth, a judge of Connecticut's Supreme Court, was leading the small states' push for equal state votes in the Senate. He argued that large states could protect themselves through the House of Representatives, which would be based on population, so the small states needed a similar means to protect themselves.

Madison restated the debate. The true division, Madison said, was between states "having or not having slaves." Government had to recognize significant opposing interests and give each a sufficient power to protect itself. If any interest in America was entitled to such "defensive power," he continued, "it ought to be mutually given to these two interests"—the slave and the nonslave. He was "so strongly impressed with this important truth that he had been casting about in his mind for some expedient that would answer the purpose."

Madison's "expedient" was simplicity itself. One house of the legislature should represent slave interests. The other should not. He explained:

> [R]epresent[ation] in one branch should be according to the number of free inhabitants only; and in the other according to the whole [number] counting the slaves as (if) free. By this arrangement the Southern scale would have the advantage in one house, and the Northern in the other.

Madison thus proposed to define the two houses of Congress in terms of slavery, imprinting the practice deep in the nation's genetic material. One part of Congress would have the specific duty of protecting slavery.

The proposal died of neglect. No one but Madison commented on it for the remaining eleven weeks of deliberations.

Why had he set off on such a quixotic initiative with no visible allies? Had he projected onto the Convention's impasse his own turmoil as an ambivalent slave owner? Such a misjudgment would be rare for Madison, who was ordinarily a perceptive political observer.

A better explanation is that Madison was picking at the scab that was irritating the entire Convention, even if no one was willing to acknowledge it. As the summer wore on, acrimony would run high between slaveholders and some northern delegates, finally driving the irascible Major Butler to bellow that southerners wanted to protect their slaves against the designs of other delegates to free them.

Were abolitionist remarks being made in taverns or in the State House corridors? Were southerners grousing among themselves about the antislavery views of Dr. Franklin, young Hamilton, and others? When Madison spoke on June 30, slavery was still the elephant in the parlor around which the delegates decorously stepped. The coming weeks would show that he correctly saw slavery as a core problem, though his remedy appealed to no one. Slavery was a nerve too raw for the Convention to confront as directly as Madison proposed. Instead, the delegates would circle the question, passing ever closer until they could avoid it no longer. The process needed more time.

This episode also illustrates how the traditional view of Madison as "Father of the Constitution" does not reflect the reality of the Convention. With his intelligence and learning, he commanded the respect of every delegate. As one wrote of Madison, admiration scrambling his syntax, "The affairs of the United States, he has the most correct knowledge of, of any man in the union."

In truth, the Virginian more often came out on the short end of contests at the Convention. By one scholar's count, "of seventy-one specific proposals that Madison moved, seconded, or spoke unequivocally in regard to, he was on the losing side forty times." Madison himself was modest about his contributions. In the year before his death, he rejected the statement that he was "the writer of the Constitution." The charter was not, he insisted, "the offspring of a single brain. It ought to be regarded as the work of many heads and many hands." Indeed it ought.

Madison's undistinguished win-loss percentage should not surprise. He was more committed than most delegates to a strong national government, as reflected in his unsuccessful crusade to give Congress the power to veto state laws. Moreover, the path of the Convention would be away from Virginia's proposals as other delegates pressed other perspectives, and then made them stick.

After Madison returned to his writing table on June 30, his proposal stillborn, the tension in the East Room continued to build. Dr. Franklin appealed for compromise with a homely image from carpentry:

> A joiner, when he wants to fit two boards, takes off with his plane the uneven parts from each side, and thus they fit. Let us do the same.

But trimming rough edges was not the spirit of that day. A New Jersey delegate raged that selecting Congress on the basis of population would create "an amphibious monster." Inspired by overheated rhetoric and annoyed by the arrogance of the large-state/slave-state allies, Gunning Bedford took to his feet. He was Delaware's attorney general. Stout and emotional, on that hot, muggy afternoon Bedford proceeded to deliver "the most intemperate speech uttered at the Convention."

Bedford challenged the large-state/slave-state allies. Georgia, North Carolina, and South Carolina ("puffed up with the possession of her wealth and her negroes") had "united with the great states." They patronized the other states, and Bedford would brook it no longer. Defiantly, he proclaimed, "I do not, gentlemen, trust you. If you possess the power, the abuse of it could not be checked; and what then would prevent you from exercising it to our destruction?" The prospect before him terrified: "Will you crush the smaller states?"

Not content with denouncing his colleagues personally, Bedford turned treasonous. "[S]ooner than be ruined" by the large-state/slave-state allies, the small states could turn to "some foreign ally of more honor and good faith, who will take them by the hand and do them justice."

His words electrified the roomful of men who had hazarded their all to fight the British Empire, who lost comrades and loved ones in that cause. Four years after that war, were the states going to turn on each other, allied with competing European powers? The prospect was outrageous.

Ellsworth of Connecticut, saddled with this woefully injudicious ally, hurriedly tendered a less explosive statement of the small states' position, but Rufus King of Massachusetts would not let the matter pass. King expressed amazement that the Delaware delegate was proposing to (in Madison's note) "take a foreign power by the hand!" The awful phrase resonated through the room. "I hope," King continued, "[Bedford] is able to excuse it to himself on the score of passion."

Fortunately, Bedford's outburst came at the end of the day, and a Saturday at that. The delegates had the next day off. Tempers could cool and fertile imaginations could search for a way out of the representation cul-de-sac. George Mason knew that the Convention was at a crucial crossroads. He wrote to a friend, "[T]wo or three days will probably en-able us to judge—which is at present very doubtful—whether any sound and effectual system can be established or not."

When the delegates reconvened on Monday, July 2, Ellsworth promptly presented a motion calling for equal state votes in the Senate. The small states had placed all their hopes on this measure, which Roger Sherman had lost on June 11 by a 6–5 margin. By Sherman's axiom, if the small states wanted to vote again, something had changed. The delegates sat anxiously as the roll call began. Massachusetts voted first, then Connecticut, then New York. Was the Convention going to make a momentous shift, or only spin its wheels again?

After ten states had voted—all the delegations through South Car-olina—nothing had changed from the vote of June 11. The count was 5–5. The two Carolinas had joined the three large states (Pennsylvania, Virginia, and Massachusetts) in voting no. Georgia had yet to vote.

The defeat of Ellsworth's motion should have been a foregone con-clusion. For the last three weeks, all four Georgia delegates had been faithful to the alliance between large states and slave states. Even though thinly settled, Georgia was growing fast and expected to be a large state soon. Its delegates supported representation based on popu-lation, along with the three-fifths ratio.

But on this morning, a good deal had changed in the Georgia dele-gation.

Two of the Georgians were also members of the Confederation Congress then sitting in New York City; the state's assembly had ap-pointed them to both bodies to save the expense of sending additional Georgians up North. Those two had just left for New York.

So only two Georgians were in the East Room on Monday, July 2. If one changed his vote, the state would shift from 4–0 against Ellsworth's motion to a 1–1 deadlock.

Suddenly, the spotlight of history fell on Abraham Baldwin, a gen-uinely obscure figure until this moment, and again ever after. A native of Connecticut, Baldwin had abandoned his training as a minister in favor of the law. He moved to Georgia only three years before the Con-vention, but rose quickly in that small community. On the morning of July 2, without offering a word of explanation, he changed the path of

Abraham Baldwin (Georgia)

the Convention by switching his position. He supported equal state votes in the Senate, deadlocking Georgia and canceling its vote.

The delegates were shocked. The final count on Ellsworth's motion was 5–5–1. Under the rules, the motion failed, but that did not matter. The small states had done it. They had stopped the large-state/slave-state juggernaut. The momentum shift was seismic. Now the stalemate was real.

In a long public career after the Convention, which included three terms in the United States Senate, Baldwin never explained his switch on July 2. The only contemporary explanation came from Luther Martin of Maryland, who ascribed it to the Georgian's belief that the small-state delegates "would go home, and thereby dissolve the convention, before we would give up the question." According to a report attributed to Jonathan Dayton of New Jersey, the small-state delegates had indeed resolved to leave if they did not prevail on the issue.

To explain Baldwin's action, even his biographer can only speculate that some form of Connecticut solidarity changed his mind.

Baldwin had spent a number of years in New Haven, where Roger Sherman was the leading citizen. Baldwin and Oliver Ellsworth boarded together in New York while they both served in Congress, and Baldwin referred to Ellsworth as his "chum." Later in July, Baldwin hoped to travel with Sherman and William Samuel Johnson (the third Connecticut delegate), though the trip fell through. Noah Webster, another Connecticut Yale man summering in Philadelphia, twice called on Baldwin and Johnson together, revealing some friendship between them.

That Connecticut connection seems to have been of prime importance on the second day of July. Somehow, Sherman and his colleagues persuaded Baldwin "to save the Convention" from the dissolution that Luther Martin thought inevitable.

But the scrum did not end with Baldwin's switch. As the tally was announced, Daniel Jenifer of Maryland entered the East Room for the first time that day. The quick-witted Rufus King immediately noted the arrival and saw an opportunity. Maryland had cast its vote with the small states, avoiding its usual intradelegation deadlock, solely because of Jenifer's absence. As Luther Martin described it, King, relying "on Mr. Jenifer to divide the State of Maryland on this question . . . requested of the President [Washington] that the question might be put again."

All eyes turned to the General. If the ballot were conducted again, and Maryland's delegation were divided by Jenifer's vote, the large-state/slave-state allies would eke out a 5–4–2 victory for proportional representation in the Senate. The small states would be turned back. The anxious room awaited the General's ruling.

Some of Washington's contemporaries liked to disparage his intellectual gifts. John Adams wrote, "That he was too illiterate, unlearned, unread for his station and reputation is equally past dispute." Only slightly more generous, Jefferson observed that the General had "neither copiousness of ideas nor fluency of words."

But Washington had solid judgment and an uncanny feel for the moment. Whether from his own sense of fair play, or because he, too, believed the small states were about to bolt the Convention, or because he knew that Jenifer had missed the vote on purpose because he (like Baldwin) wished to favor the small states, the General squelched King's maneuver. He refused to allow a second vote.

The tie left the Convention adrift, hopelessly deadlocked. Searching for words to express his "alarm," Charles Pinckney of South Carolina offered a fanciful proposal from his own constitutional plan: that the nation be divided into four equal districts, each of which would elect representatives to the Senate.

General Pinckney tepidly supported his cousin's notion, then offered a procedural evasion. The Convention might appoint a "Committee consisting of a member from each State . . . to devise and report some compromise." Sherman concurred, noting that the delegates were "at a full stop." With the tide turning against them, James Wilson and Madison opposed a committee, but they were overridden.

The delegates selected committees by ballot, the only occasions on which they voted as individuals rather than by state delegation. Both Madison and Wilson were left off the committee, whose membership augured ill for their cause. This first Committee of Eleven included aggressive small-state delegates (Paterson of New Jersey, Sherman of Connecticut, Luther Martin of Maryland, the wrathful Bedford of Delaware). The choices from the large states, though, were men of a more moderate temper on this issue (Franklin, Mason, Gerry). The tide was strong in favor of the smaller states.

With an exasperated sigh, the Convention took a three-day recess in honor of the Fourth of July holiday.

Washington dined that evening at the Indian Queen with "some of the members of the Convention." Was the General attempting to salve bruised feelings from the fierce debates? Did the diners plan strategy for the Committee of Eleven? It is impossible that the subjects did not arise.

The next day was the hottest in Philadelphia that July, and the committee's discussion was equally fiery. The chair, Gerry of Massachusetts, reported that the Senate representation issue was "so serious as to threaten a dissolution of the Convention." Martin of Maryland recalled that the delegates were "scarce held together by the strength of an hair."

Biding his time through harsh exchanges, Dr. Franklin waited for the committee members to wear themselves out. Then he spoke in his most reasonable, informal manner. He proposed an arrangement which has been called the "Great Compromise": The House of Representatives would be elected from districts of up to 40,000 persons; as a sop to the large states, that House would have the sole power to originate tax and spending legislation; and the small states would get equal votes in the Senate.

As the unquestioned senior figure at the Convention—old enough to be Washington's father, or Madison's grandfather—Franklin consciously played the role of conciliator. He disagreed with much of the final Constitution. As one biographer has noted, he was "far more comfortable with democracy than most of the delegates." He preferred a

Benjamin Franklin (Pennsylvania)

one-house legislature, a three-man executive with limited powers, and no salaries for public officials. Yet Franklin was less concerned with the specifics than that there be a Constitution at all.

A prominent Philadelphian, Dr. Benjamin Rush, described Franklin's participation in the Convention as "daily a spectacle of transcendent benevolence." Though kidney stones and other ailments sometimes kept him away from the East Room, Franklin wrote afterward that the "exercise of going and returning from the State House has done me good." Throughout the summer, he hosted dinner gatherings at which he encouraged goodwill across the state delegations.

Some of his colleagues were not sure what to make of the august octogenarian. As captured in the notes of a Georgia delegate, he was "well known to be the greatest philosopher of the present age . . . the very heavens obey him." Yet something about him did not impress. He had little physical presence. One visitor that summer described him as "a short, fat, trunched old man in a plain Quaker dress, bald pate and short white locks."

It was more than appearance. Franklin did not carry himself like a great man. He made no ringing speeches, often preferring to have James Wilson read his remarks. His first major address to the Convention (read by Wilson) proposed that public officials not be paid, a suggestion that commanded no support. In the words of the Georgian, "It is certain that he does not shine much in public council—he is no speaker, nor does he seem to let politics engage his attention."

In fact, Franklin sometimes spoke not to engage but to defuse. He suggested prayer. He compared the work of the Convention to that of a carpenter. He told jokes. Even the humorless Madison recorded Franklin's tale of how Scottish lawyers elevate to judgeships the "ablest of the profession in order to get rid of him, and share his practice among themselves." (It was probably funnier when Franklin told it; the Georgia delegate admitted that Franklin "tells a story in a style more engaging than anything I ever heard.")

At the protracted meeting of this first Committee of Eleven, Franklin waited out the younger men on the hottest day in July. Showing the pragmatic gifts he had applied to scientific and political problems all his life, Franklin sifted through the proposals before the Convention, selecting some to satisfy large states, and some for small states. Assembling them in a balanced package at the end of a day of sweltering conflict, he suggested the compromise that the committee, grudgingly, adopted.

The Convention featured powerful intellects like Wilson and Madison. Gifted orators like Hamilton and Gouverneur Morris gave passionate speeches. Deft political operators like Rutledge and Sherman crafted important alliances. Washington's presence centered the proceedings. Yet with his disarming wisdom, cheerful countenance, and benign age, Franklin contributed as much as anyone to the Convention's success.

Though Franklin persuaded the committee to accept the compromise, no one knew if the full Convention would.

At this critical point, Philadelphia's Fourth of July festivities served as a reminder of how much the nation was depending on the delegates. The city saluted American independence with parades, artillery salutes of "thirteen times three rounds," church bells, and fireworks. A local newspaper wrote that the Convention would provide "a system of government adequate to the security and preservation of those rights which were promulgated by the ever memorable Declaration of Independency."

Philadelphia offered many entertainments on the great day. General Washington visited Dr. Chavett's wax museum. Pennsylvania militia officers drank thirteen toasts, beginning with one to Congress, then to the Convention, to Louis XVI of France, all the way down to the wish that "Rhode Island be excluded [from] the union until they elect honest men to rule them."

The holiday also brought ironies. A taste near to bile might have come to delegates who attended the oration of a local law student. "Is the science of government so difficult," the student asked, "that we have not men among us capable of unfolding its mysteries and binding our states together?" The words came from someone who had never ar-

gued with Gunning Bedford or James Wilson. Though General Washington's composure was always steady, other delegates might have in-
dulged a light snort or rueful smile in response.

When Franklin's compromise came before the Convention on July
5, it was already an orphan. Those committee members who opposed
equal state votes in the Senate, Gerry told the delegates, "have only assented conditionally; and if the other side do not generally agree will
not be under any obligation to support the Report." Immediately, delegates vied to denounce the proposal.

Madison disparaged giving the "exclusive privilege of originat-
ing money bills" to the House of Representatives, the concession to
the large states. Similar limitations in state constitutions had been
easily evaded, he said, a view that Major Butler of South Carolina
shared. Madison denounced equal state votes in the Senate as an "injustice."

The excitable Gouverneur Morris provided some *post hoc* justifica-
tion for Gunning Bedford's appeal to foreign powers. Flirting with
sanctimony, Morris said he came to the Convention "as a representative
of the whole human race" but found "that we are assembled to truck
and bargain for our particular states." Many jaws clenched when Morris compared the states to serpents whose teeth must be removed, then
predicted that "[t]his Country must be united. If persuasion does not
unite it, the sword will."

Nerves strung taut by incendiary rhetoric, the delegates gave in to
peevish feelings, descending to personal comments. Bedford of
Delaware criticized Morris's choice of language; a North Carolinian
pleaded for calm, then pointed out that Gorham of Massachusetts had
been intemperate, too; Paterson of New Jersey complained of how
Madison and Morris "had treated the small states."

Delegates spoke openly of throwing in the towel and quitting the
Convention. A Georgia delegate later remembered "serious thoughts of
adjourning without doing anything."

Gerry of Massachusetts called for compromise. In the stammer that
one delegate mocked as "a profusion of those hems that never fail to
lengthen out and enliven his oratory," Gerry admitted that he had "very
material objections" to his own committee's report. He strove to put a

less offensive face on Morris's reference to swords: "If we do not come to some agreement among ourselves some foreign sword will probably do the work for us."

Mason, another committee member, spoke passionately in favor of moderation. He pleaded with the delegates to persevere. "[H]owever liable the [Committee's] report might be to objections," he said, it was "preferable to an appeal to the world by the different sides, as had been talked of by some gentlemen." The Virginian issued a personal commitment to see the Constitution-writing process through to the end:

> It could not be more inconvenient to any gentleman to remain absent from his private affairs than it was for him: but [Mason said] he would bury his bones in this city rather than expose his country to the consequences of a dissolution of the Convention without anything being done.

Most of the delegates heeded Mason's plea and stayed in Philadelphia, but they did not hurry to vote on Franklin's compromise. For the next eleven days of sizzling heat, they chewed over the representation question. Previous alliances dissolved. Leading delegates vacillated between fury over the positions taken by others and a resigned search for some other way out of the thicket in which they were snagged. Yates and Lansing of New York did leave Philadelphia, never to return. (Hamilton had already fled to meet other obligations in New York City.)

The delegates grew depressed over the lack of progress. A North Carolinian wrote that the "diverse and almost opposite interests that are to be reconciled, occasion us to progress very slowly." Rufus King wrote to a friend that the Convention had not "progressed a single step since you left us." A New Jersey delegate sounded the same note, telling Governor William Livingston that in the last ten days "we have not made the least progress in the business."

The immediate cause of these lamentations was the Convention's descent into unvarnished power politics. By allocating representatives at a rate of one per 40,000 residents, Dr. Franklin's compromise focused the delegates on exactly how many representatives each state would have in a new government. Gouverneur Morris may not have come to "truck and bargain" for Pennsylvania (after all, his home was in New York), but plenty of delegates wished to do exactly that on behalf of their states.

Growing enamored of the committee device, on July 6 the Convention appointed a five-man panel to allocate representatives to each state. Because only five delegates were chosen, the large states used their greater number of delegates to pack the committee. Its members included Gouverneur Morris of Pennsylvania, along with Gorham and King from Massachusetts and Randolph of Virginia. The fifth member, the ubiquitous Rutledge of South Carolina, would be the champion committee member of the summer, serving on five (and chairing three) before the Convention was done.

While waiting for the new committee to report, Wilson attempted to rally the large-state/slave-state alliance, but it crumbled in his hands. With two state delegations deadlocked (including Massachusetts, a large state), the Convention voted for equal state votes in the Senate. Matters looked better and better for the small states.

The committee of five proposed fifty-six members for the House of Representatives, starting with one each for Rhode Island and Delaware and progressing up to nine for Virginia. Congress could alter the allocations "upon the principles of their wealth [a concession to Rutledge and the Southerners] and number of inhabitants." Roger Sherman demanded to know "on what principles or calculations the Report was founded." He received the offhand response that the "general guide" was "[t]he number of blacks and whites with some regard to supposed wealth." Gouverneur Morris added airily that the allocations were "little more than a guess."

With a concrete proposal before them for how many representatives each state would have, the political conflicts became more fierce. Madison's diagnosis that slavery was central began to reverberate. Paterson of New Jersey challenged counting three-fifths of the slaves:

> He could regard negro slaves in no light but as property. They are no free agents, have no personal liberty, no faculty of acquiring property, but on the contrary are themselves property, and like other property entirely at the will of the master. Has a man in

Virginia a number of votes in proportion to the number of his slaves? And if Negroes are not represented in the states to which they belong, why should they be represented in the [national] government[?]

Paterson beckoned his colleagues back to "the true principle of representation," which he said was "an expedient by which an assembly . . . chosen by the people is substituted in place of the inconvenient meeting of the people themselves." Because slaves could not vote in such a meeting, they should not be represented.

Neither Paterson nor any other delegate followed the logical steps of his reasoning: just as slaves would not vote in meetings of "the people" in 1787, women could vote only in New Jersey (and in 1807 they would be disenfranchised in that state). The simple ability of wives to hold property, or even to have a legal identity, was limited at best. Equally, Paterson did not address the perversity of granting "representation" to slaves by increasing the influence of those who owned them, thus enhancing the owners' powers of oppression.

Leaping to his feet, Madison tripped Paterson up on a different point. If the gentleman from New Jersey was correct about "his doctrine of representation," Madison crowed, then that doctrine "must for ever silence the pretensions of small states to an equality of votes with the large ones." The Virginian continued, "They [the states] ought to vote in the same proportion in which their citizens would do, if the people of all the States were collectively met." It no longer mattered, if it ever had, that Madison could outthink Paterson. The Jerseyman had the votes. The states would be equal in the Senate.

Madison even tried to use Paterson's comments to revive his proposal that one legislative branch be based on only free inhabitants, with seats allocated to the second branch "according to the whole number, including slaves." Once more the Convention ignored Madison; no delegate even acknowledged his renewed suggestion.

As it adjourned on July 9, the Convention established another Committee of Eleven to reconsider the allocation of representatives among the states. John Rutledge, of course, was a member.

After another night of bargaining, the new Committee of Eleven proposed sixty-five members for the House of Representatives, adding five for northern states but only four for the southern. The South Carolinians responded with a flurry of motions to change the number of representatives assigned to specific states; all of them failed.

Having devoted most of six weeks to the question of representation, the delegates yearned to be done with it. But it was not to be. The question was about to be mingled with the explosive slavery issue; once that happened, both would simmer and boil for several more days.

The most violent outburst was triggered by a superficially innocuous provision. As the Convention limped toward adjournment on July 10, Edmund Randolph stood. As Virginia's floor leader, he wielded the prestige of the largest state. On this occasion, he moved for a regular census of the nation's population, which would provide the basis for allocating representatives as the population shifted in the future.

The suggestion seems straightforward. The people should be counted from time to time. Even the Romans did that. Yet the proposal focused the Convention on that elephant in the parlor. Which people should be counted? And how much should each count for? Three-fifths? One? Zero? The Virginian's motion inflamed the differences between slave and nonslave states.

On that evening of July 10, Washington wrote to Hamilton, who was still in New York. In the two weeks since Hamilton had left Philadelphia, matters were "if possible, in a worse train than ever; you will find but little ground on which the hope of a good establishment can be formed." The General "almost despair[ed] of seeing a favorable issue to the proceedings of the Convention."

The General confided to his former aide how frustrated he was with the "men who oppose a strong and energetic government." They were "narrow minded politicians or"—here the General tried to rein in his anger—"are under the influence of local views." The question before the Convention, he insisted, was not whether the public will or "will not accede to" the new government, but whether it was "the best form."

Washington's near-despair restrained his social life. For five of the next six nights he dined at home with the Robert Morrises and retired to his room for the evening. It was no time for conviviality.

Chapter Ten

The Small States Win

JULY 11–17

B Y WEDNESDAY, July 11, the delegates were running out of steam. As Madison remembered it, the "eloquent appeals to the members had been exhausted" since "their minds were too much made up to be susceptible of new impressions." With slavery back before the Convention and the small states near victory, emotion predominated over reason.

It started over the three-fifths ratio. Gouverneur Morris had been away from Philadelphia when the ratio was adopted. Upon returning in early July, he began to probe, sometimes painfully, for an alternative to the Wilson-Rutledge bargain. On July 12, his efforts pushed William Davie of North Carolina, a largely silent backbencher, to the breaking point. Announcing "it was high time to speak out," the future founder of the University of North Carolina was defiant:

[Davie] saw that it was meant by some gentlemen to deprive the Southern States of any share of Representation for the blacks. He was sure that North Carolina would never confederate on any terms that did not rate them at least as ⅗. If the Eastern [New England] States meant therefore to exclude them altogether the business was at an end.

General Pinckney supported Davie, as did the sixty-year-old William Samuel Johnson of Connecticut, a longtime member of Congress who would become president of Columbia College in New York. Remarkably, Johnson proposed to count slaves fully for representation, an approach that would empower slave states at the expense of his own state. The episode is sufficiently puzzling—both Davie's eruption and the Connecticut man's concession—that the suspicion arises that North and South had clashed offstage, or that Madison failed to report an angry onstage dispute.

Morris responded in kind. "It has been said that it is high time to speak out," he told the delegates, so he would. Movement and side conversations stopped as the commanding Morris scanned the gathering. He was mournful and frustrated. Just as the southerners could not agree to certain provisions, those states could not "require what the other states will never admit." He "verily believed the people of Pennsylvania will never agree to a representation of Negroes."

General Charles Cotesworth Pinckney (South Carolina)

The southerners were unmoved. Urbane General Pinckney, who only that morning had found a Morris proposal "so just that it could not be objected to," abandoned his gracious manner. He now refused to agree to anything coming from Morris, certainly not anything concerning the three-fifths ratio. "[P]roperty in slaves," he said, "should not be exposed to danger under a government instituted for the protection of property." Edmund Randolph agreed, "urg[ing] strenuously" that the three-fifths ratio would provide "security" for slavery. Always the angst-ridden slaveholder, he "lamented that such a species of property existed. But as it did exist the holders of it would require this security."

This was Virginia talking, with its wealth and many slaves, with General Washington presiding and Madison taking notes, and it was supporting the southerners' fear of action against slavery that Morris—or some other event—had triggered.

Only Rufus King supported Morris. Stressing that the South was holding the Convention hostage, the Massachusetts lawyer prophesied that the region would have ever greater power to do so in the future: "[T]here will be no point at which they will not be able to say, do us justice or we will separate." Still, the three-fifths ratio was approved again, this time by a 6–2 margin with two delegations divided.

Some external signs augured well for the following day, July 13. The hellish heat broke overnight and the morning bloomed with cool air. Even more positive, the night sky had shimmered with the aurora borealis, sheets of light flashing across the heavens. Was this the hand of Providence? Was the message approving?

Because the previous day's maneuvering had left an inconsistency in how the three-fifths ratio would be applied, Edmund Randolph moved to correct the language. While he was at it, he proposed to apply the ratio to the allocation of representatives for new states as well.

This second motion raised the volatile question of the future. It was one thing to concede political power to existing slave states; after all, they already were slave states when they helped form the Union. But now Randolph proposed to reward the spread of slavery to new lands. The delegates knew the western regions would grow fast. Settlers were flooding into the Kentucky and Tennessee territories, while speculation in Ohio lands was rampant. Growth in the West was bound to upset whatever regional balance of power prevailed in 1787. Would the future West support the slave states, or the North?

Recognizing the significance of Randolph's proposal, Morris rose once more. Starting from the Pennsylvania table at the center of the chamber, he advanced to the front with his asymmetrical, peg-legged stride. When he spoke, his walking stick rapped the plank floor for emphasis.

The recent exchanges over slavery, he said, had led him "into deep meditation." Madison's distinction between North and South had seemed to him "heretical," but now he found "the Southern gentlemen will not be satisfied unless they see the way open to their gaining a majority in the public councils." The distinction between North and South, he continued, was either "fictitious or real":

> [I]f fictitious let it be dismissed and let us proceed with due confidence. If it be real, instead of attempting to blend incompatible things, let us at once take a friendly leave of each other.

Morris noted that many expected the southern population soon to outstrip the North (an expectation that was not realized). Foreseeing a future alliance between the South and new western states, Morris warned that "every thing was to be apprehended from their [the southerners] getting the power into their hands."

Major Butler of South Carolina responded harshly the next day, as if to a slow pupil, in a statement that was redolent with southern anxiety over slavery. "The security the southern states want," he explained, "is that their Negroes may not be taken from them which some gentlemen within or without doors, have a very good mind to do."

Morris did not answer the accusation, a silence that may have been more disturbing than any words. His silence reflected the power of Butler's charge, and how politically exposed Morris was. The gentlemen of the North resented the slaveholders' arrogance. They were dismayed by the brutality of slavery, and by its contradiction of republican ideals. But they were not demanding abolition. They had come to Philadelphia to establish a new government, not a new moral order.

When the votes were counted, Morris stood alone. No state, not even Pennsylvania, opposed Randolph's motion to extend the three-fifths clause to new states.

On the final day of the week, Saturday, July 14, the large-state/slave-state allies mounted a last push. With the three-fifths ratio reinforced, Rutledge and his Deep South troops were again favoring population-based representation in the Senate. Once more, Rutledge and Wilson led the fight. Rutledge moved to reconsider the issue of equal state votes in the Senate. Wilson pressed the case. On the critical ballot, he stormed, the small states had won even though they contained only one-third of the nation's population. "What hopes will our constituents entertain," he fumed, "when they find that the essential principles of justice have been violated in the outset of the government?"

Following Wilson, Charles Pinckney proposed a diluted form of proportional representation. By assigning one senator to the smallest states and only five to Virginia, his proposal would give the smaller states more power than under a pure population-based allocation, but would recognize that the larger states were, well, larger. Wilson seconded the motion.

Delegates from New Jersey and Connecticut said no. Gerry of Massachusetts warned against creating a government acceptable only to some states. "An accommodation must take place," he said, since he was "utterly against a partial confederacy, leaving other states to accede or not accede; as had been intimated." Another Massachusetts delegate made the same point: "If no accommodation takes place, the union itself must soon be dissolved."

Madison, rarely inclined to compromise, supported Wilson and the southerners. Alarmed that per-state voting in the Senate would destroy the "proper foundation of government," Madison delivered his least persuasive remarks of the summer.

Even with per-state voting, the Virginian argued, the large states would "in some way or other secure to themselves a weight proportioned to the importance accruing from their superior numbers." In other words, the large states would have their way no matter what representation rule was applied. That argument could only reinforce the small states' demand for every possible protection against the presumably diabolical plans of the large states.

Ever the constitutional tinkerer, Madison proposed a confusing so-lution: Have the states' voting power in the Senate vary according to the subject matter before them. "In all cases where the general government is to act on the people, let . . . the votes be proportional. In all cases where the government is to act on the states as such, . . . let the states be represented and the votes be equal." The man was tired.

James Wilson closed the debate with a judgment worthy of an Old Testament prophet. He foresaw disaster from equal state votes in the Senate. "A vice in the representation, like an error in the first concoc-tion, must be followed by diseases, convulsions, and finally death."

As it turned out, the portents of the celestial lights had been in favor of the small states. Pinckney's motion for semiproportional representa-tion in the Senate was defeated. The small states had won, this time for good.

On the following Monday morning, July 16, the delegates voted one more time on the overall structure of the legislature. Dr. Franklin's com-promise was approved by the narrowest of margins, 5–4, with Massa-chusetts divided. The positive votes came from four small states (Connecticut, New Jersey, Delaware, and Maryland) and North Car-olina. Lamenting that the vote "had embarrassed the business ex-tremely," Randolph requested an adjournment to reflect on the current state of affairs.

Gloating, Paterson of New Jersey agreed "that it was high time for the Convention to adjourn," and proposed that the recess be perma-nent.

A powerful plea to finish the Convention came from an unlikely source. John Rutledge delivered his message with an unsentimental eloquence. In the recent struggles, Rutledge had prevailed on the three-fifths ratio; then he lost on equal state votes in the Senate. Refus-ing to resent his loss, he urged the delegates to move forward. Madison captured Rutledge's clipped sentences:

> [Rutledge] could see no chance of a compromise. The little states
> were fixt. They had repeatedly and solemnly declared themselves

to be so. All that the large states then had to do, was to decide whether they would yield or not. For his part he conceived that although we could not do what we thought best, in itself, we ought to do something. Had we not better keep the government up a little longer, . . . than abandon every thing to hazard? Our constituents will be little satisfied with us if we take the latter course.

Thunderstorms moved through Philadelphia that afternoon, making way for a glorious Tuesday morning. Early that morning, many of the large-state delegates met to discuss the unsatisfactory state of affairs. With palpable disgust, Madison recorded that "[t]he time was wasted in vague conversation." Too many were inclined to yield, though Madison was not.

After almost eight weeks, the great contest over legislative representation finally was over. By careful adherence to Sherman's axiom that the minority should keep talking, the small-state delegates wore down their adversaries and partly overturned the Wilson-Rutledge pact. The political triumph was remarkable. Though the small states had much more to lose if the Convention failed to produce a new government, they somehow persuaded enough delegates from the large states and slave states (though not Madison) that they might really walk out of the Convention. Containing equal parts of inspired bluff and determined advocacy, their success was singular.

Months later in the state ratifying conventions, those most opposed to equal state votes in the Senate had to defend the arrangement. They emphasized the hard political realities that forced the provision on them.

Charles Pinckney told the South Carolina conclave that "had the Convention separated without determining upon a plan, it would have been on this point." Hamilton assured New Yorkers that without the compromise, "the Convention must have dissolved without effecting any thing."

Others put a sunnier face on their loss. James Wilson told a gathering of Pennsylvanians that, upon beholding the Constitution's legislative arrangements, "my admiration can only be equaled by my astonishment, in beholding so perfect a system formed from such heterogeneous materials."

Madison went further in No. 37 of *The Federalist:* "It is impossible for the man of pious reflection not to perceive in [these provisions] a finger of that Almighty Hand, which has been so frequently and signally extended to our relief in the critical stages of the revolution." Forty years later, Madison was more candid, writing that "reconciling the larger states to the equality of the Senate is known to have been the most threatening [difficulty] that was encountered in framing the Constitution."

After the Convention adjourned on July 16, General Washington dined with his hosts, the Robert Morrises, and "drank tea" at the home of Mayor Samuel Powel. The evening excursions were pleasant and allowed him a chance to savor the Convention's recent action on a matter close to the General's heart. The delegates had been considering the future of the nation they were creating. The future, as it always has in America, meant the West.

Chapter Eleven

The Touch of a Feather

JULY 9–14

A S THE BATTLE over representation limped to its rancorous close,
America's frontier commanded the attention of both the Federal Convention and the Confederation Congress in New York
City. The Congress, with nine of its number at the Philadelphia Convention while others were absent from New York for other reasons, had
not mustered a quorum for two months. When it last had a quorum in
mid-May, it was preparing to address the development of the West,
which raised core questions about the new nation. Would the principles
of liberty and democracy extend to new territories? Would the thirteen
states share power with new states? Would slavery spread?

In 1787, the West meant the huge stretch of land between the Appalachian Mountains and the Mississippi River. Ceded by Great Britain
in the 1783 Paris Peace Treaty, the West was far larger than the thirteen
existing states. For the delegates in Philadelphia and the congressmen
in New York City, this frontier promised a wondrous expansion of
wealth and population, which would increase the nation's ability to
project power on an international scale. Also, one strategy for paying off
the nation's crushing war debt was to sell western lands.

Many Americans saw personal profit on western horizons. Leading

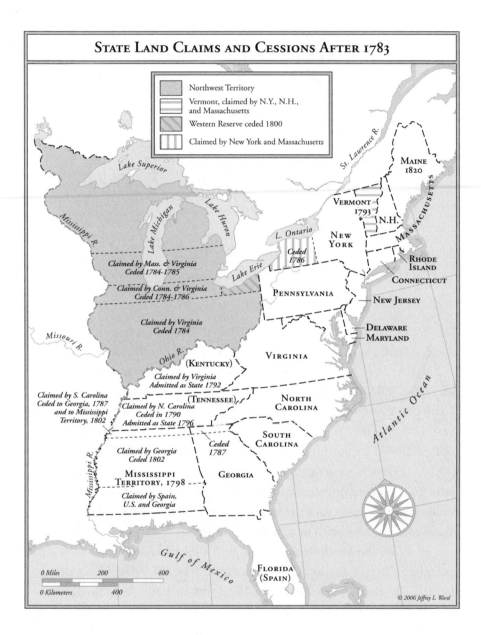

STATE LAND CLAIMS AND CESSIONS AFTER 1783

Northwest Territory

Vermont, claimed by N.Y., N.H., and Massachusetts

Western Reserve ceded 1800

Claimed by New York and Massachusetts

Lake Superior

Mississippi R.

Lake Michigan

Lake Huron

St. Lawrence R.

MAINE
1820

VERMONT
1793

N.H.

MASSACHUSETTS

L. Ontario

NEW
YORK

*Ceded
1786*

RHODE
ISLAND

CONNECTICUT

*Claimed by Mass. & Virginia
Ceded 1784-1785*

Lake Erie

PENNSYLVANIA

NEW JERSEY

*Claimed by Conn. & Virginia
Ceded 1784-1786*

DELAWARE

MARYLAND

Missouri R.

*Claimed by Virginia
Ceded 1784*

Ohio R.

(KENTUCKY)

VIRGINIA

*Claimed by Virginia
Admitted as State 1792*

*Claimed by S. Carolina
Ceded to Georgia, 1787
and to Mississippi
Territory, 1802*

(TENNESSEE)

NORTH
CAROLINA

*Claimed by N. Carolina
Ceded in 1790
Admitted as State 1796*

SOUTH
CAROLINA

*Ceded
1787*

*Claimed by Georgia
Ceded 1802*

MISSISSIPPI
TERRITORY, 1798

Mississippi R.

GEORGIA

*Claimed by Spain,
U.S. and Georgia*

Atlantic Ocean

Gulf of Mexico

FLORIDA
(SPAIN)

0 Miles   200   400

0 Kilometers   400

© 2006 Jeffrey L. Ward

citizens formed companies to press for congressional recognition of sometimes dubious land titles. At least nine of the delegates, starting with General Washington, speculated heavily in western lands before and after the Convention.

But who owned what in the West? The only certainty was that George III of England had relinquished his title. After that, six states competed for ownership with each other, with Indian tribes, and with speculators. Many settlers were simple squatters, with no legal right to the land they occupied. It would take a generation to resolve the contending claims.

Even more urgent than who owned the West, though, was the territory's impact on the fledgling nation perched on the Atlantic Coast. Some of the delegates feared westerners, portraying them as a cross between Vandals and beasts of the forest. These easterners dreaded the day when such wild creatures would outnumber the civilized residents of the thirteen states. Rufus King in 1786 worried that westward emigration would drain away people needed in the East, while future President James Monroe fretted that westerners' "interests will be opposed to ours."

Though many feared the West, even more feared losing it. The turbulent settlers might secede from the nation, might conspire with foreign powers, might foment wars with Indian nations or other countries. Cut off from the Atlantic by the tall spine of mountains, westerners felt the lure of the British (still in Canada) and the Spanish (controlling the vital Mississippi River). After he traveled through part of the West in 1784, Washington described the risk to Virginia's governor:

> I need not pose to you, Sir, that the rear and flanks of the United States are possessed by other powers—formidable ones too. . . . How entirely unconnected with [the western settlers] shall we be, and what troubles may we not apprehend, if the Spaniards on their right, or Great Britain on their left . . . should hold out lures for their trade and alliance? The Western settlers—I speak now from my own observation—stand as it were on a pivot—*the touch of a feather should turn them any way.*

In a more private letter, Washington observed that in case of conflict between the United States and Britain or Spain, the West would be "a formidable and dangerous neighbor."

Washington was right to wonder about the loyalty of westerners. Spanish archives from the era, one scholar concluded, establish the westerners' "treachery, fickleness, and untrustworthiness."

In 1784, settlers west of North Carolina formed the "state of Franklin." When the state was not immediately admitted to the Union, they threatened to secede and embarked on several Spanish "intrigues." A settlement called Cumberland (the future Nashville, Tennessee) offered to swear allegiance to the Spanish king. Future President Andrew Jackson, a recent arrival in Cumberland, joined in the scheme.

Kentucky settlers held two conventions in 1785, the second of which called for separation from Virginia and admission to the union as a state. James Wilkinson, a Revolutionary War veteran and future co-conspirator with Aaron Burr, dreamed of more drastic action. Purporting to represent Kentucky, Wilkinson in 1786 persuaded Spain to grant him a monopoly over the New Orleans trade if he could cause Kentucky to unite with Spain.

In August 1786, Congressman James White from North Carolina met in New York with Don Diego de Guardoqui, representative of the Spanish king. The congressman said that in return for the right to navigate the Mississippi, westerners would separate from the United States and accept "Spanish protection."

Washington had not overstated the danger of western separation.

Westerners' leading complaint concerned the Mississippi. For ten years and more, America had sought the right to ply its waters, since all western trade naturally flowed down them. In a sharp setback, Spain closed the river to Americans at the end of the war for independence. By 1786, John Jay of New York was representing Congress in negotiations with Spain. In return for trade advantages, including the opening of Spanish ports to American ships, Jay proposed that the United States forgo all trade on the Mississippi for twenty-five years. Southerners hotly denounced those terms, forcing Jay to abandon the negotiation. Westerners now had an even better reason to distrust the Atlantic states.

Most of the Philadelphia delegates had little experience of the West, though no place in America was far from the frontier. During Madison's boyhood, his home in the Virginia Piedmont had been threatened with Indian attack and sometimes sheltered refugees from Indian wars. Some Georgia and North Carolina delegates lived far enough inland to know the frontier well. Washington, through his youthful surveying work, his service in the French and Indian War, and his love of the woods, knew the West better than most. When Luther Martin of Maryland married the granddaughter of a legendary frontiersman (Thomas Cresap), he acquired a family lawsuit against General Washington over title to western lands, which Martin won two months before the Convention began.

The delegates' limited experience with the West reflected the twin realities of the Appalachian Mountains and eighteenth-century transportation, which combined to draw a sharp line between the thirteen states and the West. Over the mountains, travel by road was even more grueling than on the East Coast, where it was no picnic. As a modern writer has evoked the experience, a road often

> was just a tunnel in the vegetation. The traveler endured diabolical combinations of holes, mires, and tree stumps. . . . The more a road was traveled by horses and wagons, the more the surface became chewed up and rutted, and eventually the whole track would be lower than the surrounding terrain, ensuring that water would flow into it. . . . [E]ventually the track through the woods would not really be a road at all, just a linear bog.

Those "linear bogs" passed through forests that seemed infinite and impenetrable, filled with bears, wolves, mountain lions, and snakes. Many Indians were hostile, having learned that settlers were intent on taking their land. A German traveler summarized settlers' attitudes in the Ohio Valley: "The Indians are generally hated here quite as much as they are pretty well throughout America."

Westerners were a rough bunch. One contemporary described them as "about as wicked as fallen human beings can be on this side of utter perdition. Female seduction was frequent, quarreling and fighting decidedly customary—drunkenness almost universal." Some were on the run from the law, or had "outlived [their] credit or fortune" back East. One historian observed that "the cutthroat knave" and the "polished land-shark" made western settlements "veritable hells." A Frenchman wrote that frontiersmen "are often in a perfect state of war" with each other and with "every wild inhabitant of these venerable woods. . . . There men appear to be no better than carnivorous animals of a superior rank."

Despite the hardships and the hard characters, Americans kept moving westward, and at accelerating rates. A European visitor perceived in Americans a "passion for migration." In 1787, more than 900 flatboats carried over 18,000 settlers down the Ohio River. The 1790 census counted 73,000 people in Kentucky alone, with over 100,000 in the region south of the Ohio River.

Six states asserted overlapping claims to western lands, based on colonial charters that were issued when Englishmen were not sure how far North America extended. Several seventeenth-century charters declared that the colony existed from sea-to-sea, or as far as "the south seas." States clung to these grants despite their impracticality. Massachusetts and Connecticut claimed land under such clauses even though New York sat on their western borders, contradicting any claim that the New England states extended to the next ocean—so they insisted that their rights leapt over New York and resumed anew on *its* western border.

Uniquely, New York claimed western lands through its treaties with the Six Nations of the Iroquois Confederation. By assuming the Iroquois' claim of hegemony over the tribes above the Ohio River, New York claimed ownership of the land itself.

The "landless" states—Pennsylvania, Delaware, Rhode Island, New Jersey, New Hampshire, and Maryland—resented the pretensions of the others, and the argument sometimes grew bitter. Maryland, home to many investors in western lands, refused to ratify the Articles of Confederation until Virginia abandoned its most extravagant western claims. Prodded by Madison and Mason, the Virginia Assembly ceded to the new nation all land north of the Ohio River in early 1781. Satisfied, Maryland ratified the Articles.

In March 1784, Virginia gave the United States a deed for the lands north of the Ohio. Thomas Jefferson drafted legislation for Congress to carve the ceded land into the states of Sylvania, Michigania, Cherronesus, Metropotamia, Illinoia, Washington, Polypotamia, Assenisipia, and Pelisipia. Each could join the Confederation when its population equaled that of the smallest existing state. Slavery would be banned in the territory after 1800. Jefferson's legislation stalled in Congress for a year, then two, then three.

By 1787, the Confederation Congress was ready to try again. Jefferson's legislation had lost both its antislavery provision and the whimsical names for new states. The quorum that turned to the bill in early July consisted of eighteen congressmen who have ever dwelt in obscurity. America's political celebrities were in Philadelphia that summer, not in a Congress that one observer described as a body of "increasing infirmity and diminishing dignity."

Still, sitting ninety miles apart during the second week of July, the Confederation Congress and the Convention began a beguiling pas de deux on the West—and then, unexpectedly, on slavery. Through parallel actions on western lands, those two bodies embraced a policy of republican expansion that the world had never before seen. Then by contradictory actions on slavery, they left that refractory problem for later generations. Those parallel and conflicting actions have lured some historians down the road to conspiracy theory, searching for connections between the Confederation Congress and the Convention in this crucial period.

In Philadelphia, the delegates had to decide how new states would be admitted to the Union. Not only western lands promised new states: Vermont would join the Union as soon as New York abandoned its claim to that territory, while Maine was expected to separate from Massachusetts and seek statehood. Still, the great growth would be in the West, which troubled many delegates. On July 6, Rufus King of Massachusetts cautioned that equal state votes in the Senate would give as many as ten votes to new states in the Northwest Territory even though all those states together would have fewer people than Pennsylvania.

Three days later, Nathaniel Gorham of Massachusetts rose. Gorham, who had an anxious side, was anxious about the West. If the new government allocated one representative for every 40,000 people, he warned, western states might one day "out-vote the Atlantic." The Atlantic states should keep the government "in their own hands, [so they] may take care of their own interest." Gouverneur Morris echoed Gorham the next day, urging the original thirteen states to "keep a majority of votes in their own hands."

Two days later, George Mason fought back on behalf of states yet to come. He spoke plainly:

> Ought we to sacrifice what we know to be right in itself, lest it should prove favorable to states which are not yet in existence. [T]he western states . . . [must] be treated as equals, and subjected to no degrading discriminations. They will have the same pride . . . which we have, and will either not unite with or will speedily revolt from the Union if they are not . . . placed on an equal footing.

Morris responded by sharing his dislike of all things western. Though he was the sturdiest challenger to slavery at the Convention, the aristocrat did not mince words in belittling the frontier. Having seen backcountry representatives in Pennsylvania's Assembly, Morris was sure they were not "equally enlightened":

> The busy haunts of men, not the remote wilderness, was the proper school of political talents. If the Western people get the power into their hands they will ruin the Atlantic interests. The back members are always the most averse to the best measures.

Madison tore into this patronizing twaddle. Morris, he chided, "determined the human character by the points of the compass." All men having power, not just westerners, "ought to be distrusted to a certain degree," but Madison was "clear and firm in opinion that no unfavorable distinctions" should apply against westerners.

On that day, July 11, the revitalized Confederation Congress in

New York City took up what would become the Northwest Ordinance. The legislation called for three to five states to be established in the lands north of the Ohio River (the future Ohio, Michigan, Indiana, Illinois, and Wisconsin). The new states would join the union "on an equal footing with the original states."

The bill guaranteed to residents of the territory many rights that would be left out of the Constitution, including the right to "peaceable worship," to due process of law, and to be protected against cruel and unusual punishments. Only after ratification of the Bill of Rights in 1791 would Americans in the Atlantic states possess similar rights. Uniquely, the legislation also declared that "the means of education shall forever be encouraged"; on slavery, the bill was silent.

Two days later, on Friday the thirteenth, the states present in Congress amended the bill and approved it by an 8–0 vote, confirming the historic promise that states carved from the Northwest Territory would be admitted on "an equal footing." The four southern states from Virginia through Georgia all voted aye, joined by New York, Delaware, Massachusetts, and New Jersey.

In Philadelphia on the thirteenth, twenty-four hours away by express coach, the identical proposition ran into heavy weather. Gouverneur Morris was again trying to pull up the ladder behind the thirteen states. He predicted—accurately, as it turned out—a future alliance between southerners and westerners who would foment a war with Spanish America.

This time a fellow Pennsylvanian, James Wilson, challenged him. "The majority of people wherever found," he insisted, should govern "in all questions." By denying that principle, Great Britain had lost its American colonies. Surely the new nation should not make the same mistake by denying the rights of westerners.

The next day, Saturday the fourteenth, the Massachusetts delegates unveiled a proposal to contain the malignant influences of the West. Elbridge Gerry said he would welcome western states "on liberal terms," but he could not support "putting ourselves into their hands." Upon gaining power, westerners will, "like all men, abuse it," then will "oppress commerce, and drain our wealth into the Western country."

Gerry's solution, seconded by Rufus King, was a guarantee that the original thirteen states together would *always* have more representatives than all other states combined. The measure, he noted modestly, would "secure the liberties of the states already confederated."

Gerry's motion missed passage by a single vote. Four states voted in favor, five were opposed, and one (Pennsylvania) divided. By a hair, the thirteen states declined to retain control over the government for all time.

The principle of equal treatment for new states—embraced unanimously by Congress in New York, and more reluctantly by the Philadelphia Convention—was novel. Beginning with Rome and continuing through Venice, republics had grown by conquest and colonization, but did not extend equal status to their new lands. America would take a different approach. New states would stand equal to their predecessors. On this issue, Mason, Wilson, and Madison held the delegates to their republican ideals. The former colonials would not become colonizers.

Westerners had to be encouraged by the decisions of the second week of July. In both New York and Philadelphia, the feather's touch had been applied, and the pivot turned decisively in the direction of fairness and equality for the West.

On slavery, the outcome would be far less clear.

Chapter Twelve

The Ipswich Miracle

JULY 13

IT MIGHT BE CALLED the "Ipswich Miracle," because the men most responsible for it—Nathan Dane and Manasseh Cutler—came from that small town north of Boston, hard by the sea. Few know of the miracle, and those who do often question it, or try to connect it to the Constitution. Even Dane never expected Congress to adopt his antislavery amendment to the Northwest Ordinance. Like any miracle, the explanations for it do not quite satisfy.

In the summer of 1787, Dane represented Massachusetts in the Confederation Congress. A farm boy, he had entered Harvard at age twenty-one, supporting himself by teaching school. Studious rather than martial, Dane was graduated in 1778 and read law, never soldiering in the Revolutionary forces. After serving in the State Assembly for three years, in 1785 he won a seat in Congress.

In the following year, Dane served on a committee on the Northwest Territory, which functioned at Congress's vagarious pace. In June of 1787, however, the committee received a jolt from Rev. Manasseh Cutler, a fellow Ipswich resident and an unlikely candidate to become one of America's first and most effective lobbyists.

A man of broad interests and impressive achievements, Rev. Cutler held degrees from Yale and Harvard. His several careers marked him as a small-scale version of Dr. Franklin.

He read law and was admitted to the bar, but in 1771 he became a Congregational minister and was called to the pulpit of an Ipswich church, where he was pastor for the next fifty years. When the town's doctor volunteered for the army, Cutler took up the study of medicine, which was interrupted by brief service as an army chaplain. He completed his medical training while also studying astronomy, meteorology, and botany. He produced the first classification of New England plant life and ran a school in his home for twenty-five years.

By June of 1787, this renaissance man had taken on a project of an entirely different color. At the end of the war, almost 300 Continental Army officers petitioned Congress for "bounty lands" in the Northwest Territory, which had been promised as a reward for their military service. In early 1786, the group's leaders met at the Bunch of Grapes Tavern in Boston to form an association to pursue the land claims. They named Rev. Cutler to the managing committee of the new Ohio Company of Associates. Though the founders were prominent men who

Rev. Manasseh Cutler

themselves knew many congressmen, they chose this lawyer-minister-physician-scientist-educator to represent them. It proved an inspired choice.

Over a five-week period in July and August of 1787, Cutler transformed the drifting land scheme into reality, and in the process recorded a riveting account of his tour through every corridor of power that the new nation had to offer. Of the prominent Americans located between Boston and Philadelphia that summer, only General Washington evaded the irrepressible Rev. Cutler.

The Ohio Company aimed to buy 1.7 million acres of government land around the current Marietta, Ohio, at a price of $1 an acre. Because the company would pay with devalued loan certificates issued during the war, the true price would be far lower. As the deal was consummated, the Ohio Company paid 8 cents an acre.

To complete this attractive transaction, the Ohio Company needed two actions from the Confederation Congress. First, Congress had to approve the deal. Second, by establishing a stable government in the Northwest Territory, Congress would provide essential reassurance to prospective settlers. For more than two years, Congress dithered on both counts. Enter Rev. Cutler.

A tall man of generous proportions, yet "extremely light on his feet," the reverend's easy bonhomie won the trust of congressional representatives in New York, including his hometown representative, Nathan Dane. A Virginia congressman described Cutler as "an open, frank, honest New Englander—an uncommon animal." Though a pastor, Cutler was no ascetic. A family member recalled him as fond of fencing, never without his snuffbox, and the possessor of "a well-stock[ed] liquor cabinet."

In early May, congressional committees addressed the Ohio Company's application to buy the lands, considering at the same time an early version of the Northwest Ordinance. As suddenly as this forward motion had started, it stopped. Several congressmen left for the Philadelphia Convention; others went absent. For almost two months, Congress was becalmed by the lack of a quorum.

Arriving in New York on July 5, Rev. Cutler was a whirlwind in his trademark black velvet suit, with silver buckles at the knees and on his shoes. So many strands of history came together over the next ten days, with Rev. Cutler's hands near most of them, that historians struggle to find the narrative that accounts for all of them.

On July 6, a Virginian introduced Rev. Cutler on the floor of Congress, which then met on the second level of New York's City Hall. After greeting Dane and some congressmen, the minister from Ipswich dined with other congressmen, then supped with still more. He attended a lecture by a prominent divine on the subject of "Hypocrisy." With unwavering good cheer, Cutler called the talk entertaining "notwithstanding the dryness of the subject, the badness of [the speaker's] delivery." What, one wonders, was the good part?

For two days, he joined Dane at meetings of the congressional committee that was preparing the Northwest Ordinance and the land contract for the Ohio Company. Rev. Cutler formed an alliance with another land syndicate, led by William Duer of New York. As luck would have it, Duer was president of Congress's Treasury Board, and several of his investors were members of Congress. Duer impressed the minister-lobbyist. The New Yorker "lives in the style of a nobleman," Cutler wrote, putting out "not less than fifteen different sorts of wine . . . besides most excellent bottled cider, porter, and several other kinds of strong beer." Duer would be a valuable ally.

On the tenth, Rev. Cutler gave the committee his comments on the legislation, along with several proposed amendments. Years later he confided to his son, who was then an antislavery politician in Ohio, that he gave Dane an amendment to bar slavery in the Northwest Territory. It was needed, Rev. Cutler explained, because he "was acting for associates, friends, and neighbors, who would not embark in the enterprise, unless these [antislavery] principles were unalterably fixed."

The amended bill received its first reading in the Confederation Congress on the next day, July 11, but Cutler was not there to hear it. With Congress turning to the Northwest Ordinance—rather than the far more important matter (to him) of the land contract—the Ipswich cleric "thought this was the most favorable opportunity to go on to Philadelphia." He arrived there on the evening of the twelfth, preceded by a letter of introduction from the governor of Massachusetts to Elbridge Gerry.

The purpose of his jaunt to Philadelphia, where he stayed for only two days, is not entirely clear. By the account in his journal, he was no more than a hyperactive tourist, sleeping little and gobbling up the city's sights in great gulps that leave the reader breathless but exhilarated. Some have searched for a deeper purpose in his trip that would explain why he left New York just as Congress was taking up the Northwest Ordinance, one of the two matters he cared about.

According to his journal, Rev. Cutler did not waste a moment in Philadelphia. Within an hour of arriving at the Indian Queen, he was meeting with the two Massachusetts delegates who lodged there (Gorham and Caleb Strong), and assembling a supper party. Gerry left his family's lodgings to join the meal, along with Madison and Mason from Virginia, two North Carolinians, and two South Carolinians (John Rutledge and a "Mr. Pinckney," very likely Charles). The ease of assembling the party on such short notice suggests that it was a slow evening in the City of Brotherly Love; then again, perhaps it reflects some special agenda that Rev. Cutler wished to pursue.

The reverend stayed up until "half after one" with the three Massachusetts delegates, gossiping about home-state matters. After a short night, he breakfasted at five-thirty with Strong and Gerry, then enjoyed a carriage tour of Philadelphia and its country houses. Afternoon dinner was spent with Dr. Benjamin Rush, one of Philadelphia's first citizens, with whom he discussed botany and the cataloging system of Linnaeus. Then it was off to Charles Willson Peale's home to review the painter's gallery and Mrs. Peale's fossil collection. Surrounded by Peale's patriotic canvases, Rev. Cutler exclaimed in his journal, "I fancied myself introduced to all the general officers that had been in the field during the war."

Rev. Cutler moved on to the State House, a "noble building," which had the only doors in the city that were closed to him: "[S]entries are planted without and within—to prevent any person from approaching near—who appear to be very alert in the performance of their duty." Next came the future University of Pennsylvania, where Cutler examined both the facilities and the faculty.

The high point of his visit came that evening, when Gerry and the reverend called on Dr. Franklin, "the wonder of Europe and the glory of

America." Rev. Cutler lingered there for five hours. He and the doctor slipped away from a larger gathering to review scientific "curiosities" and a massive botany text. "The Doctor seemed extremely fond," Rev. Cutler wrote, "of dwelling on philosophical subjects, while the other gentlemen were swallowed up with politics. This was a favorable circumstance for me." The Ipswich minister enthused that Franklin "has an incessant vein of humor, accompanied with an uncommon vivacity which seems as natural and involuntary as his breathing."

Rev. Cutler's own charms induced Dr. Franklin to begin telling of a recent Convention incident, a story that started when the sage produced a two-headed reptile, an evocative political metaphor. Sadly, someone present invoked the Convention's secrecy rule and halted Franklin's tale in mid-recitation.

Returning to the Indian Queen at 10 P.M., Cutler joined a "sumptuous table" with a half-dozen delegates. When the others discovered that Rev. Cutler had an early appointment to view the botanical garden of the Bartrams, a general clamor arose to join him. Madison, Rutledge, Mason and his son, and two North Carolinians enlisted for the 5 A.M. departure to the garden, which lay across the Schuylkill River, about four miles away. (These episodes raise the suspicion that the delegates endured great tedium when Rev. Cutler was not around.) In a rare laconic touch, the reverend noted Mr. Bartram's surprise at receiving the august company at that early hour.

Rev. Cutler, though, had not lounged abed until the 5 A.M. departure. Possibly the heat disturbed his rest, but the reverend rose even earlier to take in the famed Philadelphia market, which he reported as a wonder, attended by so many people that it was "like the collection at the last day." Upon leaving Bartram's garden, Cutler toured the gardens at Gray's Tavern and visited Philadelphia hospitals with Dr. Rush. He departed for New York in the evening, leaving an exhausted city in his wake.

So what was this effervescent minister up to during his frenetic forty-eight hours in Philadelphia? The available answers represent rank speculation, that most entertaining historical exercise. One hypothesis is that he hurried to Philadelphia to block Gouverneur Morris and the

Sketch of Bartram's garden, Earl of Derby's Estate

Massachusetts delegates from limiting the rights of future western states, which would have disrupted the Ohio Company's settlement plans.

This speculation imagines the following chain of events. In the first week of July, several Convention delegates traveled to New York to discharge their simultaneous duties as members of Congress. Though bound by the secrecy rule, a delegate-congressman somehow indicated that the Convention might not accord equal treatment to the West. Or maybe the news came from two congressional representatives who had been in Philadelphia over the Fourth of July. However delivered, the news triggered a flying trip to Philadelphia by the Ohio Company's representative extraordinaire, and hurried meetings with Convention heavyweights like Gerry, Rutledge, and Madison.

That Rev. Cutler never recorded such a purpose counts heavily against this speculation, particularly since he was not delicate about preserving details of his lobbying in New York. In any event, the challenge to equal treatment of the West came from exactly those Massachusetts delegates with whom Rev. Cutler spent the most time. Indeed, it was after the morning trip to Bartram's garden on July 14 that Gerry and Rufus King pressed their proposal that the thirteen states should always have a majority in Congress. If Rev. Cutler aimed to persuade them to treat westerners fairly, he was singularly unsuccessful in the effort.

Others have tried to link Rev. Cutler's trip to the Ipswich Miracle, which took place in New York on July 13, while the reverend was away. That was the day Congress approved the Northwest Ordinance. At the very last minute of floor debate, Nathan Dane moved to add a sixth article to the ordinance, which provided: "There shall be neither slavery nor involuntary servitude in the said territory." It imposed unequivocal abolition, the bugbear of every southerner and the provision that Cutler claimed to have written. As a concession to slave owners in other parts of the country, Article Six included a "fugitive slave provision," requiring the return of escaped slaves to their masters. Dane's Article Six was approved by unanimous vote and became an honored part of the nation's founding documents.

Describing the event in a letter to Rufus King, Dane's surprise and delight were palpable:

> When I drew the ordinance . . . I had no idea the States would agree to the sixth Article prohibiting Slavery—; as only Massachusetts of the Eastern States was present—; and therefore omitted it in the draft—; but finding the House favorably disposed on this subject, after we had completed the other parts I moved the article—; which was agreed to without opposition.

Those states supporting Dane's Article Six included slave-owning stalwarts: Virginia, North Carolina, South Carolina (!), and Georgia.

How did this miracle happen? More particularly, how did it happen at the same time that Major Butler of South Carolina was threatening to lead southern delegates out of the Philadelphia Convention because he suspected northerners wanted to abolish slavery?

Congressman Nathan Dane (Massachusetts)

More than forty years later, Dane offered a simple explanation that fits both the Ohio Company's efforts to bring settlers to the Ohio Valley and Rev. Cutler's version of events. In the 1780s, Dane wrote, the Northwest Territory was expected to be "principally for New England settlers," so Article Six "more especially had reference to them." Only three days after the ordinance was adopted, Dane made that point in his letter to Rufus King, observing that the northwest lands would "no doubt be settled chiefly by Eastern [New England] people."

Since the New Englanders had no slaves, Dane continued in his 1830 letter, Article Six provoked no controversy. Southerners in Congress had little reason to preserve slavery in the Northwest Territory; indeed, they might prefer to funnel antislavery settlers there, away from areas where slavery had been introduced. Dane followed parallel reasoning when he supported North Carolina's requirement that slavery be legal in the western lands it ceded to the United States (which became Tennessee). In those lands, Dane concluded, "slavery had taken root" already.

Timothy Pickering of Massachusetts, a future secretary of state, had made that argument to King in 1785:

> To suffer the continuance of slaves, till they can be gradually emancipated, in states already overrun by them, may be pardonable because unavoidable without hazarding greater evil; but to introduce them into countries where none now exist, countries which have been talked of, which we have boasted of, as asylums for the oppressed of the earth, can never be forgiven.

William Grayson, a Virginia representative in Congress, offered another explanation for approval of the abolition clause. He wrote to James Monroe that the southern members agreed to the provision "for the purpose of preventing tobacco and indigo from being made on the N.W. side of the Ohio." Although that explanation seems strained, Grayson had little reason to dissemble to Monroe on the subject of squelching competitors in tobacco and indigo markets. Grayson added, however, that the southerners had "several other political reasons" for supporting the slavery ban. He did not elaborate on those.

One political reason might have grown from the dispute with Spain over the Mississippi. If northerners felt greater kinship with western settlers, the theory goes, then they would be more concerned about the Mississippi, which was critical to the South and the West. By accepting abolition in the Northwest Territory, where slavery was unlikely to flourish, southerners could hope to tie New Englanders more closely to the West.

Almost seventy years after the Convention, another explanation came from Edward Coles, who had been a personal secretary to Madison. Writing in 1856, Coles attributed to Madison the statement that Congress and the Convention executed a coordinated compromise on the "distracting question of slavery." The coordinated compromise, according to Coles, required northerners to accept fugitive slave provisions in both the Constitution and the Northwest Ordinance to ensure that southerners could retrieve their escaped property. That agreement supposedly "creat[ed] the great unanimity by which the [Northwest] Ordinance passed" with its ban on slavery, and also made the Constitution "more acceptable to the slave holders."

With some effort, Coles's story might be shoehorned into a conspiratorial view of Rev. Cutler's visit to Philadelphia. Cutler's dinners at the Indian Queen and the excursion to Bartram's garden *could* have been occasions for thrashing out the slavery compromise Coles described almost seventy years later. Though the notion of a coordinated slavery settlement has some intuitive appeal, the evidence for it is wafer-thin. Indeed, no congressman or delegate who was there ever said there was such a deal.

Although the Framers were guarded in later remarks about the Convention's debates, they did explain most key decisions. But never—not even during bitter debate over the Missouri Compromise in 1819 and 1820, with Rufus King and Charles Pinckney on opposite sides in the Congress, and with Madison watching from the sidelines—did any suggest there had been a coordinated settlement over slavery. Indeed, while Coles's version would gratify the human desire to organize facts into patterns, his hearsay report came far too late to command much regard.

More important, after mid-July of 1787 the Convention delegates did not act as though there had been a coordinated settlement on slavery. If there had been such a deal, John Rutledge had no need to maneuver for additional proslavery protections in his Committee of Detail in early August, nor did Gouverneur Morris have to deliver his thundering jeremiad in response, nor would disputes over the slave trade have raged at the end of that month. A great many of the principal delegates acted for the next several weeks as though there were no coordinated settlement on slavery.

The first question recurs: How *did* the Ipswich Miracle happen in New York on July 13? How did those anonymous nobodies in Congress achieve abolition (albeit geographically limited) when the celebrated Framers in Philadelphia—Washington, Franklin, Madison, Hamilton— prudently declined to raise the issue? The very obscurity of Congress may provide some answer. Being eclipsed by the Convention may have given it the latitude to do the right thing. That the northwest lands held very few slaves and were largely unsettled certainly enhanced that freedom to act.

After 1787, the two men from Ipswich gave the nation long years of service, though they would never again be so near the center of events. For ten years, Dane served in the Massachusetts government, until deafness drove him from public life, and finally from law practice. He devoted his last two decades to compiling a digest of American law that was the leading legal text of its time. Dane never lost his taste for moral betterment. In 1813, he helped form the first antiliquor organization, the Massachusetts Society for the Suppression of Intemperance.

Rev. Cutler won his land contract later in the summer of 1787, after a furious lobbying campaign. The cleric found that "matters went on much better" after he endorsed the president of Congress, General Arthur St. Clair, as the first governor of the new territory. Rev. Cutler had little to learn from twenty-first-century practitioners of the lobbying arts:

> In order to get at some of [the congressmen], so as to work powerfully on their minds, [we] were obliged to engage three or four persons. . . . In some instances we engaged one person, who engaged

a second, and he a third, and so on to a fourth, before we could effect our purpose.

The minister traveled west in 1788 with the second group of Ohio Company settlers. There he studied unusual mounds of earth, which he concluded had been built by Native Americans, and wrote a book about his travels. After serving in the state legislature and two terms in Congress, he retired to literary pursuits and his ministry in Ipswich. He never lobbied again.

Although Rev. Cutler escaped from Philadelphia after only two days, the Convention delegates had more than two months to go. They had decided on a two-house legislature, with one house based on proportional representation and the other granting equal votes to the states. They also had resolved to treat the West fairly. But what should the executive be like? What powers should Congress have, or the states, or the president, or the courts? And how might a president be chosen?

Time was running out, and tempers were fraying.

Chapter Thirteen

The Presidential Muddle

JULY 17–26

WHEN HE ROSE as the first speaker on Thursday, July 26, George Mason intended to settle the Convention's meandering deliberations surrounding the presidency. To Mason's way of thinking, the delegates had chased their tails on this issue for far too long. He meant for them to reaffirm the Virginia Plan's prescription that Congress should choose the president for a single term of seven years.

Not a large man, Mason commanded attention with his erect posture, formal manner, and sharp insights. From the Convention's first days, he strode eagerly into the debates, sometimes in the pointed language for which he was known. But he had not yet tried to dictate the docket. Men like Wilson and Madison and Rutledge had framed most initiatives. Though younger than Mason, they had walked on the national stage in years when he stayed close to his Gunston Hall estate.

After two months in Philadelphia, Mason was comfortable in this larger arena. He was ready to do more. On this day, with a heavy rain drumming against the windows of the State House, he was reaching for the reins on the presidency question, a subject that had occupied much of the last ten days. How should the president be chosen? How long should he serve? Should he be eligible for more than one term? The delegates seemed no closer to answering those questions than they ever had been.

Through the debates on the presidency, the delegates had divided along lines now familiar. Southerners feared being swamped by the more populous North. Small-state delegates worried that only large-state candidates would become president. Still, the exchanges lacked the blazing intensity of the fights over representation. Though that contest had left psychic bruises and lingering resentments, Franklin's compromise was holding. No delegation had stalked out since the New Yorkers departed in early July.

Then good news arrived on July 23. Two New Hampshire delegates materialized, bringing the Convention's numbers back to eleven state delegations. With one more state represented, one more table occupied, the delegates' spirits lifted.

Almost as important, the heat broke. Providential cool reigned in the Delaware Valley through the third week of July. The gentle weather helped everything, including Alexander Hamilton's efforts to avert a duel between a Georgia delegate and a British merchant. When Hamilton presented the merchant's apology for his conduct, the Georgian professed himself satisfied and withdrew his challenge.

Still, Mason's timing was not the best. July 26 was getaway day, the Convention's last session before an eleven-day break the delegates had granted to themselves. During that recess, five of their number would meet as a Committee of Detail, though the committee would address much more than details. While other delegates gamboled through summer days, the chosen five would create a charter of government from the disparate resolutions the Convention had adopted and amended and reamended and readopted.

Mason was not on that committee. Again, younger men were chosen. But before the delegates scattered and the committee turned to its labors, he had work for them to do.

One overriding factor reduced the urgency of discussions about the presidency: the tall man who presided over them. Every delegate, and most Americans, assumed that George Washington would be the first president.

That expectation shaped the debates, which in some sense involved writing the General's future job description. When the delegates first sat as the Committee of the Whole in early June, they found it awkward to talk about the presidency in his presence. Would some remark give unintended offense? What unhappy consequence might flow from that? Both Rutledge and Madison commented on the early "shyness" of the delegates on the subject. Dr. Franklin urged the delegates to "deliver their sentiments" on the presidency because "it was a point of great importance."

In the ensuing seven weeks the delegates had shed their shyness, but the General was still a powerful presence. No delegate would question Washington's fitness to be the first president. His war leadership had entered national mythology. The delegates' challenge was imagining the president *after* George Washington. They had to design a presidency for that mere mortal.

A North Carolinian touched lightly on this concern on July 17. Though current Americans, he warned, knew all the "distinguished characters" who might serve as president, in the future "this will not always be the case." Major Butler of South Carolina thought the delegates granted the president too much power because

> many of the members cast their eyes towards General Washington and shaped their ideas of the powers to be given to a president by their opinions of his virtue. So that the man, who by his patriotism and virtue contributed largely to the emancipation of his country, may be the innocent means of its being, when he is laid low, oppressed.

The issues about the presidency seemed straightforward at first blush, but became daunting when examined closely. Most delegates wanted a presidency with vigor, energy, and vitality, or whatever word expressed their frustration with the weakness of Congress under the Articles. But the president should not be too strong. That would risk monarchy and oppression. The goal was easily stated, difficult to achieve.

Where were the examples to copy? Few nations in the eighteenth century had nonhereditary executives. The Netherlands, supposedly a republic, was led by the stadtholder of the House of Orange, a hereditary office. Switzerland chose no overall leader. The delegates viewed with disgust the corrupted election processes for the Holy Roman emperor and the king of Poland.

The thirteen state constitutions offered no consensus on the best way to select a chief executive. In many states, the legislature made the choice, but several allowed the people to elect the governor directly. Pennsylvania used a more complicated method, having the people vote for members of an Executive Council, with the Assembly selecting a president from that council.

The Convention focused on a few features of the presidency: how he would be chosen, for how long, and whether he could seek additional terms. Also important were how to remove a bad president from office and whether he should have the power to veto legislation.

The answers to these questions were interconnected, so changing one answer could change the answers to others. If the president's term in office was long, should he be confined to one term? If he could serve multiple terms, shouldn't the selection process protect against corrupt scheming for extra terms? How he could be removed from office would matter to every question.

Whatever the reason—the reassuring presence of General Washington, the limited real-world models, or the interdependence of the factors to be balanced—the Convention struggled with the presidency. Madison found the debates on the issue "tedious and reiterated." James Wilson, who proposed the convoluted elector system that the Convention adopted, remembered that the delegates "were perplexed with no part of this plan so much as with the mode of choosing the President."

When the delegates took up the presidency on Tuesday, July 17, they started with the report of the Committee of the Whole. That report specified that a single individual would head the executive branch; that much survived the coming debates. The report also proposed that Congress choose the president for a seven-year term with no second term possible, but many delegates would grow to doubt those arrangements.

Mason and Dr. Franklin successfully argued for removal of the president by legislative impeachment, an English practice for discharging the king's ministers. Having no political ambitions and little concern about offending the General, Mason put the matter frankly: "Shall any man be above justice? Above all, shall that man be above it who can commit the most extreme injustice?" Without impeachment, Franklin urged, the only way to remove an unjust leader was assassination. Impeachment permits "regular punishment" or "honorable acquittal."

Having decided how to remove a president, the delegates struggled with how to choose one.

Gouverneur Morris demanded that the people vote directly for the president. Though far from a man of the people, Morris scorned giving Congress that power. Congressional selection, he insisted, "will be the work of intrigue, of cabal, and of faction: it will be like the election of a pope by a conclave of cardinals; real merit will rarely be the title to the appointment."

Others complained that popular election would ensure bad presidents, or that they came always from a populous state. Mason insisted that the people could not be trusted. Popular elections are "unnatural," he said, like "refer[ring] a trial of colors to a blind man."

Morris's motion for popular election was buried by a 1–9 vote, but he was not discouraged. Two days later, the Pennsylvania delegate moved for reconsideration. The president, he argued, would be "the guardian of the people, even of the lower classes, against legislative tyranny." But if selected by Congress, he would be "the tool of a faction, of some leading demagogue." The people should choose their guardian.

Though he still drew little support, the debate revived Wilson's idea from early June: The people could vote for "electors," whose sole duty would be to choose the president. The electors would be wise, or so the argument proceeded, where the masses were ignorant and easily misled. Madison applauded the approach as providing more influence for southern states. Those states would suffer under popular elections "on the score of the Negroes"—since their slaves could not vote—but slaves could be counted when allocating electors.

The delegates voted for an elector system, but then prescribed that state legislatures, not the people, would choose the electors. Wilson deplored this distortion of his idea. He never intended for the states to have that power. Still, it was early for despair; the protean debate over the presidency was just warming up.

On the next day, July 20, the Convention adopted a suggestion by Gerry of Massachusetts and Ellsworth of Connecticut. For the first election under the new Constitution, each state would have one, two, or three electors, based on its size, which would sharply favor the smallest states. But the concession was largely meaningless, since Washington was certain to be elected by acclamation in the first election. After the first election, each state would have the same number of electors as it had members of the House of Representatives. That approach gave southerners the benefit of the three-fifths ratio, which determined how many seats they had in the House. That solution held up for four days.

On July 24, a New Jersey delegate moved to restore congressional selection of the president. His reason? "[T]he improbability that capable men would undertake the service of Electors from the more distant states." The delegates began to air their misgivings about the presidency. The discussion ricocheted among ill-considered ideas that carried unpredictable consequences.

A North Carolinian proposed to divide the nation into three districts, with each electing a chief executive. That would protect North and South from each other, and would protect against a single executive becoming "an elective king." The sponsor thought it "pretty certain . . . that we should at some time or another have a King," but he wished to "postpone the event as long as possible." For the stony-faced presiding officer, talk of monarchy was awkward, even offensive. Another King George for America?

Gerry of Massachusetts wanted to deploy a battery of public officers in selecting the president. State legislatures would choose electors; if no candidate commanded a majority of electors, then the House of Representatives would select two candidates from the four with the most electoral votes; the Senate would choose the president from the two finalists. In Gerry's process, only state governors would play no role. According to Madison, "The *noes* were so predominant" that the roll of states was not called.

With that, the delegates voted by a 7–4 margin to restore to Congress the power of selecting the president, setting off a fresh round of worry that Congress would dominate him. If congressmen held the key to his second term, the president might become "the cringing dependent of influential men." Would a longer term help? A president with a lengthy term would be less tempted to make improper deals with Congress.

Luther Martin of Maryland championed the idea of a longer term. He suggested eleven years. Inspired, Gerry proposed fifteen years. Mocking the auction-house atmosphere, Rufus King called out "Twenty years!" adding, "This is the medium life of princes." Even Madison cracked a smile, recording that the remark "might possibly be meant as a caricature of the previous motions."

James Wilson of Pennsylvania had a new scheme up his sleeve. Why not select a small number of congressmen by lot, "not more than 15," and have those fifteen "retire immediately and make the election" of the president? Because no one would know which fifteen would pick the president until the lots were drawn, "intrigue would be avoided . . . and the dependence [of the President on Congress] would be diminished." With a shrug, Wilson admitted his scheme "was not a digested idea and might be liable to strong objections."

Dismayed by the rambling debate, Gouverneur Morris pleaded that the issue be postponed. The executive was the most important subject before them, he insisted, since the president could make himself "the despot of America":

> It is the most difficult of all rightly to balance the executive. Make him too weak: the legislature will usurp his powers. Make him too strong: he will usurp on the legislature.

Recognizing that they were making no progress, the delegates agreed to the postponement.

Thunder and rain rolled through Philadelphia the following morning, and a heavy fog still clung to the Convention's deliberations. Remarkably, the delegates had concocted more schemes for presidential selection.

Ellsworth of Connecticut moved that Congress elect the president *except* when an incumbent sought reelection. In those cases, the state legislatures should choose electors, who would pick the president, thus removing the incumbent's motive to pander to Congress. Gerry denounced the approach, suggesting that state governors select the president (thereby proposing to use the only state or national officials omitted from his earlier notion).

The Convention had lost its rudder on the issue. Madison stepped away from his writing desk and assumed his earnest, thoughtful posture. The delegates knew by now what to expect from him: close reasoning, thorough analysis, no fireworks. As a Georgian remembered, Madison was always "the best informed man of any point in debate," although "he cannot be called an orator." Another observer called Madison "cool," with "rather too much theory."

Madison began deliberately. "There are objections against every mode that has been, or perhaps can be, proposed." Nevertheless, presidents must be chosen. State officials must do it, or national officials, or "the people themselves." Painstakingly, the Virginian reviewed each method of selection. For him, the true choice was between "appointment by electors" and "appointment by the people."

Although the use of electors might succeed, Madison said, popular election was better. He acknowledged that candidates from large states could have an edge in such contests, and that southern states would be disadvantaged since their slaves would not vote. Those problems, he insisted, were small compared to the objections to the other alternatives.

Once again the delegates ignored a lucid Madisonian appeal to reason. Mason reaffirmed his preference for selection by Congress, while Major Butler of South Carolina supported electors. Gouverneur Morris, astoundingly, endorsed Wilson's scheme for a lottery to pick fifteen congressmen who would then choose a president.

How about, a North Carolina delegate broke in, having each citizen vote for *three* candidates? That way small-state candidates would have a better chance of success.

Elbridge Gerry erupted again, in his stuttering way, widening and squinting his eyes in turn. The suggestion from North Carolina was "radically vicious." The "ignorance of the people" would allow men "dispersed through the Union and acting in concert to delude them into any appointment." Gerry pointed to the Society of the Cincinnati as potential election conspirators. The example struck uncomfortably close to General Washington, who recently headed that organization of former army officers.

Despite its patronizing and antidemocratic ring, Gerry's lament about the ignorance of the people reflected the limited communications of 1787. Information could be hard to come by. There were about eighty newspapers in the country, many of them weeklies of two or four pages, concentrated in urban areas. Indeed, the Convention's roots led back to the Mount Vernon Conference of 1785, where as privileged a character as George Mason had no idea that he had been appointed to negotiate the Potomac River compact with Maryland.

John Dickinson of Delaware stepped forward with an idea for addressing the information problem: each state's voters could name a "favorite son" for president, since they would know the men in their own state; then Congress or electors could select from among those thirteen choices.

Upon adjournment that Wednesday afternoon, the delegates were dizzy with alternatives, none of which commanded significant support. Most questions surrounding the president remained open as they set off for dinner.

And so Mason took the floor the next morning, getaway day, eager to put this meandering debate out of its misery. The Virginian's views were tart. As Jefferson observed, his language was "strengthened by a dash of biting cynicism when provocation made it seasonable." On this day, Mason felt provoked.

Noting the "difficulty of the subject and the diversity of the opinions concerning it," he ticked off seven proposals before the Convention, each of which he rejected. Although presidents should be selected by those who know the candidates best, popular election would assign it to "those who know least." Of Wilson's lottery proposal, he observed dryly that "the tickets do not appear to be much in demand."

All of these bad ideas, Mason concluded, demonstrated the wisdom of the structure adopted by the Committee of the Whole: election by

George Mason Memorial, Washington, D.C.

Congress for a seven-year term, with no right to run again. Only this approach, Mason said, would serve the "pole star" of his own political beliefs, "the preservation of the rights of the people."

With little discussion, the delegates did exactly as Mason urged, by a 6–3–1 vote. The deadlocked state, this time, was Virginia. Madison specifically recorded that he and General Washington opposed Mason's motion.

Emboldened by his success, Mason sprang up with more proposals. He moved that no one should serve in Congress unless he owned "landed property" and had no "unsettled accounts" with the government. Too many debtors, he explained, were entering state assemblies to "promote laws that might shelter their delinquencies," and "this evil had crept into Congress."

The delegates reacted warily. John Dickinson objected to "interweaving into a republican constitution a veneration for wealth." Madison did not like requiring "landed" property; what of men of business who owned no land? Several thought it unfair to bar those who had claims against the government, or were defending claims by the government; that would allow bureaucrats (darkly referred to as "the auditors") to exclude men from Congress by delaying settlements.

Mason tried to salvage the proposal by pointing out that when the British Parliament imposed similar conditions during "the reign of Queen Anne," they were "met with universal approbation." But it was now seventy years later in a new republic on the other side of the Atlantic. In this new time and very different place, property qualifications had little appeal. One by one, the Convention stripped out Mason's conditions until his proposal was no more.

Undeterred, the Virginian moved to a third item. The national capital, he argued, should not be in the same city as any state capital. In its thirteen years, Congress had resided in many places, including New York, Philadelphia, Annapolis, Trenton, Princeton, and Lancaster, Pennsylvania. Mason warned that having state and national governments in the same place "tended to give a provincial tincture to the national deliberations."

Again the delegates were leery. They had not yet explored the question. Many factors figured in locating the capital. Moreover, that eleven-day recess could start any minute now, as soon as the Convention adjourned. Most delegates had made plans for the break.

Perceiving the tepid reception for his motion, Mason withdrew it "for the present." He had won on the big one, the presidency. He might find openings for raising the other issues after the recess. All in all, it had not been a bad day's work.

With passionate unanimity, the Convention sped through its remaining business. It referred to the Committee of Detail all nineteen resolutions it had adopted in reviewing the Virginia Plan, plus Charles Pinckney's initial plan for the government and the rejected New Jersey Plan. Then the Convention adjourned for eleven days, leaving behind the five members of the Committee of Detail.

When they returned on August 6 to review the committee's draft Constitution, the delegates would scarcely recognize the document. That committee's bold actions would change the Convention's focus on many issues. The Convention also would reconsider the presidency, returning again and again to that nagging question.

For Mason, too, the recess would be a watershed. On the other side of that divide began his disillusion with the emerging Constitution. Though he would repeatedly reach for the reins in August and in September, he would not hold them again. Ultimately, he would jump off the wagon altogether.

Chapter Fourteen

Rutledge Hijacks the Constitution

JULY 27–AUGUST 6

As the Convention neared its late July recess, John Rutledge could feel the moment approaching, and he intended to make the most of it.

The private conversations among the delegates started in mid-July. After deliberating for six weeks and more, the Convention had produced only refinements of the Virginia Plan's resolutions, now numbering nineteen statements of principle that did not make up a constitution. As Baldwin of Georgia wrote, the Convention had produced "foundations, cornerstones, and all the rest of the stones," but needed "workmen to put it together."

Someone had to link the resolutions to each other, to fill in the gaps between them, to create a true charter of government. Thirty or forty men sitting around the East Room could not do the job right. A small committee could. Noting agreement "on the principles and outlines of a system," a North Carolina delegate thought a committee could render the system "properly dressed." They would call it the Committee of Detail and put Rutledge in charge.

Over eleven days, the lawyer from South Carolina would hold the Constitution in his hands. With strength of mind, with care and attention to the four other men on the committee, he could shape the nation and its future.

A commanding figure, the tall, slender Rutledge did not shy from challenges. When he was governor of South Carolina in 1778, the legislature adopted a constitution that denied him a veto over legislation. Rutledge calmly vetoed the new constitution, then resigned his position. He returned to office in triumph the following year under a constitution that gave him a veto. Many shared the view of the French diplomat who called him "the proudest and most imperious" man in America.

But Rutledge had gifts beyond sheer force of character. He could be a gracious host and charming companion. He understood men. He could take the measure of his committee members, judge what was important to each and what was not, gauge whether to use flattery or cajolery, reason or intimidation. At close quarters, he was as irresistible as a forest fire.

The geographic balance of the Committee of Detail was so perfect that the slate must have been hammered out in advance. From North to South, the members were:

> From Massachusetts, Nathaniel Gorham
> From Connecticut, Oliver Ellsworth
> From Pennsylvania, James Wilson
> From Virginia, Edmund Randolph
> From South Carolina, John Rutledge

Rutledge was chairman, probably because he commanded the most votes in the balloting.

The committee's work was the most important single undertaking of the summer: writing the first draft of the Constitution. The task called for many skills: balanced judgment to apply the compromises embodied in the nineteen resolutions adopted by the Convention; vision and imagination to extend those skeletal resolutions to a genuine plan of government; a lawyer's facility with words to achieve precision where agreement was clear, equivocation where it had been elusive.

The nineteen resolutions were only 1,200 words long; the Rutledge Committee's draft would be three times longer, extending for twenty-three articles containing forty-one sections. Missing parts would have to be drafted, ambiguities dispelled, the whole thing knitted into a coherent document.

The five committee members left only a modest trail behind them. From one perspective, their draft was a remarkable cut-and-paste job, reaching beyond the nineteen resolutions to borrow provisions from the despised Articles of Confederation, from state constitutions, and even from Charles Pinckney's almost-forgotten plan.

But they did much more. They added provisions that the Convention never discussed. They changed critical agreements that the delegates had already approved. Spurred by Rutledge, they reconceived the powers of the national government, redefined the powers of the states, and adopted fresh concessions on that most explosive issue, slavery. It is not too much to say that Rutledge and his committee hijacked the Constitution. Then they remade it.

With the exception of Nathaniel Gorham, the committee members were hardworking lawyers of distinction. Four would be leading legal figures in the new government. Randolph was the first attorney general. Wilson, Ellsworth, and Rutledge served on the new Supreme Court. Even Gorham, a nonlawyer without much formal education, was a state court judge.

From their time in the Confederation Congress, all five knew each other and the weakness of that government. Ellsworth and Randolph served in the Confederation Congress in 1782, while all except Randolph were in the next year's Congress when the Confederation's fiscal problems grew acute. Wilson and Rutledge were friendly enough for the South Carolinian to stay with Wilson when he first arrived in Philadelphia. Randolph was only thirty-four years old; the others were between forty-two and forty-nine.

All had been conspicuous at the Convention. Randolph presented the Virginia Plan. Wilson and Rutledge crafted the compromise on the three-fifths ratio. Ellsworth helped lead the small-state drive for per-state voting in the Senate. Gorham, chair of the Committee of the Whole, repeatedly called for compromise during the acrimonious debate over representation.

The committee members had been more than merely active; they had been constructive. Each had demonstrated a commitment to *finishing* the Constitution. They had raised objections and questions, but they had also found solutions. When their motions were rejected, they did not sulk; they negotiated and demanded, then moved for reconsideration.

Some omissions from this committee were glaring, none more so than Madison. No delegate had greater knowledge of constitutions. None had worked harder to achieve the Convention's mission. Yet Randolph was the Virginian on the committee.

Perhaps the other delegates had heard one too many lecture from the didactic Madison, or maybe his labors over the Convention's notes were thought to place sufficient demands on his time. Perhaps Madison, "in the grip of a great intellectual passion" for the Constitution, seemed a poor choice for the work of compromise and conciliation. Whatever the reasons, it must have galled him to watch others bend to this critical job.

Other omissions are more easily explained. For all his brilliance, Gouverneur Morris had missed three weeks of the Convention in June. General Washington's Olympian gifts were ill suited to the committee's task, while age and ailments removed Dr. Franklin from contention. Roger Sherman was hurrying back to New Haven for his daughter's wedding. Prickliness likely disqualified Mason of Virginia and Gerry of Massachusetts.

The committee had much to do in eleven days, so it set promptly to work. The five committee members likely convened on the second floor of the State House, in the Library Room, sometimes used by the Pennsylvania Assembly. They also could meet in James Wilson's parlor on Market Street, or in the rented rooms of another committee member.

For Rutledge, the committee was a perfect venue. In the intimacy of the committee room, what mattered was not oratory, but persuasive power and personal relationships. Equally important, Rutledge knew what he wanted: a weaker central government and watertight protections for the South and its slave system. The boldest portions of the committee's draft reflected his goals.

James Wilson brought the greatest learning to the panel. As one delegate wrote, he "can trace the causes and effects of every revolution from the earliest stages of the Grecian commonwealth down to the present time." Yet Wilson had demonstrated on the floor of the East Room—and in the battle of Fort Wilson in 1779—that he was no academic milquetoast. Wilson relied on powerful reasoning rather than polish, and he was Rutledge's equal in the former, though by no means in the latter. As one lawyer recalled the Scot,

[Wilson's] manner was rather imposing than persuasive, his habitual effort seemed to be to subdue without conciliating, and the impression left was more like that of submission to a stern than a humane conqueror.

As tough-minded as Rutledge and Wilson were, each esteemed that quality in the other. Perhaps fitting for two such unsentimental figures, neither left behind correspondence between them, nor with any other Framer on political matters. We are left to speculate on the chemistry, and patriotism, that allowed these two hard-driving lawyers to work so well together.

The other three committee members merit notice on their own. Though dubbed "endless Ellsworth" for his prolix speech, and at times parodied for enthusiastic snuff-taking, Connecticut's Oliver Ellsworth was no man to trifle with. In debate and publication, he employed a heavy-handed mockery, the residue of the obstreperous adolescent who had been dismissed from Yale for pranks that included poisoning the communal bread.

Writing after the Convention, Ellsworth's essays supporting the Constitution were such bare-knuckled exercises that a biographer calls them "truly venomous." Ellsworth referred to one Convention delegate as a liar and another as subject to madness. A ghoulish side emerges in a letter to his wife on July 21, just three days before his appointment to the Committee of Detail. After viewing an Egyptian mummy, he confided that "[t]he flesh which I tried with my knife, cuts and looks like smoked beef kept till it grows hard." Perhaps he was joking.

A strong proponent of states' rights, Ellsworth sought to fence in the powers of the new national government. He would play a significant role after the recess as well.

Randolph and Gorham brought milder dispositions to the committee. Randolph, in particular, was all nerve endings, hypersensitive to shifting political winds. That sensitivity would serve him ill in the Convention's closing days, when he agonized over whether to sign the Constitution, then decided not to, only to reverse himself months later. With charity, a biographer refers to the trait as Randolph's "uncanny talent for identifying the 'middle position.' "

Contemporaries judged him more harshly. In a portrait that only a relative could draw, the acid John Randolph of Roanoke compared his cousin Edmund to "the chameleon on the aspen, ever trembling, ever changing." Another Virginian wrote in 1788 that Randolph was "by nature timid and undecided." Viewing Randolph's twists and turns on the Constitution, one historian observed simply, "No one was sure what side he was on."

The least accomplished of the committee members, Gorham of Massachusetts, left the least record behind. His portrait shows a jowly mien consistent with a contemporary description of a "lusty" fellow with an "agreeable and pleasing manner." He parlayed those endowments into the presidency of the Congress in 1786–87, where he struck James Monroe as "greatly overrated." Gorham left little mark on the committee's final product.

None of the five members wrote down a description of the committee sessions, so the story must be pieced together from limited records. Three central documents survive: a first outline in the handwriting of Randolph (with edits by Rutledge), extensive notes and a second draft by Wilson (again, with Rutledge's edits), and the final report presented to the Convention. This evidence places the drafting pen in the hands of those three men.

Randolph's initial outline reads like a joint product, as though the committee members worked through its provisions while the Virginia governor took down their thoughts in outline form. The outline began with two rules for drafting "a fundamental constitution": that it should include "essential principles only," avoiding minor provisions that would change over time; and that it should be stated in "simple and precise language."

Wilson's draft, a far more polished effort, included the first attempt at what became the ringing preamble of the final document ("We the People of the United States . . ."). In this first try, Wilson managed only the more prosaic "We the People of the States of New Hampshire, Massachusetts, Rhode Island," and so on. Judging from the appearance of Wilson's draft, the committee jointly crawled through it in some steamy room, weighing each word and comma, along with what was implied by words and commas omitted. On Wilson's draft, the disciplined regularity of an elegant cursive is periodically brutalized by insertions in Rutledge's barely legible scrawl.

Beginning with Randolph's outline, the committee added numerous provisions that the Convention had never discussed but which were not likely to be very controversial. They might be called "details," even if sizable ones. Examples include the Speech and Debate Clause, which grants immunity to congressmen for comments made in their jobs, and provisions organizing the House of Representatives and the Senate.

More ambitious was the committee's decision that the Senate should negotiate treaties with foreign countries and should name ambassadors. No delegate had ever suggested those arrangements, which reflected the committee's hopes that the Senate would attract "respectable characters" who would be more trustworthy than the president. That change also reinforced the power of the smaller states, which would have greater influence in the Senate. Though the final Constitution would reduce the Senate's role to providing the president with "advice and consent" on treaties and ambassadors, even that reduced role has enabled the Senate to block compacts as important as the Kyoto Protocol on global warming and the Treaty of Versailles after World War I.

Some of the Rutledge Committee's innovations did not survive. The committee designated the president of the Senate to succeed a

John Rutledge (South Carolina)

president who died in office, but the Convention created the vice presidency instead. The committee reversed the Convention's decision that the national government should pay congressmen, replacing it with payment by the states; Ellsworth later led the effort to change it back, freeing national legislators from "too much dependence on the States."

Three of the Rutledge Committee's changes fundamentally reconstituted the new government. Two dealt with the core problem of how to balance power between the states and the national government, though those transformations prompted no dissent from other delegates. The third tore open the divide between North and South.

Led by Rutledge, the committee's first change went to the heart of the matter: the powers of Congress.

In the Convention's early days, Rutledge objected that the Virginia Plan gave Congress open-ended powers; he called for "an exact enumeration" of them. Though Rutledge wanted a stronger national government, he had no interest in an all-powerful one. He insisted that only specific powers should be assigned to the new government. Edmund Randolph responded in late May that Congress's powers could not be defined better, a contention that Wilson echoed.

In mid-July, Rutledge again demanded a "specification of the powers" for Congress. Randolph now agreed with him. Without such a specification, Randolph protested, Congress could "violat[e] all the laws and constitutions of the states." Nevertheless, the Convention approved a resolution giving Congress broad power to legislate

> in all cases for the general interests of the Union, and also in those to which the States are separately incompetent, or in which the harmony of the United States may be interrupted by individual legislation.

In the committee room, Rutledge drove straight to the point. Though convinced that the flimsy Confederation was "not worth a farthing," the South Carolinian feared a Congress with such indefinite powers. With Ellsworth also a strong supporter of states' rights, Rutledge held Randolph to his newly announced position in support of state prerogatives.

The committee did not waste time modifying the broad language approved by the Convention just two weeks before. Randolph's outline ignored that provision, replacing it with eighteen "enumerated" powers, many drawn from the Articles of Confederation. Those eighteen powers began with the power to impose taxes, continued through making war, and finished with declaring what constitutes treason. By this transformation, the committee made the new national government one of limited powers, and did so without any indication that the Convention desired the change.

Not every committee member was as devoted to the states as Rutledge was. James Wilson was skeptical of state governments, and he was nowhere near as malleable as Randolph. The Randolph outline threatened Wilson's vision of a vigorous central government. Esteem Rutledge though he might, Wilson would not be stampeded from his principles. The Scot took responsibility for producing the next draft of the charter. Working with pen and paper at his quiet writing desk, Wilson inserted more critical changes.

Though he retained the enumeration of congressional powers, Wilson added a momentous one: the power to "make all laws that shall be necessary and proper" to carry out Congress's responsibilities. Two years before, Wilson had argued that the Articles effectively granted Congress power to act "when no particular state is competent" to do so. Now he wrote a similar power into the Constitution. This provision would operate as a "catchall," loosening Rutledge's enumerated-powers structure. As secretary of the treasury, Alexander Hamilton would make brilliant use of this clause to defend his policy initiatives, including paying off the war debts of the states and establishing a national bank.

In a second revision, Wilson imposed eight limits on the states, barring them from entering into treaties, issuing bills of credit or currency, taxing imports, or engaging in war. These provisions, which offset Rutledge's limits on Congress, also had no basis in the resolutions approved by the Convention.

Wilson repaired the Supremacy Clause adopted by the Convention, which purported to make national law "supreme" over inconsistent state laws. Wilson's suspicions may have been triggered because the clause was written by Luther Martin of Maryland, a staunch defender of the states. In the calm of the committee room, Wilson noted that Martin's language made national law supreme over state *statutes*, but was silent on state constitutional provisions—a silence that would allow state constitutions to contradict federal law. By eliminating that loophole, Wilson created the tool that courts would use to block state actions that violated the Constitution.

When Rutledge presented the committee's report to the full Convention, no disputes arose over the transformation of the government into one with only the powers specifically named, or over Wilson's restrictions on the states. Perhaps the Convention's silent acquiescence was due to the countervailing impact of the changes, one limiting the national government, the other restraining the states. Perhaps, based on private conversations and the tenor of the debates, the committee had judged well the balance between state and federal powers that would satisfy the delegates.

Rutledge and Wilson thus achieved a creative resolution of the one novel question before the Convention: how to reconcile federal and state powers in an effective structure? Their resolution left both governments sovereign, both separate, both intertwined, one superior. It was a complex and dynamic resolution, and one that every generation has redefined, but it stands as a signal achievement of the Convention.

The committee's third transformation of the Constitution was far less successful. In fact, it would trigger an insurrection in the East Room.

The committee members fabricated three brand-new provisions that were dear to southerners. First they guaranteed that the importation of slaves could never end. Then they banned any taxes on exported goods. Finally, they required that "navigation acts" (that is, legislation concerning interstate and foreign trade) be approved by a two-thirds vote of each house of Congress.

No prior action by the Convention even implied these three provisions. They so completely favored the South that one scholar, in resentful tribute to Rutledge's skills, called them "a monument to Southern craft and gall." The guarantee of the slave trade could help only the southern states, while the ban on export taxes would protect southern tobacco, rice, and indigo.

The two-thirds vote requirement for trade legislation reflected southern anxiety that such laws would force goods into American ships and thereby raise freight costs for planters. Before the Revolution, southerners had suffered under Britain's "navigation acts," which had excluded shipping competitors and driven up freight costs. Those acts also were synonymous with the heavy taxes imposed by the British that played a large part in starting the Revolution. As a further bonus for the South, the two-thirds vote requirement would allow that region to block any legislation on the trade in slaves.

There had been a single preview for these startling provisions. As the delegates prepared on July 23 to create the Committee of Detail, the courtly General Pinckney had delivered an undisguised threat:

[He] reminded the Convention that if the Committee should fail to insert some security to the Southern States against an emancipation of slaves, and taxes on exports, he should be bound by duty to his state to vote against their report.

Though the delegates had not debated these issues, Rutledge's committee proposed to give General Pinckney and the southerners everything they wanted. What accounted for this epic giveaway?

The triumph plainly was Rutledge's, though the committee was stacked in his favor, starting with Randolph. However much the Virginia governor might bemoan slavery, he represented a state premised on slavery. To protect his political future, Randolph had to return home with meaningful protections for slavery.

Rutledge was fortunate in the northerners on the committee, particularly the absence of Gouverneur Morris. Wilson, the Pennsylvanian, was no abolitionist. He not only had sponsored the three-fifths ratio and its enhancement of the South's political power, but also owned a slave who labored every day in the Wilson kitchen just two blocks from the State House. In the coming weeks, Ellsworth of Connecticut would prove consistently solicitous of southern concerns. The Connecticut delegate would argue against any attempt to disturb slavery. Gorham of Massachusetts supported the three-fifths ratio and never criticized slavery through the summer.

The economic provisions of the southern giveaway—the ban on export taxes and the limit on navigation laws—seem not to have troubled either Wilson or Ellsworth. That their states exported many goods may have made them receptive to those provisions.

The biggest losers under the navigation-law provision were those states dependent on shipping, and they were lightly represented at the Convention. New York's delegates had gone home, while Rhode Island never sent any. Gorham represented commercial Massachusetts, but he was no match for Rutledge. Upon his death, Gorham would be eulogized for a temper that was "mild and conciliating, accompanied with patience and prudence"; wonderful qualities for many purposes, but not for resisting the forceful man from Charleston.

While the Rutledge Committee wrote the Constitution, Washington went fishing. Because his carriage needed repair, he set off with Gouverneur Morris, "in his Phaeton with my horses," to the neighborhood of Valley Forge.

On their first day out, "whilst Mr. Morris was fishing," the General visited the ghosts of that place where he and his army had spent the bitter winter of 1777. Finding the works "in ruins," he did not write down the powerful feelings the visit must have stirred. He did record his conversation with local farmers about their buckwheat, which was "excellent food for horses" and also "to lay on fat on hogs."

A few days later, Washington and Morris again escaped the city. This time they traveled to Trenton with the Robert Morrises. Their first fishing day was "not very successful," but on August 4 the General "fished again with more success (for perch)."

Many delegates fled Philadelphia during the recess. Roger Sherman and William Samuel Johnson left several days early, intent on reaching New Haven in time for the wedding of Sherman's daughter. Elbridge Gerry and Major Butler visited their families in New York. General Pinckney took his new wife to Bethlehem, Pennsylvania, in search of cooler air. Delegates from New Jersey, Delaware, and Maryland could reach their homes fairly easily.

As the recess drew to a close, the delegates returned to some of the hottest days of the summer. The sweet anticipation of finishing their work mingled with dismay over Philadelphia's infernal heat. They would soon see the draft Constitution produced by the Rutledge Committee. The great business would take a major stride forward. They had grappled with and resolved so many difficult issues. What challenges remained to derail them?

Chapter Fifteen

Back to Work

AUGUST 6

THE TANG OF fresh ink hung in the air of the East Room on Monday, August 6. With some delegates still making their way back from the recess, attendance was thin that morning. Only eight states had enough delegates present to vote.

The men were eager to see what Rutledge's committee had produced, hopeful that they were entering the home stretch of the effort. Some, though, feared the Convention was headed in the wrong direction, toward a national government with too much power. All of the delegates were disappointed that Philadelphia seemed hotter and muggier than they remembered, the threat of rain that morning adding a charge to the heavy atmosphere.

When General Washington recognized John Rutledge as the first speaker, all eyes turned to the South Carolina table at the edge of the room. Head thrown back and drawn up to his full height, the proud South Carolinian announced that his committee had completed its work. With a dignity equal to the moment, he strode to the front of the chamber and handed the committee's report to the Convention's secretary. Freshly printed versions, with broad margins for notes, were distributed. Over the weekend the delegates had heard scraps of news about the report. Now they fell on their copies, searching out the provisions each cared about most.

As Rutledge returned to his seat, the secretary read the report aloud, droning through the seven pages of the draft Constitution. For Rutledge and the others on his committee, it was a moment of sharp satisfaction. Now the Convention would work from *their* draft. Better than anyone else, the five committee members would know what was in that draft and what was not. From this point forward, four of them—Rutledge, Wilson, Ellsworth, and Gorham—would act as the Convention's sheepdogs, herding the delegates through debates, explaining provisions, proposing alternative language, nudging the Convention to get on with it. Edmund Randolph, in contrast, would thrash back and forth, increasingly uncertain about the plan of government.

Rutledge was the head sheepdog, starting on that first day back, August 6. After the report was read, several delegates proposed to take an extra day off "in order to give leisure to examine the Report." The suggestion was defeated handily.

In the coming days, Rutledge watched with dismay as the delegates repeatedly wrestled with difficult issues only to postpone voting on them. By August 15, he could stand no more. After all, in mid-July Rutledge had despaired that he already had been in Philadelphia twice as long as he expected.

Washington recognized the South Carolinian. According to Madison's laconic summary, Rutledge again "was strenuous against postponing." He "complained much of the tediousness of the proceedings." Fellow committee member Ellsworth joined him "in the same language," predicting, "If we do not decide soon, we shall be unable to come to any decision."

Three days later, Rutledge's patience ran out once more. Hoping to inject a sense of urgency, he "remarked on the length of the session, the probable impatience of the public and the extreme anxiety of many members of the Convention to bring the business to an end." He proposed to add an hour to the daily schedule. They should meet "precisely at 10" in the morning and adjourn "precisely at 4," and "no motion to adjourn sooner [would] be allowed." Chastised, the delegates agreed.

Only four days later, a movement was under way to eliminate the longer sessions. Rutledge managed to defeat that effort, but after two more days he relented. The extra hour was causing resentment among delegates who were tired, hot, and hungry for their dinners. The Convention reverted to its former hours, adjourning at 3 P.M.

The Rutledge Committee's report moved the Convention into a new phase. The nineteen resolutions of the Virginia Plan had carried a tinge of the theoretical. They were no more than an outline of proposals and concepts. The new report added specifics and depth. For men accustomed to working with state constitutions and the Articles of Confederation, the report's structure was familiar and unmistakable. This was a constitution.

The delegates' reactions were as diverse as the delegates themselves. A North Carolinian blithely concluded that "as the great outlines are now marked," he could leave Philadelphia, since the "residue of the work will rather be tedious than difficult." Several expressed the hope that the Convention would finish its work by early or mid September. The diligent Madison suggested that it could take "months" more to finish the job—a view that would have dismayed his colleagues.

In truth, time was running out and the delegates knew it. The nation would not wait indefinitely, nor could the delegates afford to sojourn in Philadelphia for many more months. Not only Rutledge was on edge. By the third week of August, General Washington wrote with exasperation to his old Army colleague, Henry Knox, that the Convention's progress was "slow," and he wished he could add "sure." If no good came from the deliberations, he commented sardonically, "the defects cannot with propriety be charged to the hurry with which the business has been conducted."

To break out of the cycle of amendment and reconsideration and amendment and reconsideration, Rutledge would persuade the delegates to turn again to their pet procedural ploy—referring difficult matters to committees. Rutledge's own Committee of Detail continued to meet until early September, resolving a variety of new issues. Four more Committees of Eleven would be established, culminating in an ultimate catchall panel, the Committee on Postponed Parts, a bureaucratic title of disarming candor. A final five-man panel, the Committee of Style, would produce Gouverneur Morris's masterful final draft of the Constitution.

The process for selecting committee members remains somewhat mysterious. Under the rules of the Convention, each delegate voted for committee members, a practice that gave greater influence to the states that sent more delegates—Pennsylvania with eight, Virginia with five (two had gone home), and (ironically) tiny Delaware with five.

But *how* did the delegates agree on the committee members? That process could determine the committee's product, as illustrated by the pro-South report of Rutledge's committee. Did a few power brokers like Rutledge and Roger Sherman of Connecticut step into the corridor to agree on a "slate"? For Committees of Eleven, did a form of courtesy allow each delegation to designate who from that state would serve on a committee? Did a consensus on candidates develop informally on the floor of the East Room? Or was particular influence wielded by the New England states because they voted first in the North-to-South sequence?

Without knowing the exact procedure for choosing committee members, we know the selection criteria had to vary for each state. For small delegations, the choices were few; if one New Hampshire delegate was serving on an active committee, then the other one had to go on the next committee. For some states, like Connecticut, the delegates' views were largely the same, so it mattered little who was selected. But for delegations like Pennsylvania, which contained diverse personalities, the choice could make a significant difference: Dr. Franklin for compromise; James Wilson for a strong central government and hard work; Gouverneur Morris for creativity; one of the others to muffle Pennsylvania's voice. We know that the delegates' personal qualities were considered; after the Convention, Ellsworth wrote that Luther Martin of Maryland was left off many committees because of his "endless garrulity."

But before the committees could operate, the delegates had to digest the draft Constitution. The most complete record of that first effort comes from an overlooked delegation, Maryland. The Rutledge Committee report hit the fractious Marylanders like a thunderbolt.

• • •

Maryland did not send her most distinguished citizens to the Convention. Of the first five delegates selected by the state assembly, four declined to go, preferring to remain home for a battle over the state's issuance of paper money. That political struggle delayed the naming of the state's delegation until May 22, eight days after the Convention's scheduled starting date.

Once appointed, Maryland's five delegates won no prizes for diligence. None attended the entire Convention, though Daniel Carroll and Daniel Jenifer came close. Ranging in age from twenty-eight (John Francis Mercer) to sixty-four (Jenifer), they included two members of the planter aristocracy (Jenifer and Carroll), the tumultuous attorney general (Luther Martin), an Irish-born physician from a merchant fam-

Luther Martin (Maryland)

ily (James McHenry), and the little-known Mercer, who had moved from Virginia only the year before.

On August 6, for the first time, all five were in the East Room of the State House simultaneously. Dr. McHenry, having missed June and July because of a family illness, recorded the Marylanders' responses to the Rutledge Committee report. Though McHenry was a close aide to General Washington during the war, the Irishman failed to impress at least one delegate, who wrote:

> [McHenry] is a man of specious talents, with nothing of genius to improve them. As a politician there is nothing remarkable in him, nor has he any of the graces of an orator.

Nevertheless, McHenry's notes afford a view of delegates off the Convention floor, a glimpse of that portion of their lives that, like an iceberg, lies concealed below the waterline of the past.

For the Marylanders, the committee report was a revelation of what the new government would be; it was not a welcome revelation. At McHenry's suggestion, the delegation met at 5 P.M. on the day they received the report. They convened at Carroll's lodgings in nearby Germantown. McHenry wanted the delegation to "prepare ourselves to act in unison," since unity had been elusive for the Marylanders. It would continue to be so.

Through many weeks before the recess, only Jenifer and Martin had attended the Convention. With Jenifer supporting a strong government and Martin opposed, the two canceled each other out on eighteen separate ballots, including whether there would be per-state voting in the Senate, and the choice between the New Jersey and Virginia plans. The deadlocks took a toll on collegiality, which was chafed further by Martin's bumptious ways. As one delegate put it, he was "so extremely prolix that he never speaks without tiring the patience of all who hear him."

Having an uneven number of Maryland delegates present would end the stalemates, but the Marylanders still were arguing over whether the Convention should only amend the Articles or should write a new Constitution. Mercer, newly arrived, asked whether the state's people would support the entirely new government outlined by Rutledge's committee. Martin predicted they would not, then wheeled on Jenifer, his nemesis through many hot weeks. With Jenifer's support, the attorney general sputtered, they might have prevented the Convention from undertaking a completely new Constitution.

Twenty-five years senior to Martin, Jenifer had negotiated with George Mason at the Mount Vernon Conference two years before. By this point in the summer, Jenifer could not abide Martin's belligerence. He answered icily that supporting Martin would have been "in vain."

McHenry "begged the gentlemen to observe some order." He sympathized with Martin and hoped Maryland could lead the Convention back to the one-state/one-vote structure of the Articles. If that effort failed, McHenry urged, "we should then agree to render the system reported as perfect as we could."

Carroll objected, insisting that merely amending the Articles would not be enough. Still seeking consensus, McHenry countered that amendments might "sufficiently invigorate it for the exigencies of the times," prompting Martin and Jenifer to disagree from different perspectives. Jenifer echoed Carroll's position, while Martin wanted very little amendment of the Articles. Americans needed only a "confederation [that could] act together on national emergencies." With agreement on the big issues impossible, McHenry proposed they meet again to address specific questions about the committee report.

At the Convention on the following day, McHenry showed the others some specific amendments to the committee report. (They were already down to four Maryland delegates, since Martin left for New York that morning.) McHenry's propositions expressed Maryland's interests as a small slaveholding state with a lively trade through the port of Baltimore.

He wanted the Senate to have an equal power to originate legislation on tax and spending matters ("money bills"), even though Dr. Franklin's compromise over the Fourth of July had confided that power exclusively to the House of Representatives. Also, he proposed that no "navigation act" be enacted unless two-thirds *of each state's representatives* voted in favor of it; this proposal would raise the obstacles to such legislation even higher than the standard inserted by Rutledge that trade laws be enacted by two-thirds majorities of each house of Congress.

Reacting positively to McHenry's propositions, the Marylanders agreed to try another meeting that evening.

Without the combative Martin, the second meeting went more smoothly. McHenry arrived first, finding Carroll alone at 5 P.M. The two men agreed that giving the House the exclusive right to raise and spend money would so harm the small states that it would destroy the Union. They also agreed on the need to strengthen the restrictions on navigation laws in order to protect Maryland's "dearest interest of trade." The Marylanders "almost shuddered" at the idea of a Congress with unfettered power to tax and regulate commerce. They could never support that provision. They greatly feared that Virginia would secure legislation requiring that ships call at Norfolk before proceeding into the Chesapeake Bay.

When Jenifer arrived, he agreed to support McHenry's propositions, as did Mercer when he came. Mercer insisted, though, that he "did not like the system" before the Convention. Having attended the Convention for two whole days, the young man was certain "he would produce a better one."

McHenry recorded no more Maryland conferences, perhaps because their results proved so inconsequential. He never presented his proposals to the Convention, most likely because they were so far out of step with its direction. Franklin's compromise on representation was still holding, while the final Constitution would strengthen, not weaken, the national government's power over commerce, a move that must have driven the Marylanders beyond shuddering and directly to shivering and shaking.

Maryland's only concrete contribution to the Constitution came on the last day of deliberations, when McHenry and Carroll moved to allow states to impose import taxes to pay for harbor and navigation improvements, which were needed for the Chesapeake. As he had at the Mount Vernon Conference two years before, George Mason supported them. The motion carried.

That achievement did not conceal Maryland's disarray. Neither Mercer nor Martin signed the Constitution, though the other three did.

The hard feelings from their days of deadlock were captured in a late exchange between Martin and Jenifer.

Of the final Constitution, Martin told Jenifer, "I'll be hanged if ever the people of Maryland agree to it."

"Then I advise you," Jenifer replied, "to stay in Philadelphia, lest you be hanged."

Jenifer was vindicated. The Maryland state convention ratified the Constitution by a wide margin.

Above the waterline of history, on August 7 the delegates dutifully turned to the Rutledge Committee's draft. As they had with the Virginia Plan, they started at the beginning and trudged through each provision, debating and voting on amendments, then voting on each provision as it was or was not amended. Many questions were worthy of days of analysis, but there was no time. If a dispute resisted resolution, they passed over it. Only scholars need catalog every issue addressed through August, but several remain of sharp interest, beginning with just how democratic the new government would be.

On August 7, Gouverneur Morris demanded a property qualification for voting in national elections. Only landowners should vote, he said, as was true for many state elections. His reasoning was tortuous: true democracy, he said, required denying the vote to those without property, who otherwise "will sell them [their votes] to the rich."

From the Rutledge Committee, both Wilson and Ellsworth opposed Morris, as did Dr. Franklin. Rutledge brought the discussion to a thumping halt when he called Morris's motion "very unadvised," because it "would create division among the people and make enemies" of those denied the vote.

Yet three days later the South Carolinians began to agitate for property qualifications for those *holding* national office. Charles Pinckney insisted that the president should have $100,000 of property, with judges and congressmen having half that amount. That would ensure that those officials would be "independent and respectable." Rutledge seconded, explaining that his committee had not included such a provision, "being embarrassed by the danger on one side of displeasing the people by making [the requirements] high, and on the other of rendering them nugatory by making them low."

Dr. Franklin deflated the proposal with humor. He had observed, he said, that "possession of property increased the desire of more property," and that "some of the greatest rogues he was ever acquainted with were the richest rogues." South Carolina's motion was "rejected by so general a *no*" that the roll of states was not called.

More poignant was James Wilson's battle, on behalf of immigrants like him, to limit residency requirements for holding office. The committee report required only three years of residence for members of the House of Representatives and four for senators. George Mason challenged the provision on August 8. Although he favored "opening a wide door for emigrants," Mason did not wish to have "foreigners and adventurers make laws for us and govern us." All but one state supported a seven-year requirement for the House of Representatives.

On the following day, Gouverneur Morris insisted on fourteen years of residence for senators. Major Butler of South Carolina, an Irish immigrant, offered surprising support. Had he held office upon arriving in America, he told the delegates, "his foreign habits, opinions and attachments would have rendered him an improper agent in public affairs."

Wilson made the question personal. Noting that he was an immigrant—a fact always plain from his accent—Wilson was distressed that he might be "incapacitated from holding a place under the very Constitution which he had shared in the trust of making." While living in Maryland, Wilson related, his immigrant status had placed him "under certain legal incapacities, which never ceased to produce chagrin." Even if one does not wish public office, "to be incapable of being appointed [is] mortifying."

When the fourteen-year proposal was defeated, Rutledge insisted that the Senate residency requirement had to be longer than the seven years approved for the House. Accordingly, a nine-year requirement was imposed.

Wilson would not relent. Four days later, he moved to reduce the House requirement to four years. Supported by Madison and Hamilton (another immigrant), Wilson pointed out that all of Pennsylvania's generals during the Revolution had been foreign-born, as were three of its Convention delegates. He read from the Pennsylvania Constitution, which granted full rights to immigrants after two years of residence. He made no headway; the residency requirements stood unaltered.

Another crusade ended in failure that August. For weeks, Madison had argued unsuccessfully that Congress must have the power to veto state laws. Young Charles Pinckney took up that cause on August 23. To avoid an immediate vote on the controversial provision, Madison suggested it be referred to a committee for study. The opponents of the measure needed no further study. George Mason asked if every road or bridge in the nation should be subject to congressional veto? John Rutledge was categorical. By binding states "hand and foot," this provision "would damn and ought to damn the Constitution." By a narrow margin, the delegates refused to refer the question to a committee.

This refusal did not mean that states could ignore the new Constitution. By giving federal courts "the judicial power" to apply the Constitution, the Convention assigned to those courts the task of reviewing state laws for constitutional violations. State courts already applied state constitutions to those laws, and most delegates (though not all) expected the federal courts to perform a comparable review.

On two issues, the bedazzling elements of money and power led the delegates down circuitous paths. The first was broached by that inveterate stirrer-of-pots, Gouverneur Morris. On Thursday, August 16, the Pennsylvania delegate proposed to remove Congress's power to "emit bills on the credit of the United States." Though the phrase is murky to modern readers, Morris aimed to bar the national government from issuing paper money. A few delegates opposed the idea, but most competed to applaud it. Major Butler was "urgent" in his support, while a New Hampshireman preferred rejecting the Constitution to retaining the words "and emit bills." A Delaware delegate declaimed that those three words, if not deleted, "would be as alarming as the mark of the Beast in Revelations."

Having adopted Morris's motion, many delegates surely thought they had barred the national government from issuing paper money. It did not turn out that way. Having removed Congress's power to issue paper money, the Convention did not actually *prohibit* it from doing so.

The Convention took that extra step for the states, denying them the power to issue money in a vote intended, in the words of Roger Sherman, to "crush paper money." By not denying that power to Congress, the delegates left open the claim that the power was contained within the authority to take "necessary and proper" actions (inserted by Wilson in the committee's draft). Ninety-seven years later, that was exactly what the Supreme Court held, allowing the "mark of the Beast" into American wallets.

The second intersection of money and power focused on whether the House of Representatives should have exclusive power to originate tax and spending bills. That exclusive power was part of the compromise brokered by Dr. Franklin in the first Committee of Eleven; it was intended to compensate large states for accepting per-state voting in the Senate. Giving the House authority over "money bills" would empower the larger states, which should dominate that branch of the Congress.

The confusion started on Wednesday, August 8, when young Charles Pinckney moved to eliminate the money-bill provision, "as giving no peculiar advantage to the House of Representatives and as clogging the government." Madison and Wilson, leaders of the large states, supported the South Carolinian. Madison dismissed the provision as "a source of injurious altercations between the two Houses" of Congress, and it was dropped by a 7–4 vote, with the support of Virginia, Pennsylvania, and South Carolina, former members of the large-state/slave-state alliance.

Other large-state delegates grew alarmed. Randolph of Virginia demanded that the money bill provision be reconsidered. Admitting that he did not much care for it, he insisted that the large states should at least get what they had been promised in the Franklin compromise. Mason advanced a more principled argument. The House of Representatives, like the House of Commons, would be elected by the people and should control money matters.

Wilson and Madison shunned Randolph's demand. John Rutledge descended to slang in calling the provision an attempt to "bubble" the public and "a mere tub to the whale," referring to a sailors' practice of flinging a tub into the water to divert a whale from harming their ship.

South Carolina had such a requirement, he said, and it was ineffective. In his state, if "the amendment of the Senate is pleasing to the other House, they wink at the encroachment; if it be displeasing, then the Constitution is appealed to."

John Dickinson of Delaware noted that eight state constitutions had such a provision, as did Great Britain. Appealing to the common-law training shared by many delegates, he insisted, "Experience must be our only guide. Reason may mislead us."

Dickinson added a political point. In the contest over ratification, "[a]ristocracy will be the watchword; the shibboleth among its adversaries." By favoring the democratic House over the aristocratic Senate, the money-bill provision would reassure the people.

Reason trumped experience. On August 13 the money-bill provision lost by a 4–7 vote. Notably, Virginia now supported the provision, General Washington joining with Randolph and Mason to outvote Madison.

But two days later, Randolph had Rutledge's support for the provision, having persuaded him that it was neither a bubble nor a tub-to-the-whale. The Convention postponed the issue. Like so many others, the question would end up before the Committee on Postponed Parts.

As August crawled by, the pro-South provisions in the Rutledge Committee's report began to emerge as a major obstacle to the Convention's progress. The southerners' every wish had been gratified, but the contest was not over. The same elephant remained in the parlor, but something had changed. Now the delegates from the nonslave states wanted to confront it.

Chapter Sixteen

The Curse of Heaven

AUGUST 8–29

A S IT HAD BEFORE, slavery came up in a sideways fashion. On the second day of debate over the Rutledge Committee report, the Convention was addressing the allocation of seats in the House of Representatives. A North Carolinian wanted to clarify how the three-fifths ratio would be applied. His motion was adopted.

The General recognized Rufus King of Massachusetts. King was angry; the three-fifths ratio, he spat out, was "a most grating circumstance."

King was one of nature's lucky ones. Of middle size, he was darkly handsome and well spoken. Having been born to a wealthy merchant family, he married into a wealthier one. Though only thirty-two, the Harvard-educated lawyer had already earned high regard at the Convention. One delegate recorded that there was "something peculiarly strong and rich in his expression, clear and convincing in his arguments." From his time in the Confederation Congress, King was known to oppose slavery. His efforts to exclude slavery from the Northwest Territory helped lay the groundwork for the Ipswich Miracle. By nature pragmatic, King ordinarily took thoughtful positions. But on Wednesday, August 8, after absorbing the pro-South provisions of the draft

Constitution, King was as hot as the brick walkways outside the State House.

He told the delegates that he had been willing to accept the three-fifths ratio as the price of creating a strong national government. The Rutledge Committee's report "put an end to all these hopes" by ensuring the continued importation of slaves and banning export taxes. The result had "so much inequality and unreasonableness" that "Northern states could never be reconciled to it."

King stopped short of abolitionism. His complaint was that the South was getting too much: the three-fifths ratio increased its power; banning export taxes protected its economy; and preserving the slave trade ensured its oppressive social system. It was more than he could stand. King had hoped "that at least a time would have been limited for the importation of slaves. *He never could agree to let them be imported without limitation and then be represented in the National Legislature.*"

Though he spoke strongly, King signaled that he was willing to deal. Perhaps, he added, the three-fifths ratio could be dropped, or exports made taxable.

Roger Sherman attempted to calm the waters. The gawky Connecticut delegate conceded that the slave trade was "iniquitous." Of course it was. Still, he urged, the Convention had long ago adopted the three-fifths ratio; it should not be challenged now.

Sherman's soft words did not work on Gouverneur Morris. Prodded by King's outburst, the Pennsylvanian reared up on his peg leg, brimming over with rage and righteousness. He moved that representatives be allocated according to the number of "free inhabitants," expunging the three-fifths ratio. Then, declaring that he "never would concur in upholding domestic slavery," he delivered the first abolitionist speech in American political life.

Slavery, he proclaimed, was a "nefarious institution—it was the curse of heaven on the states where it prevailed." Contrasted with the prosperity and order of nonslave states, slavery brought "misery and poverty" to "the barren wastes of Virginia, Maryland, and the other states having slaves." He bitterly summarized the effect of the three-fifths ratio:

[T]he inhabitant of Georgia and South Carolina who goes to the Coast of Africa, and in defiance of the most sacred laws of humanity tears away his fellow creatures from their dearest connections and damns them to the most cruel bondages, shall have more votes in a government instituted for protection of the rights of mankind, than the citizen of Pennsylvania or New Jersey who views with a laudable horror so nefarious a practice.

And what were the northern states to receive in return, he asked? Because of the risk of slave uprisings, northern militias must defend southern states against "those very slaves." Northerners will pay import taxes, while southerners import more slaves, duty-free, so "their votes in the national government [will be] increased" and their untaxed exports grow. With a flourish, he announced that he would sooner pay a tax to purchase every slave "than saddle posterity with such a Constitution."

Gouverneur Morris (Pennsylvania)

Only one voice supported Morris. Jonathan Dayton of New Jersey, the youngest man in the room, seconded Morris's motion.

Roger Sherman again tried to defuse the situation, employing illogic that approached nonsense. He assured the delegates that the three-fifths ratio meant only that "the freemen of the Southern states" would be represented "according to the taxes paid by them, and the Negroes are only included in the estimate of the taxes." No one pointed out the twin fallacies of Sherman's remark—that slaves were not taxes, and that the freemen of the North would receive no representation for taxes *they* paid.

The question was called on Morris's motion. The defenders of slavery did not need coherent arguments. Only New Jersey voted yes.

The storm over slavery subsided for the moment, but the northerners were not done. John Rutledge had driven his committee to give the South everything it wanted. His nature would not allow him to try for less than complete victory. But he had overreached, violating the basic rule of this Convention: no one would get everything he wanted.

By concentrating his fire on the slave trade, Morris attacked the most vulnerable of the pro-South provisions. The brutality of the passage from Africa, and the high mortality rate among the enslaved, were widely reviled. While the Convention sat, a Philadelphia magazine carried an emotional depiction of the journey:

> The rolling sea hurries the heaving hearts: the sighing souls escape! . . . The groans of a hundred men, the sighs of a hundred women, the cries of a hundred youths are one! . . . Silence prevails, and the dead bodies are thrown to the watchful sharks, whose ravenous jaws are glutted with the flesh of men! The markets in the west are full of slaves. The fathers of oppression are there: their flinty hearts regard them as beasts of burden.

Also, challenging the slave trade was an easier political position than abolition. It did not threaten slave owners with immediate economic loss, nor did it raise the confounding challenge of what to do with black ex-slaves in a society that defined itself as white. Finally, cutting off the slave trade might slow the spread of slavery until some policy could be contrived to reverse it.

Even in the South, the politics of the slave trade were complex. By the summer of 1787, only Georgia and North Carolina allowed slave imports. Just three weeks before the Convention began, Philadelphia's *Evening Chronicle* reported that South Carolina had banned slave imports for two years. After losing many slaves during the Revolution, planters there had plunged deep into debt to restock their plantations. When indigo prices fell, the planters defaulted on their debts and merchants were ruined. Largely to repair the state's battered credit and balance of trade—and to save the planters from themselves—state legislators pushed for an end to slave imports.

Not that the slave trade lacked for defenders. General Pinckney would speak for many in 1788 when he declared his commitment to it:

> [W]hile there remained one acre of swamp-land uncleared of South Carolina, I would raise my voice against restricting the importation of negroes. I am as thoroughly convinced as that gentleman is, that the nature of our climate, and the flat, swampy situation of our country, obliges us to cultivate our lands with negroes, and that without them South Carolina would soon be a desert waste.

In the same remarks, General Pinckney stressed that many Convention delegates opposed the slave trade, which he attributed to "the religious and political prejudices of the Eastern and Middle States," while Virginia "was warmly opposed to our importing more slaves."

Despite the vulnerability of the slave trade, and despite Morris's incendiary words, many days lapsed without further mention of it. Almost two weeks passed before the delegates reached the ban on export taxes in the Rutledge Committee report.

Tuesday, August 21, was a hot rainy day from Philadelphia's seemingly limitless supply of sultry weather. When several delegates moved to soften the ban on export taxes, southerners replied with harsh ultimatums. Major Butler "strenuously opposed" export taxes, while a North

To BE SOLD, on board the Ship *Bance-Yland*, on tuesday the 6th of *May* next, at *Ashley-Ferry*; a choice cargo of about 250 fine healthy NEGROES, just arrived from the Windward & Rice Coast. —The utmost care has already been taken, and shall be continued, to keep them free from the least danger of being infected with the SMALL-POX, no boat having been on board, and all other communication with people from *Charles-Town* prevented.

Austin, Laurens, & Appleby.

N. B. Full one Half of the above Negroes have had the SMALL-POX in their own Country.

Advertisement for slave sales (1770)

Carolinian predicted that giving Congress the power to levy such taxes would "destroy the last hope of an adoption of the [Constitution]." The five slave states and their Connecticut allies defeated a proposal to allow Congress to impose such taxes with a two-thirds vote.

Having preserved the export tax ban, the southerners were sandbagged by one of their own. Back from his trip to New York, Luther Martin was firmly established as the delegate least concerned about irritating his colleagues. At the end of the session on August 21, he started talking like a northerner. He argued in favor of taxing slave imports, or eliminating the slave trade. Trafficking in humans, he insisted, "was inconsistent with the principles of the revolution and dishonorable to the American character."

Rutledge flew to the defense of slavery. The intensity of his response reflected the risk posed by Martin's motion. Rutledge did not address moral principles. That was not his style, and it was far from his strongest ground. Instead, Rutledge talked hard politics and hard money. "Religion and humanity have nothing to do with this question," he said, defiantly challenging each delegate.

> Interest alone is the governing principle with nations. *The true question at present is whether the Southern states shall or shall not be parties to the Union.* If the Northern States shall consult their interest, they will not oppose the increase of slaves which will increase the commodities of which they will become the carriers.

Rutledge pushed the delegates away from the morality of slavery to a brutal realpolitik. The other states had to choose. If they wanted South Carolina in the Union, they must back off on slavery. If they did so, they would make money.

Connecticut once again supported the South. Oliver Ellsworth approved Rutledge's cold-eyed view. "The morality or wisdom of slavery," he said, "are considerations belonging to the states themselves." The national government need not be concerned with slavery.

The last speaker of the day, Charles Pinckney, agreed that South Carolina would never join a nation that banned the slave trade (despite the suspension of the trade then prevailing there). If left "at liberty on this subject," he added, the state might ban the trade on its own.

In the cooler air of the following morning, August 22, the delegates began a notable exercise in group hypocrisy. The attack on the slave trade resumed from yet another unexpected quarter. George Mason of Virginia, owner of several hundred slaves, took to his feet to denounce the trade, "this infernal traffic." Echoing Morris's jeremiad, Mason told the delegates that the slave trade risked "the judgment of heaven" against America:

> As nations cannot be rewarded or punished in the next world they must be in this. By an inevitable chain of causes and effects [P]rovidence punishes national sins by national calamities.

Betraying no embarrassment over his own slaveholdings, Mason blamed the British and the New Englanders for their "lust of gain" which sustained "this nefarious traffic."

Those supple men from Connecticut, Roger Sherman and Oliver Ellsworth, strained to deflect the attack. Sherman piously repeated his disapproval of the slave trade, but denied that the "public good" required that it end. Donning rosy-hued lenses, he predicted that "the good sense of the states" would lead them to abolish slavery "by degrees." Ellsworth repeated that assertion, foreseeing that in the future slavery "will not be a speck in our country." Completely misunderstanding human nature, Ellsworth predicted that fear of slave insurrections would cause owners to extend "kind treatment of the slaves."

Slavery's defenders would not yield the high moral ground to Mason, a slaveholder. Ellsworth suggested that if the question were viewed in "a moral light" (which Ellsworth had no wish to do), then the Convention "ought to go farther and free those already in the country." General Pinckney pointed out that Virginia already had so many slaves that a ban on slave imports would actually benefit Virginians, who could sell excess slaves in other states for higher prices.

Angry, Charles Pinckney slipped the bounds of reason so far as to defend slavery as a positive public good. "If slavery be wrong," he proclaimed, "it is justified by the example of all the world." Both ancient and modern states allowed slavery, and "in all ages one half of mankind have been slaves."

His cousin, General Pinckney, insisted flatly that "South Carolina and Georgia cannot do without slaves." John Rutledge once more drew a line in the sand:

> If the Convention thinks that North Carolina, South Carolina and Georgia will ever agree to the plan, unless their right to import slaves be untouched, the expectation is vain. The people of those states will never be such fools as to give up so important an interest.

The southern threats did not have the desired effect. For the first time that summer, delegates from the rest of the nation roused themselves on slavery. They insisted that the new government must have power over the slave trade.

The respected John Dickinson of Delaware rose. His words had special force. After inheriting thirty-seven slaves, Dickinson had freed them all just one year before; under Delaware law he not only lost the value of the slaves, but also had to post a bond for each he set free. Dickinson told the delegates it was "inadmissible on every principle of honor and safety that the importation of slaves should be authorized."

Realizing that their ultimatums were not working, the South Carolinians began casting about for an accommodation.

General Pinckney offered the first crack in southern intransigence, admitting that maybe imported slaves could be taxed. Northerners responded indirectly. James Wilson criticized the exemption of slaves from any import tax, while Rufus King of Massachusetts called that exemption "an inequality that could not fail to strike the commercial sagacity of the Northern and middle states."

The South Carolinians got the message. General Pinckney and Rutledge suggested a committee should consider taxes on slave imports. Leaping at the opening, Gouverneur Morris proposed that the committee also address the ban on export taxes and the two-thirds vote requirement for navigation acts. "These things," he said, "may form a bargain among the Northern and Southern states."

At this key juncture, another ambivalent slaveholder from Virginia entered the fray. While serving on Rutledge's committee, Edmund Randolph helped produce the package of prosouthern provisions. Ever changeable, Randolph now announced that he could never agree to a Constitution that exempted slave imports from taxation, which would "revolt the Quakers, the Methodists, and many others in the states having no slaves." Then again, he added, striking the clause might drive South Carolina and Georgia from the Union. A committee would have to find some middle ground. Randolph surely could not.

The Convention chose a Committee of Eleven to address *both* that issue *and*—as Morris proposed—Congress's power to regulate commerce. The mood for compromise dictated the committee members selected. From Virginia, the delegates picked not the combative Mason, but Madison, whose strongest desire on the slavery issue was for it to go away. From South Carolina came neither the aggressive Rutledge nor the blustery Major Butler, but the popular General Pinckney—described by one contemporary as "frank, manly, and liberal." The delegates passed over Wilson and Morris from Pennsylvania, picking the largely invisible George Clymer, a merchant. The choice from Connecticut was neither Sherman nor Ellsworth, whose alliance with the southerners was increasingly open, but the affable William Samuel Johnson.

After the day's intense exchanges, many delegates retired to the banks of the Delaware River to observe a test of a newfangled steamboat designed by John Fitch of Connecticut. At this stage of the Convention, any diversion was a godsend. King and Gorham of Massachusetts had whiled away a recent evening reviewing heraldry treatises in a local library, "looking for the coats of arms of most of our acquaintances."

Fitch's boat, the *Perseverance,* preceded by almost two decades the Robert Fulton vessel that is often acclaimed as the first steamboat. It was a narrow, odd-looking affair, propelled by steam-driven racks of paddles on either side. A tireless promoter, Fitch had met previously with several Convention delegates, including Washington, Madison, and William Houston of New Jersey. He had failed in his top goal of enlisting the support of Dr. Franklin, the nation's leading inventor. For steamboats, Dr. Franklin favored a form of jet propulsion over Fitch's design.

Fitch's steamboat

By August, the *Perseverance* was reaching speeds of four miles an hour when steaming up the Delaware River with a full load. The inventor offered a ride to Johnson of Connecticut and any delegates who dared. The response was enthusiastic. Most delegates attended the demonstration, Fitch recalled, though not Washington. (The General's absence may be explained by his endorsement of a competing steamboat design of James Rumsey, who never achieved commercial service.) Fitch added that "Governor Randolph with several of the Virginia members were pleased to give it any countenance they could." In 1790, Fitch ran regular boats between Philadelphia and Trenton, though he shut down the service after losing money on every trip.

Fitch's boat only briefly distracted the delegates from the thorny questions of slavery and trade. Governor William Livingston of New Jersey, appointed to head the new Committee of Eleven, stepped from the Convention's shadows to the center of the controversy.

Born to a powerful New York family, Livingston had retired to New Jersey in middle life, but then was drawn into Revolutionary politics. He became that state's first governor in 1777, holding the office until his death in 1790. Like other New Jersey delegates, he was antislavery.

Livingston had joined the New York abolition society two years before. In 1786, he pushed through the New Jersey legislature a ban on the slave trade and a bill freeing his own two slaves. Slavery, he wrote, "is utterly inconsistent with the principles of Christianity and humanity, and in Americans, who have almost idealized liberty, [it is] peculiarly odious and disgraceful." With John Dickinson and Luther Martin also on the new committee, General Pinckney was going to have his hands full.

After the Convention, both Martin and General Pinckney provided descriptions of the Livingston committee. Martin's version carried his irreverent edge:

[T]he eastern states, notwithstanding their aversion to slavery, were very willing to indulge the Southern states, at least with a temporary liberty to prosecute the slave trade, provided the southern states would, in their turn, gratify them, by laying no restriction on navigation acts; and after a very little time the committee, by a great majority, agreed on a report.

General Pinckney's version had less edge:

> "Show some period," said the members from the Eastern States, "when it may be in our power to put a stop, if we please, to the importation of this weakness [slaves], and we will endeavor, for your convenience, to restrain the religious and political prejudices of our people on this subject." The Middle States and Virginia made us no such proposition; they were for an immediate and total prohibition.

Livingston presented the committee's report on Friday, August 24, just two days after the panel was named. General Pinckney had given ground on several points. Using a euphemism for slaves ("such persons as the several states . . . shall think proper to admit"), the slave trade would continue until 1800, but thereafter Congress could stop it. Moreover, slave imports would be taxed like other imports. Finally, no two-thirds majority requirement would apply to navigation laws.

When the Convention turned to this report on the following day, a Saturday, General Pinckney already was renegotiating it. Seconded by Gorham of Massachusetts, he moved to add eight years to the protection for the slave trade, to 1808. "Twenty years," Madison grumbled, "will produce all the mischief that can be apprehended from the liberty to import slaves." The sectional division on the vote was stark. Three New England states joined four southern ones in voting aye, with Virginia and the middle states on the short end. Then the delegates capped the tax on imported slaves at $10 apiece.

With the substance of the new deal taken care of, the politicians in the room turned to appearances. Gouverneur Morris tugged on southern whiskers, moving to substitute "slaves" for "such persons," then to specify that slave imports were authorized only for North Carolina, South Carolina, and Georgia, since only those states wanted them. George Mason agreed to the word "slaves," but opposed naming the three states "lest it should give offense." Sherman opposed Morris on both points, finding his proposed language "not pleasing."

Sherman's sensibilities also led him to object that taxing slave imports would "acknowledg[e] men to be property." General Pinckney waved away the objection, considering it a small price for gaining twenty years of slave imports. The Convention postponed addressing the two-thirds vote requirement for navigation laws.

The South Carolinians were not finished. Three days later, at the close of the session on Tuesday, August 28, General Pinckney and Major Butler proposed to add a requirement that "fugitive slaves and servants be delivered up like criminals." Congress had included that provision in the Northwest Ordinance, the price for the Ipswich Miracle.

The delegates greeted the Fugitive Slave Clause doubtfully. Wilson complained of the expense of tracking down fugitives and delivering them up. Sherman "saw no more propriety in the public seizing and surrendering a slave or servant, than a horse." The South Carolinians withdrew the motion, but they were busy that night with Sherman and the New Englanders. To secure the Fugitive Slave Clause, they agreed to give up the two-thirds requirement for navigation acts.

Next day, General Pinckney offered a cloying tribute to "the Eastern States." He noted New England's commercial losses during the Revolution, its "liberal conduct" toward South Carolina at the Convention, and "the interest the weak Southern states had in being united with the strong Eastern ones." He laid the flattery on with a spatula:

> He had himself, [General Pinckney] said, prejudices against the Eastern States before he came here, but would acknowledge that he had found them as liberal and candid as any men whatever.

In view of what capital fellows the New Englanders were, General Pinckney announced, he would abandon the two-thirds vote requirement for trade laws.

Supporting the deal, John Rutledge appealed to national goals, not regional interest. Any single navigation act might "for a little while" harm the South, he said, but "[a]s we are laying the foundation for a great empire, we ought to take a permanent view of the subject and not look at the present moment only."

In the final vote, South Carolina joined six states north of Maryland to reject the two-thirds requirement for navigation laws.

South Carolina promptly moved to collect on its part of the deal.

Major Butler renewed his fugitive slave motion; it passed unanimously, without discussion.

In the Convention's last week, John Rutledge tied down one last loose end on slavery, securing a provision that the twenty-year extension of the slave trade could never be amended. It was the only provision in the Constitution with that protection.

Slavery was the original sin in which the nation was conceived. Gouverneur Morris and Rufus King knew it, and said so. John Dickinson and William Livingston knew it; they had freed their slaves. The delegates who belonged to abolition societies—Franklin, Hamilton, and Livingston—certainly knew it. Oliver Ellsworth, who steadfastly stood by his southern allies, reminded the delegates that if the matter were viewed "in a moral light," then every slave should be freed; he knew it. Roger Sherman called the slave trade iniquitous; he knew it. Each of those ambivalent Virginians—Mason and Madison and Randolph and the General himself—all knew it. The men from South Carolina surely knew it. Charles Pinckney said he would vote against the slave trade within his own state; John Rutledge would not discuss the morality of slavery, an argument he knew he could only lose.

When he returned to South Carolina, General Pinckney boasted of the protections for slavery that he and his colleagues had won:

> [W]e have secured an unlimited importation of negroes for twenty years. . . . [T]he general government can never emancipate them, for no such authority is granted; . . . We have obtained a right to recover our slaves in whatever part of America they may take refuge, which is a right we had not before. In short, . . . we have made the best terms for the security of this species of property it was in our power to make. We would have made better if we could; but, on the whole, I do not think them bad.

Northerners were less cheerful on the subject. James Wilson claimed that the slave trade provision would "lay the foundation for banishing slavery out of this country; . . . though the period is more distant than I could wish." With regret, he added, "It was all that could be obtained. I am sorry it was no more."

Fifteen years after, Rufus King's regret focused on the three-fifths ratio and the "preponderance which it has given to the slave-holding states over the other states." It was one of the Constitution's "greatest blemishes." The nonslave delegates, he said, "injudiciously" agreed to the ratio because they thought that it would mean the South would pay extra direct taxes. But the national government—reflecting the South's extra power under the three-fifths ratio—rarely imposed direct taxes, so the North never got the financial advantage it sought.

Madison blamed South Carolina and Georgia for preserving the slave trade, adding, "Great as the evil is, a dismemberment of the union would be worse." McHenry made the same point, insisting that most delegates wanted to ban the trade outright, a view that Madison echoed in private correspondence years later.

The Convention's proslavery actions had grim consequences. The twenty-year extension of the trade allowed as many as 170,000 more Africans to be imported. The additional eight years of slave trade that General Pinckney wheedled from the Convention (from 1800 to 1808) was no small thing. South Carolina imported 75,000 Africans between 1804 and 1808, when Congress finally abolished slave imports.

For seven decades after the Convention, the three-fifths ratio gave southern politicians extra power they wielded to protect the slave system, following the example set by Rutledge and General Pinckney. The Fugitive Slave Clause proved an important link in the chains of American slavery, making freedom even more elusive for southern slaves and leaving blacks in free states always vulnerable to seizure and enslavement. In a lawsuit over the fugitive slave provision, the *Dred Scott* case, the Supreme Court declared in 1857 that enslaved humans were property—the assertion from which even Connecticut's Roger Sherman recoiled.

Rufus King and James Madison lived well into the nineteenth century, long enough to see slavery conflicts grow more and more bitter. Rueful over the actions of the summer of 1787, their responses bore striking parallels.

In 1819, the retired Madison sketched out a detailed plan to sell off western lands and use the proceeds to buy slaves and ship them to Africa. In 1833, when he was eighty, he became president of the American Colonization Society, which aimed to send blacks to Africa. Eight years earlier, then-Senator King introduced a resolution to spend the proceeds from the sale of public lands to emancipate slaves and move them to empty parts of the nation.

But King and Madison had grown old and their solutions were fanciful. The problem that defied resolution in 1787 had only become more intractable. When southern guns fired on Fort Sumter in April 1861, a grandson of John Adams wrote in his diary, "We the children of the third and fourth generation are doomed to pay the penalties of the compromises made by the first."

Chapter Seventeen

David Brearley's Presidency

AUGUST 24–SEPTEMBER 7

I N THE THIRD WEEK of August, David Brearley of New Jersey complained that "[e]very article is again argued over, with as much earnestness and obstinacy as before." Brearley, chief justice of his state's supreme court, would soon have greater reason to regret that pattern.

Four days after Brearley wrote his letter, the delegates reached the presidency article of the Rutledge Committee report. It was Friday, August 24, almost too late to revise the elements George Mason pushed through on the last day before the recess: that Congress would choose the president for a single seven-year term. The report named the president commander in chief, describing his major powers as executing the laws and appointing government officers.

On that hot Friday morning, the Convention avoided the flights of near-fancy that infected its discussion of the presidency a month before. No one proposed a lottery to select congressmen to pick the president, or three regional chief executives, or fifteen-year terms. Still, no consensus emerged on the presidency and no one attempted to shape the debate. Mason, so forceful on the issue on the day before the recess, was silent.

The opening exchanges were familiar, even depressingly so. Supported by Wilson, Daniel Carroll of Maryland proposed election of the president "by the people." The motion lost by a thumping margin.

The small and large states arm-wrestled for advantage. Rutledge won approval for both houses of Congress to elect the president by joint ballot, which would dilute the small states' advantage in the Senate. Dayton of New Jersey countered that each state should cast one vote when Congress voted on the president, which would nullify Rutledge's motion. Dayton's motion lost by one vote.

Staunchly opposed to congressional selection of the president, Gouverneur Morris revived Wilson's idea that the people could vote for electors who would choose the president. On the "abstract question" of using electors, the Convention's gears locked up tight; four were in favor, four against, two states divided, and Massachusetts absent. A motion to send the question to a committee yielded a different deadlock, 5–5, one state divided. Despairing of forward motion, the Convention abandoned the subject "at the instance of the deputies from New Jersey."

In the absence of William Paterson, who had gone home, Chief Justice Brearley was leading the Jerseymen, rising several times on the twenty-fifth. Long lost to memory, the forty-two-year-old Brearley had served eight years on the state's highest court. The scanty records about him sketch a thoughtful, steady personality, with little flash or affection for the limelight.

The recorded impressions of the man represent faint praise, though not quite damnation: "[A] man of good, rather than of brilliant parts," was one; another reported, "Although hardly a brilliant figure, he was capable and respected." The *New Jersey Journal* was more generous, granting him "perspicuity of argument and persuasive eloquence which carried conviction with it."

Though he missed only two days of the Convention, Brearley spoke fewer than a dozen times. A fellow delegate observed that "as an orator he has little to boast of," which may account for his reticence. His contributions were larger offstage, beginning with the crafting of New

David Brearley (New Jersey)

Jersey's failed alternative to the Virginia Plan. Brearley's longest address, delivered in the early stages of the small-state rebellion, had recommended dividing the nation into states of equal size, a mocking proposal designed to illustrate the futility of the large states' quest for equality in representation.

Brearley's revolutionary credentials were impeccable. His father, also David Brearley, had led land riots against New Jersey's royal proprietors in 1747. After being jailed for high treason, the elder Brearley was liberated by a crowd of neighbors. He lived to see his sons help drive the British from the country.

The younger Brearley rose to the rank of colonel of militia in three years of fighting, including the battles at Brandywine and Monmouth. His principles were firm. Shortly after becoming chief justice, he vacated two convictions for trading with the British. Only a few months from combat duty, Brearley ruled that the state constitution overrode a statute that allowed a jury of only six (not twelve) to hear trials of such treacherous conduct. Even to prosecute traitors, Brearley would permit no shortcuts. The decision marked the first time an American court found a statute unconstitutional.

Cool and rainy conditions greeted the delegates on Monday, August 27. They were an impatient group. After three weeks of slogging through the Rutledge Committee's report, they had yet to address twelve of its twenty-three articles. To accelerate, the delegates continued to refer contested issues to committees, or postpone them outright. Time was pressing on them. They needed to make progress.

The twenty-seventh began with presidential impeachment. When Gouverneur Morris raised a concern, the topic was dropped. The loquacious Morris could stall forward movement for hours.

The delegates took up who would succeed a president unable to complete his term. Morris objected again, so that issue was skipped, too. They had to keep moving.

By the end of that last week of August, the acceleration strategy had worked, after a fashion. As the hour for adjournment drew nigh on Friday, August 31, the delegates had reached the end of the committee report, Article 23, which prescribed the procedure for ratifying the Constitution. Increasingly disaffected, George Mason supported postponing the question, declaring great unhappiness with the draft Constitution. To undo the mischief caused by the Convention, he insisted, a second Convention might be required. Provoked, Gouverneur Morris fired back. He had "long wished for another Convention," he announced, "that will have the firmness to provide a vigorous government."

Brushing aside the theatrics, the delegates approved an amended version of the ratification clause. They had reached the end of the Rutledge Committee draft, but there was no time for elation. A month's agenda of hard questions had been sent off to committees and remained unresolved.

The Rutledge Committee was considering additional powers for Congress, whether to preserve the rights of habeas corpus and freedom of the press, and a proposed Executive Council to advise the president. Two committees chaired by Livingston had finished their work (on, respectively, the slave trade and the assumption of state war debts), but a panel headed by Roger Sherman was considering equal treatment of American ports.

Then there were the many postponed questions, starting with the presidency. For these, the Convention established the Committee on Postponed Parts.

The members chosen for this committee reflected the delegates' impatience. They wanted decisions, not debate. The nation eagerly awaited the new government charter; the delegates' personal obligations clamored for attention; the cooler weather, with its promise of changing seasons, reinforced the need for dispatch.

The Committee on Postponed Parts bristled with brainpower. Rufus King was there from Massachusetts and Roger Sherman from Connecticut. Gouverneur Morris represented Pennsylvania, with John Dickinson of Delaware. For Virginia, Madison finally sat on a crucial committee.

Improbably, at the head of these luminaries sat David Brearley, with his "good, if not brilliant parts." Perhaps his months of quiet enterprise had earned respect from his peers that history has forgotten. Perhaps his sober competence was the right tool for forging agreement among the more brilliant. Whatever the reason, New Jersey's chief justice assumed heavy responsibilities.

The committee's agenda was fearsome. It had to define Congress's powers to impose taxes and to make war, to decide whether to authorize copyrights and patents, and to plan for the seat of the new government. How should relations with Indian tribes be conducted? Brearley's committee even had to grapple with the endless dispute over whether the House of Representatives should have exclusive power over money bills. The presidency, however, dwarfed the other issues. The Convention still had not agreed on the structure of an entire branch of government.

After less than one hundred hours, Brearley presented the committee's report on the presidency. Standing "in his place" in the East Room on Tuesday, September 4, the Jerseyman showed a touch of pride by reading the report aloud before handing it to the secretary for a second reading. Pride was not entirely out of order. Meeting only when the Convention was in recess, Brearley's committee comprehensively reworked the presidency.

John Dickinson left the only account of the committee's deliberations. In a letter written fifteen years later, Dickinson took credit for prodding the committee to adopt the elector system that Wilson had proposed in June. That Wilson started his legal career as a clerk in Dickinson's law office adds symmetry to the tale.

On the morning of Monday, September 3, Dickinson arrived late to a committee meeting. Prone to migraines, Dickinson admitted he was "much indisposed during the whole time of the Convention." An air of fragility always clung to him. More than a decade before, John Adams penned a memorable portrait of the cadaverous lawyer:

> He is a shadow—tall, but slender as a reed—pale as ashes. One would think at first sight that he could not live a month. Yet upon a more attentive inspection, he looks as if the springs of life were strong enough to last many years.

Upon entering the Library Room on the second floor of the State House, Dickinson "found the [committee] members upon their feet,"

John Dickinson (Delaware) by Charles Willson Peale, from life, 1782–83

ready to leave. As a courtesy, they read him the minutes of their session, including their decision "that the President should be chosen by the legislature."

Dickinson objected in his quiet but insistent manner. The president would have such great powers, he said, that he must be "in a strict sense of the expression, *a man of the people.*" The Constitution might be rejected if the people had no role in choosing the president.

Gouverneur Morris responded warmly. "Come, gentlemen," he said, "let us sit down again, and converse further on this subject." Dickinson continued the story:

> We then all sat down, and after some conference, James Madison took a pen and paper, and sketched out a mode for electing the president agreeable to the present provision [in the Constitution]. To this we assented and reported accordingly.

The roles attributed to the delegates are familiar: the garrulous Morris, always willing to talk over issues one more time; Madison, the constitutional tinkerer, scratching the outlines on paper.

As read by Brearley on September 4, the new article on the executive took up five sections instead of two, and embodied a many-sided compromise. The committee shortened the president's term from seven years to four and freed him to seek reelection. They created a vice president, whose only responsibility was to preside over the Senate and succeed a president who could not complete his term. The election machinery, the heart of the provision, was elaborate.

Each state would have as many electors as its total number of senators and members of the House of Representatives, with each state legislature deciding how to choose that state's electors. Meeting in their states, electors would cast two ballots, at least one for a person from another state. The person with the highest total of elector votes would be president *if* he had a majority; the second-place finisher would be vice president. If no candidate held a majority, the Senate would choose the president and vice president from the top five vote-getters.

The committee had blended many elements to draw the widest possible support. Using electors would appeal to Wilson and Morris, who wanted a role for the people and feared skullduggery if Congress alone made the choice. Having the number of electors equal the total of all senators and congressmen would please the large states; it also gave extra electors to slave states through the three-fifths ratio. To gratify small states, each state cast an equal vote when the Senate decided elections.

Brearley's committee changed the presidency in two other ways. It transferred important powers from the Senate to the president, who now would make treaties and appoint ambassadors and Supreme Court justices (subject to Senate approval). Also, the committee moved impeachment trials from the courts to the Senate, making them more political.

Having delivered his report, Brearley sat mute during the next three days of debate, content to have Morris and others explain and defend the proposals. During that debate, the delegates never touched on flaws that emerged as soon as the nation began electing presidents. Instead, they focused on the Senate.

In most elections, the delegates thought, the electors, being "strangers to the several candidates," would winnow the field of candidates down to five; the Senate then would choose the president. "[N]ineteen times in twenty," George Mason predicted, "the President would be chosen by the Senate," which he thought "an improper body for the purpose." That prospect also troubled Elbridge Gerry of Massachusetts and Alexander Hamilton (who had returned from New York for the Convention's final days).

James Wilson replied that the electors would know the candidates. "Continental characters will multiply as we more and more coalesce," Wilson said, though he did not much like the Senate's role either. By the next day his discomfort had grown. He attacked the powers of the Senate as creating "a dangerous tendency to aristocracy." The Senate could approve treaties, try impeachments, and approve executive and judicial appointments. The result, he said, was that

[t]he President will not be the man of the people as he ought to be, but the minion of the Senate. He cannot even appoint a tide-waiter [a minor customs official] without the Senate.

Some proposed to shift the choice of president to the House of Representatives, or to both houses sitting together. The small states objected, fearing they would lose power. Roger Sherman assembled a hybrid solution: the House would choose the president when no candidate commanded a majority of electors, but each state delegation would have a single vote. Worn down, the delegates embraced the solution by a 10–1 vote.

The delegates spent two days more on the executive branch. Some disliked having the vice president preside over the Senate, fearing his influence over that body. Ever practical, Sherman replied that without that duty, the vice president "would be without employment." Sherman anticipated the view of John Adams, the first vice president, who called the job "the most insignificant office that ever the invention of man contrived."

George Mason was troubled by the impeachment provision. Concerned that the listed offenses of treason and bribery were too limited, he moved to add to it "high crimes and misdemeanors." The delegates agreed, adopting a seventeenth-century phrase that was already archaic in 1787 and has grown more opaque in the years since.

But the delegates never returned to the intricate electoral process they had created. Soon enough, that process would prove clumsy and vulnerable to manipulation, requiring repair after only four elections under it. The Twelfth Amendment, adopted in 1803, solved the most acute problems, but the elector system still produces presidents who have won fewer votes than their "losing" opponents.

The delegates' efforts on the presidency do not compare well to their detailed outline for Congress, or their simple and effective arrangement of the national judiciary. When he read the Constitution, Thomas Jefferson called the presidency "a bad edition of a Polish king." Indeed, both presidential terms and succession were the subject of twentieth-century amendments.

The verdict of Madison, who served two terms in the office, was mixed. Noting that the "final arrangement" of the presidency occurred "in the latter stage of the session," Madison admitted in 1823 that "it was not exempt from a degree of the hurrying influence produced by fatigue and impatience." Secure with the prospect of General Washington as first president, lacking precedents for electing a national executive, and pressed for time, the delegates' efforts on the executive branch fell short.

History has not been generous to David Brearley, often ignoring his role in the creation of the American presidency. Asked to solve the most difficult problem remaining before the Convention and to do so on an impossible timetable, his committee produced a solution that the Convention could accept. Major flaws could be repaired in the future, and still might be. Brearley could take satisfaction in discharging a difficult duty that fell to him rather than to those with more glittering reputations.

Chapter Eighteen

The Loyal Opposition

AUGUST 31

FOR THOSE delegates most skeptical of the draft Constitution, frustration mounted through August. That resentment burst loose on Friday, August 31, a cool and pleasant day, when the Convention reached the end of the Rutledge Committee report. Luther Martin, the Convention's self-appointed wild card, started it.

Gouverneur Morris was demanding that the state ratifying conventions must be assembled "speedily." Though the people would initially favor the Constitution, he warned, state officials would "intrigue and turn the popular current against it," imperiling ratification.

Martin of Maryland, the most adamant opponent of the Constitution still in Philadelphia, saw his opening. Twisting Morris's point, Martin agreed that the people would not ratify "unless hurried into it by surprise."

The other dissidents may have planned to announce their opposition that day, or they, too, may have been provoked by Morris's suggestion that the people should not be given much time to consider the Constitution. Whatever prompted them, three prominent delegates seized the moment to challenge the nascent charter.

Elbridge Gerry of Massachusetts spoke first. In his hesitating, tic-ridden delivery, the wealthy merchant announced his agreement with Martin. The new system, he said, was "full of vices." Insisting that the Convention had no authority to replace the Articles of Confederation, Gerry moved to postpone the ratification article.

George Mason seconded the motion. Never one to mince words, Mason left no doubt as to his feelings, pledging to "chop off his right hand" rather than sign the current draft of the Constitution. Without revisions, he insisted, the only proper course would be "to bring the whole subject before another general Convention."

The unpredictable governor of Virginia added his voice to the chorus of dissent. If the Constitution continued to be unacceptable, Edmund Randolph proclaimed, the state conventions should propose amendments to it, which should be submitted to another general convention.

Could these dissidents be serious about another convention? The prospect sickened many hearts in the East Room.

They *were* serious, and they commanded the Convention's attention. Having reached painful compromises to quell the revolt of the small states and then to paper over the slavery issue, the delegates now were hearing fundamental objections to the entire constitutional structure.

Others had raised the same objections. Luther Martin had denounced the draft Constitution as intended "to abolish and annihilate the state governments," but he could be dismissed as an annoying (if intelligent) windbag. Some dissidents had been won over, while others abandoned the Convention. The conservative New Yorkers, Lansing and Yates, had left seven weeks before. Mercer of Maryland's cameo appearance in Philadelphia lasted only eleven days.

But these three dissenters were not easily ignored. They were respected delegates, having played central roles through the summer. Randolph had presented the Virginia Plan, then sat on the pivotal Rutledge Committee. Gerry chaired the Convention's first committee, which adopted Franklin's compromise to resolve the large-state/small-state impasse. Mason was the topper: General Washington's friend, respected elder statesman, moving force at the Mount Vernon

Conference at the beginning of the road to Philadelphia. He had impressed everyone at the Convention. A Georgia delegate applied no qualifications when he called Mason "undoubtedly one of the best politicians in America."

Though they were only three, the dissidents reflected the views of many Americans who feared a strong central government would lead to rule by aristocracy, or even monarchy. But in a turnabout worthy of fiction, their dissent would play a major role in the ultimate success of the Constitution they doubted.

Earlier in August, many delegates were flirting with the idea of dissenting from the Constitution. By presenting a true draft charter, the Rutledge Committee report stirred up a host of concerns. As recalled by Luther Martin, Gerry convened meetings among those who thought the report had "a tendency to destroy the rights and liberties of the United States." Gerry and Mason hosted several sessions of the doubting, attended by delegates from Connecticut, New Jersey and Delaware, Georgia and South Carolina. This dissident caucus, Martin wrote, aimed to amend the draft "to render it less dangerous."

The existence of the dissident caucus was no secret to delegates who lived and worked in such close quarters. Convention leaders like Wilson and Rutledge, Madison and Morris, knew how to count votes. They listened to the concerns of the doubters, reasoned with them, pointed out the importance of reaching agreement, and worked out accommodations. But Mason, Gerry, and Randolph resisted. Each reached the point of dissent by a different path.

Randolph's opposition was the least firm, the least principled, and the least respected. After the Convention, Madison wrote tactfully that the Virginia governor did not sign the Constitution so he would be "at liberty to be governed by further lights on the subject." Randolph's biographer suggests the governor was "covering all his options so that he could support the position that seemed most popular once the document had been made public." Bluntly, Randolph hedged his bets, leery of angering Virginians while Patrick Henry and others were poised to attack the Constitution. To the Convention's last day, Randolph insisted he might support the Constitution at some future point.

Randolph voiced specific objections to the Rutledge Committee draft. He insisted that the Convention give the House of Representatives the exclusive power to originate money bills. Rejecting that provision would endanger "the peace of this country." He pressed the issue on August 13, in dramatic language:

> We ha[ve] numerous and monstrous difficulties. Surely we ought not to increase them. When the people behold in the Senate, the countenance of an aristocracy; and in the president, the form at least of a little monarch, will not their alarms be sufficiently raised without taking from their immediate representatives a right which has so long been appropriated to them.

Later in August, Randolph told the Convention that he "would sooner risk the Constitution" than agree to the provision approved by the Rutledge Committee (on which he served) perpetuating the slave trade and banning taxes on slave imports. Yet Randolph loathed the recommendation of the Livingston Committee to eliminate the two-thirds vote requirement for navigation laws. Here was an issue that mattered to Virginia voters, and it prompted Randolph's threat on August 29 that

> there were features so odious in the Constitution as it now stands that he doubted he should be able to agree to it. A rejection of the motion [requiring a two-thirds vote for navigation laws] would complete the deformity of the system.

Gerry shared Randolph's mistrust of the Senate, but particularly detested the prospect of a national military and a standing army, a concern few others shared.

In the Convention's early days, the experience of Shays' Rebellion had made Gerry hostile to democracy. In Massachusetts, he reported, "the worst men get into the legislature." They were, he continued, "men of indigence, ignorance and baseness, [who] spare no pains however dirty to carry their point against men who are superior to the artifices practiced." He expressed nostalgia for the America of only a decade before:

> At the beginning of the war we possessed more than Roman virtue. It appears to me it is now the reverse. We have more land and stock-jobbers than any place on earth.

By mid-August, though, Gerry had reversed himself. Now he was concerned that the exclusive Senate would be too powerful. The draft Constitution, he complained on August 14, "is as complete an aristocracy as ever was framed."

The Massachusetts delegate pressed his military concerns on Friday, August 17, as the Convention debated whether the national government might send troops to oppose a rebellion even if no state government asked for help. After the battles with Captain Shays and his compatriots, the question was hardly academic. Without a state request

Elbridge Gerry (Massachusetts)

for troops, Gerry opposed "letting loose the myrmidons of the United States"; the Convention ignored his objection.

Next day, Gerry questioned an omission by the Rutledge Committee. Nothing in its report barred standing armies in time of peace. At this point, tradition reports two lighter moments, though the straitlaced Madison recorded neither. Drawing on phallic imagery, Gerry is supposed to have compared a standing army to a "standing member," which was "an excellent assurance of domestic tranquility but a dangerous temptation to foreign adventure." From Gerry, the metaphor had particular impact. In the words of Rev. Manasseh Cutler, "Few old bachelors . . . have been more fortunate in matrimony than Mr. Gerry." Though Gerry was forty-three years old and of modest appearance (so modest that Rev. Cutler estimated his age at fifty-five), his wife was described as "young, very handsome, and exceedingly amiable."

After scoring with his ribaldry, Gerry demanded that any standing army be limited to 3,000 men, a demand that brought a riposte from an unlikely source. The sober General Washington, it turned out, was paying attention. The General suggested in an aside that Gerry's motion should be matched with a provision that "no foreign enemy should invade the United States at any time with more than three thousand troops." Thus deflated from the presiding chair, Gerry lost the argument.

By August 21, Gerry was leaning toward opposing the Constitution, confiding to his wife that "*entre nous,* I do not expect to give my voice to [it]." Still, he did not leave the fight. Two days later, he bitterly opposed giving the national government power over state militias, which he called "a system of despotism." Gerry turned sarcastic:

> Let us at once destroy the state governments, have an executive for life or hereditary, and a proper Senate, and then there would be some consistency in giving full powers to the [national] government.

Five days later, Gerry shared with his wife his fears for the future. "I am exceedingly distressed at the proceedings of the Convention," Gerry wrote, "and almost sure they will if not altered materially lay the foundation of a civil war." By August 29, he wrote, "I have been a spectator for some time, for I am very different in political principles from my colleagues." Gerry remained in Philadelphia, he explained three days later, only "to prevent my colleagues from saying that I broke up" the Massachusetts delegation.

Mason seemed to reach dissident status later than the others. Like Randolph and Gerry, the Virginian disliked the aristocratic Senate, expressing his view on August 8 with a household metaphor:

> An aristocratic body, like the screw in mechanics, working its way by slow degrees, and holding fast whatever it gains, should ever be suspected of an encroaching tendency.

Yet two days later, on August 10, Mason pronounced the draft Constitution to be "founded on sound principles." Through August, Mason engaged in floor debate on the money-bill issue, militias, the use of paper money, and limitations on the offices that congressmen could hold. Though occasionally acerbic, the Virginian never openly despaired of the outcome of the Convention. During the slave-trade debate, he warned that national sins are punished by national calamities, but returned to a more measured tone in the following days.

Mason's attitude changed after the Second Livingston Committee made its recommendation to jettison the two-thirds vote requirement for navigation laws. In challenging that measure, Mason sounded for the first time like a parochial Virginian:

> Is it to be expected that [the southern states] will deliver themselves bound hand and foot to the Eastern states, and enable them to exclaim, in the words of Cromwell on a certain occasion—"the lord hath delivered them into our hands"?

Mason could not be accused (unlike Randolph) of pandering to a Virginia electorate he had no intention of ever facing. Yet when he joined the dissidents two days later, other delegates had to wonder at it. After all, the Virginian had announced in early July that he would sooner "bury his bones" in Philadelphia than leave without a constitution.

In a conversation with Jefferson just a week before he died in 1792, Mason said the turning point for him was the deal over the slave trade and navigation laws. Until then, according to Jefferson's notes, Mason would have "set his hand and heart" to the Constitution. The alliance between New England and South Carolina, for him, changed "the great principles of the Constitution."

The three dissidents continued to dispute matters large and small as the Convention wound to a close in September. (Luther Martin left Philadelphia on September 5 and did not return.) When the Brearley Committee proposed that the Senate choose the president if no candidate commanded a majority of electors, Randolph warned that some parts of the plan "made a bold stroke for monarchy," while this provision would "do the same for an aristocracy." Mason agreed, announcing that he would "prefer the Government of Prussia" to this arrangement, which would "fix an Aristocracy worse than absolute monarchy." Mason and Gerry objected to the office of vice president, while the Massachusetts delegate continued to denounce a standing army.

Through the final days, Mason and Gerry served on Convention committees. They sometimes presented coordinated amendments, trying to bend the charter to their views. Mason won insertion of "high crimes and misdemeanors" into the impeachment clause and added authority for the states to impose export duties to defray inspection costs.

On September 10, Gerry moved for reconsideration of the procedure for amending the Constitution. Rutledge's committee had authorized only one method of amendment—if two-thirds of the states asked, Congress would convene a convention to consider amendments. The delegates now added a second mechanism, restoring the Virginia Plan's provision that Congress could propose amendments, to be ratified by two-thirds of the state legislatures. That essential, last-minute revision created the mechanism by which all twenty-seven amendments have been adopted.

Despite these successes, the dissidents endured lonely times. They were standing apart from three dozen colleagues with whom they had worked for four months. They were dissenting from a crucial national initiative that was supported by America's greatest figures, General Washington and Dr. Franklin. Would Americans honor them for their convictions, or would they be disparaged as vain and egotistical? What would history say?

The Convention's last days brought personal friction as well. With the finish line in sight, the delegates became less tolerant of discussion. Writing afterward, Madison described Mason in the final days as "in an exceeding ill humor indeed," due to "a number of little circumstances arising in part from the impatience which prevailed towards the close of the business."

At the last possible moment, though, the dissidents' diligence was rewarded. In an inspired action, they created a precious legacy for the nation.

By September 12, a Wednesday, the effort seemed largely complete. A five-man Committee of Style had delivered the final draft of the new Constitution. Gouverneur Morris was working on the cover letter to Congress that would accompany the new charter. It was surely too late for major changes. Perhaps minor points could be tidied up.

A North Carolina delegate raised a problem. Although the Constitution guaranteed trial by jury in criminal cases, it was silent about juries in civil trials. Gerry pounced. The question should be referred to the Committee of Style, he said, to prepare an extension of the right to a jury trial. Agreeing that civil jury trials should be guaranteed, Mason saw a larger opportunity:

> He wished the plan had been prefaced with a Bill of Rights, and would second a motion if made for the purpose. It would give great quiet to the people, and with the aid of the State declarations [of rights], a bill might be prepared in a few hours.

Gerry made the motion, and Mason provided the promised second. They knew a bill of rights could be prepared quickly; Luther Martin had drafted one before leaving Philadelphia the week before, though it had not been presented to the Convention.

Only Sherman of Connecticut spoke against the motion. He supported "the rights of the people" but was sure that state constitutions adequately protected them. Every state delegation voted against a bill of rights.

There were reasons to defeat the Mason-Gerry motion. It was well beyond late, and the motion smelled like a delaying tactic. State constitutions protected many rights, and those might be enough. Months later, James Wilson insisted that a bill of rights was not needed "since liberty may exist and be as well secured without it." Moreover, he asked, why enumerate rights when any right left out "will be presumed to be purposely omitted"?

These reasons, though, had easy refutations. The "supreme" federal charter would override state constitutions, as Wilson knew; after all, he wrote that part of the draft Constitution. And if a bill of rights was superfluous, why had Pennsylvania and seven other states adopted them, while other state constitutions listed specific rights as inalienable?

The omission of a bill of rights was a political blunder of the first magnitude. Of the many criticisms of the Constitution during the fight over ratification, none was so telling as the absence of protection for individual rights. How could the leaders of the Revolution, having fought the British to vindicate American liberty, forget to include those rights in the Constitution?

When the dissidents explained their refusal to sign the Constitution, they marshaled many objections, beginning with the lack of a bill of rights. All three denounced the aristocratic Senate. They all feared Congress's power to make laws "necessary and proper for carrying into execution" its other powers. Randolph and Gerry objected to the power to raise armies without limit, while Randolph and Mason insisted on a two-thirds vote requirement for navigation acts. Mason could not stomach the continuation of the slave trade.

The dissidents forecast great turmoil. "The sovereignty or liberty of the states will be destroyed," Gerry wrote, while Randolph predicted the Constitution "would end in tyranny." Mason could not decide between two evil outcomes:

This government will set out a moderate aristocracy: it is at present impossible to foresee whether it will, in its operation, produce a monarchy, or a corrupt, tyrannical aristocracy; it will most probably vibrate some years between the two, and then terminate in the one or the other.

Although the dire predictions proved wrong, the dissidents could take satisfaction in the power of their last-minute demand for a bill of rights. That demand became the great rallying point for opponents of ratification. As Patrick Henry told the Virginia ratifying convention:

> You have a Bill of Rights to defend you against the State Government, which is bereaved of all power; and yet you have none against Congress, though [it is] in full and exclusive possession of all power! You arm yourselves against the weak and defenseless, and expose yourselves naked to the armed and powerful.

From France, Jefferson agreed that a bill of rights was essential: "what no just government should refuse."

In addressing the ratifying convention in South Carolina, Charles Pinckney was bracingly candid about why he did not support a bill of rights. "Such bills generally begin with declaring that all men are by nature born free," he stated. "Now, we should make that declaration with a very bad grace, when a large part of our property consists in men who are actually born slaves."

Though the states ratified the Constitution without a bill of rights, several voted for amendments they wanted to add. Virginia proposed a Declaration of Rights with twenty elements, while Massachusetts proposed nine amendments, New Hampshire twelve, and New York more than thirty. North Carolina called for a twenty-clause Declaration of Rights plus twenty-six amendments. The First Congress responded to this tsunami of popular demand. By September 25, 1789, it approved twelve amendments to the Constitution. Ten of them took effect as the Bill of Rights two years later.

Those ten amendments include the rights Americans cherish most, and most associate with the Constitution—freedom of speech, worship, and the press; protection against unreasonable searches; the right to jury trials in criminal and civil cases; the guarantee of due process of

law; the promise of just compensation if the government takes property; the ban against cruel and unusual punishment. Many hands and
many voices brought those rights into being, and many more have labored through the centuries to preserve them. The first, though, were
those of George Mason and Elbridge Gerry.

Chapter Nineteen

With All Its Faults

SEPTEMBER 8–17

ALMOST ABRUPTLY, by the end of the first week of September the job was close to done.

On Saturday, September 8, with the presidency questions resolved, the momentum to finish was strong. That morning, of seven amendments offered on the making of treaties, only one was approved.

The pace continued brisk. The delegates turned to Brearley's final report, which offered a compromise on the nagging money-bill issue. The committee proposed to give the House of Representatives exclusive power to originate money bills, but to allow the Senate to make any amendments it wished. The compromise rendered the House's power far from exclusive. With little discussion, it was adopted. The small states won again.

It was time to catch a breath. Once more someone had to assemble a draft Constitution, stitched together from the Rutledge Committee's draft, from the reports of the five committees that worked through August, and from the Convention's amendments. To do the job, the delegates selected a five-man Committee of Style. In naming this last committee, the delegates made no pretense of balancing geographic regions, or small states and large states, or those seeking a strong central government and those favoring states' rights.

The committee's chairman was a senior, conciliatory figure, Johnson of Connecticut. The other four members, however, were all in their thirties, all unfriendly to state powers, and all from larger, cosmopolitan states. Those looking for the influence of General Washington would note that three were his protégés. Also, all four were brilliant.

Three had found much common cause during the summer. James Madison, Rufus King, and Gouverneur Morris had earned their places with diligent labor, often jointly pushing to strengthen the national government. The last committee member, though, was a surprising choice.

Alexander Hamilton had been away from Philadelphia more than he had been there, returning only three days before this committee appointment. He could not even cast a vote; with two New York delegates still boycotting the Convention, the state had no delegation officially present. Hamilton's daylong speech in the third week of June stood as an embarrassing failure. Indeed, on the Convention's final day he remarked that "no man's ideas were more remote from the [Constitution] than [my] own." Yet, owing to his undoubted talents and commitment to the new nation, he was placed on this final committee.

The delegates entrusted the committee to these younger men, ignoring political considerations, because the job seemed largely ministerial. Madison wrote that their task was "to revise the style of and arrange the articles which had been agreed to by the House." According to Dr. McHenry's notes, the panel was supposed to "revise and place the several parts under their proper heads."

After the long summer of conflict, the Convention's imminent climax loomed huge. The prospect of leaving Philadelphia was intoxicating. Randolph, Gerry, and Dayton of New Jersey each wrote home to announce they would be there soon. Even General Washington allowed himself that much, admitting, "I am quite homesick."

A New Hampshire delegate expected the Constitution would bolster the value of public debt and paper currency. In an eighteenth-century version of insider trading (though for the benefit of public entities), he urged his state's governor to get a jump on the market by having towns buy back their devalued bonds and notes; otherwise, the towns "will be obliged to buy [them from] brokers, hawkers, speculators and jockeys at six or perhaps eight times their present value."

William Livingston of New Jersey struck an ironic tone in letters to his son-in-law, John Jay. On September 4, he advised Jay that the "mountains will bring forth before long," warning that the Convention's delays made it "less to be feared that the birth will be . . . a ridiculous mouse, than a *monstrum horrendum ingens.*" A week later Livingston complained that his departure date had been "clouded by reason of there being certain creatures in this world that are more pleased with their own speeches than they can prevail upon anybody else to be."

Although the delegates could not leave until the final document was prepared, they had more time to themselves now and their hearts were lighter. The fresher air of September helped. Old Roger Sherman spent an afternoon on the banks of the Schuylkill River with a New Hampshire delegate and two Philadelphia liverymen.

General Washington started to get around town again. On his Sunday ride, he stopped at Bartram's botanical gardens. He visited Dr. Franklin to examine a "mangle," a machine "for pressing, in place of ironing, clothes from the wash." To the General's practical eye, the device would work well with "tablecloths and such articles as have not pleats and irregular foldings and would be very useful in all large families." Washington dined one day at Mrs. House's establishment, probably to confer with Madison and other delegates who lodged there, and drank tea with the elegant Binghams. Twice he met socially with Don Diego Guardoqui, the newly arrived representative of the king of Spain, who might hold the key to commerce on the Mississippi. The Philadelphia Light Horse staged a dinner for the General, and others were mounted by Dr. Franklin and by Charles Biddle, Pennsylvania's vice president.

While some began to relax, Madison's appetite for work remained sharp. Writing to Jefferson on September 6, the Virginian reported that it was "the first day which has been free from committee service, both before and after the hours" of the Convention. Though still under the rule of secrecy, Madison offered an overview of the new government, assuming that the Constitution would be public long before his letter could reach France. Still disappointed that Congress would have no power to veto state laws, he grumbled that the plan would not "prevent the local mischiefs which everywhere excite disgusts against the state governments."

Madison wrote nervously about the nation beyond the East Room of the State House. "Nothing," he assured Jefferson, "can exceed the universal anxiety for the event of the meeting here. Reports and conjectures abound concerning the nature of the plan which is to be proposed." The hunger for news can be seen in a late August report in a Philadelphia paper. Wishing to reassure its readers despite having no information to convey, the paper was reduced to praising the delegates' work habits:

> The punctuality with which the members of the Convention assemble every day at a certain hour, and the long time they spend in the deliberations of each day (sometimes seven hours) are proofs, among other things, how much they are entitled to the universal confidence of the people of America.

Madison acknowledged to Jefferson that the public was "certainly in the dark" as to the new Constitution, but he was more troubled that "[t]he Convention is equally in the dark as to the reception which may be given to it." Would it be acclaimed or reviled? Though "certain characters will wage war against any reform," Madison hoped Americans would accept "anything that promises stability to the public councils and security to private rights." Still, he added, "if the present moment be lost, it is hard to say what may be our fate. . . ."

The Committee of Style turned out to be Gouverneur Morris's opportunity to redeem his volatile performance through the summer. As he allowed years later, the Constitution "was written by the fingers which write this letter." Madison confirmed the claim. Committee chairman Johnson, Madison wrote in 1831, "with the ready concurrence of the others," asked Morris to prepare the final draft.

Why Morris? At first blush, the selection seems risky. He had been out-of-step with the Convention on many points. To the southerners, he had been an irritant, denouncing slavery in the harshest terms. He opposed equality for westerners, as well as the small states' demand for equal votes in the Senate. His loquacity—he spoke more often than anyone else, despite missing three weeks in June—must have annoyed more than a few delegates.

Nevertheless, two of Morris's qualities suited him to the job. As Madison acknowledged years later, the Pennsylvania delegate had a gift for expressing himself clearly, a gift Madison keenly appreciated as the Convention's scribe. "The correctness of [Morris's] language," Madison wrote, was "particularly favorable to a reporter." After amendment and counteramendment, key provisions of the Rutledge Committee report wore crusted layers of language that could confuse rather than illuminate. Morris would be equal to the task of unkinking snarled sentences and reorganizing the entire document.

Equally important was Morris's willingness to work with those who had bested him. Madison noted that to the "brilliance of his genius," Morris added

> what is too rare, a candid surrender of his opinions when the lights of discussion satisfied him that they had been too hastily formed, and a readiness to aid in making the best of measures in which he had been overruled.

Morris's cooperative spirit was essential at this stage. It was too late for the sort of hijacking that John Rutledge had mounted through the Committee of Detail. This draft had to be faithful to the Convention's actions. Morris could be trusted to do that.

With the entire Convention waiting on him, Morris worked quickly. The Committee of Style first met on the evening of Saturday, September 8, and the printed Constitution was distributed to the delegates four days later, on the morning of Wednesday, September 12.

Because his true home was in New York, even though he was a delegate for Pennsylvania, Morris was lodging at Mrs. Bailey's on Market Street. Seated at his writing desk in his rented room, Morris's critical eye took in the tangled structure of the Rutledge Committee report. It had twenty-three articles. Morris tossed out the first two as surplus, then consolidated the next seven. Once under way, the work developed its own rhythm.

Moving related sections together, imposing a simple structure, Morris condensed twenty-three articles into seven. He devoted one article each to the Congress, the executive, and the judiciary. Article IV described how the government would interact with individuals and states, while Article V addressed amendments. Article VI established the supremacy of the national government, assumed the debts of the Confederation, and banned religious tests for holding office. The final article announced that the Constitution would take effect when nine states ratified.

The new structure streamlined the charter, an effect that Morris reinforced with rigorous editing. A good example was the allocation of seats in the House of Representatives. The final compromise was complex: each state had a specific number of representatives for the first election, but future allocations would be based on census totals. Rutledge's committee outlined the compromise in three sections that extended for 268 words; Morris placed it in one section with 100 fewer words.

Morris also wrote a new preamble. Paeans have been written to his transformation of the opening from "We the people of the States of New Hampshire, Massachusetts" and so on, to "We the People *of the United States*. . . ." By not referring to each state, Morris proclaimed a new government based on the consent of the people. Here, theorists declaim, popular sovereignty stands foursquare.

A practical reason helps explain the change. Listing the states would have been presumptuous, even foolish, since ratification by every state was no foregone conclusion. Indeed, Rhode Island and New York were still absent.

Greater consensus surrounds the balance of Morris's preamble, which distills the purposes of government: "to establish justice, insure domestic tranquility, provide for the common defense, and secure the blessings of liberty to ourselves and our posterity." Many constitutions have been written since. France has had more than ten, while almost two hundred are now in place around the globe, not to mention supernational statements like the Universal Declaration of Human Rights and the draft Constitution for the European Union. Yet none surpasses—and few rival—Morris's preamble. Madison approved of "the talents and taste stamped by the author on" the Constitution: "A better choice [than Morris] could not have been made, as the performance of the task proved."

On a single point, the Committee of Style departed from the Convention's efforts. On August 28, Rufus King had pressed to bar states from interfering with private contracts, but the Convention never voted on his motion. Reviving the issue in the committee room, King met greater success. Morris inserted a clause that a state may make no law "altering or impairing the obligation of contracts."

Morris produced two documents in addition to the Constitution. The first included two resolutions outlining the ratification process by conventions "chosen in each state by the people." Once nine states ratified, the resolutions set forth the steps for choosing a Congress and presidential electors, and establishing the new government. Even a so-

Hamilton, Wilson, and Madison with Dr. Franklin under his mulberry tree

phisticate like Morris must have felt a thrill as he set down those measures.

Morris's last document, a letter for transmitting the Constitution to the Confederation Congress, was a more humble affair. It admitted that "[i]ndividuals entering into society must give up a share of liberty to preserve the rest." Though always difficult "to draw with precision the line between those rights which must be surrendered and those which may be reserved," the difficulty had been greater at the Convention because of the "difference among the several states as to their situation, extent, habits and particular interests." This Constitution, Morris stressed, was one of compromises:

> Each state [was] less rigid on points of inferior magnitude than might have been otherwise expected. And thus the Constitution which we now present is the result of a spirit of amity and of that mutual deference and concession which the peculiarity of our political situation rendered indispensable.

Even though he composed the final draft, Morris was restrained in praising the Constitution. "I not only took it as a man does his wife, for better, for worse," he wrote, "but what few men do with their wives, I took it knowing all its bad qualities."

On Wednesday, September 12, the Convention received the Morris revision. Over the next two days, the push to finish strengthened, though a few struggled against the powerful tide. George Mason delivered an ill-timed lecture "on the extravagance of our manners, the excessive consumption of foreign superfluities, and the necessity of restricting it." Eager to silence the Virginian, the delegates appointed a committee of the five oldest delegates ("without debate") to consider the need for "sumptuary regulations" of the sort Henry VIII had used to restrict the clothing worn by different classes of people. Wisely, this committee never reported to the Convention, nor is there a record that it ever met.

Matters grew testy when Morris quibbled over how to count the days for the president's "pocket veto." The vote was begun while Morris was in mid-peroration, a "number of members being very impatient."

The delegates denied Congress power to build canals, to establish corporations, or to charter a national university. They rejected guarantees of jury trials in civil cases, or freedom of the press. In dismissing the last motion, Roger Sherman of Connecticut insisted that "the power of Congress does not extend to the press."

The final avalanche of activity came on a very long Saturday, September 15. In more than two dozen votes, the delegates approved only one change, adding the second method of amending the Constitution through congressional action and state ratification.

Then there were no more motions. The man who started the deliberations, Edmund Randolph, rose from Virginia's table in the center of the room. Admitting "the pain he felt at differing from the body of the Convention," he urged again that states be allowed to propose amendments for a second convention. Supporting him, Mason stressed the secrecy of the Convention's proceedings, which meant that the Constitution was "formed without the knowledge or idea of the people. A second convention," he said, "will know more the sense of the people and be able to provide a system more consonant to it." Charles Pinckney regretted "these declarations from members so respectable," but every state voted against Randolph's motion.

It was almost 6 P.M. The delegates had been in session for eight hours without a break. Tired and unfed though they were, the solemnity of the moment was unmistakable. With deliberation, the secretary called the final roll on "the Constitution, as amended." New York and Rhode Island did not answer. Nor did North Carolina, its delegates perhaps having left in search of dinner. Each of the remaining ten states voted yes.

All that was left was to incorporate the last changes in the document and to sign it. The delegates had Sunday to make their travel plans.

In the public mind, two delegates stood head and shoulders above the others. With sardonic resentment, John Adams summarized the popular version of the nation's birth:

[T]hat Dr. Franklin's electrical rod smote the earth and out sprung General Washington. That Franklin electrified him with his rod and thence forward these two conducted all policy, negotiation, legislation, and war.

Though the General and the doctor were the most conspicuous delegates, through the summer they mostly avoided the push-and-pull of the Convention. As a North Carolina delegate wrote in July, they conducted themselves "with inconceivable circumspection," aware of the special impact of their actions and words.

When it came to imagining the government structure, analyzing counterproposals, striking compromises, muscling through deals, the Convention's leadership had come from John Rutledge and James Wilson, from James Madison and Gouverneur Morris, and from Oliver Ellsworth and George Mason. Washington sat at the front of the room, grave but silent, while Franklin was an infrequent participant. Yet on the Convention's last day, with the work done, Dr. Franklin and the General stepped comfortably back to their natural places at center stage. They played the roles that only they could play, and they played them flawlessly.

Over the preceding month, Dr. Franklin had spoken little, most often in support of the dissidents. When George Mason pleaded for an Executive Council to advise the president, Franklin warmly endorsed the motion. When Randolph urged that state conventions be allowed to propose amendments for a second Convention to consider, Franklin seconded the motion.

Having been on the short end of many votes, and appreciating his role as the eldest delegate, Franklin resolved to help close wounds suffered during the long summer. After the secretary read the final Constitution on Monday, September 17, Franklin rose "with a speech in his hand." As he had before, Franklin asked Wilson to read it; he also delivered a copy to Madison to ensure its preservation for history. In its wisdom, humility, and vision, it was worth preserving.

Franklin started by saying that "there are several parts of this constitution which I do not at present approve." With a slightly befuddling set of negatives, he added, "I am not sure I shall never approve them." Through a long life, Franklin had been forced by better information or fuller consideration to change opinions . . . which I once thought right, but found to be otherwise. It is therefore that the older I grow, the more apt I am to doubt my own judgment, and to pay more respect to the judgment of others.

After indulging two quips, Franklin insisted, "I agree to this Constitution, with all its faults, if they are such, because I think a general government necessary for us." No second convention would do better because men always bring with them "all their prejudices, their passions, their errors of opinion, their local interests, and their selfish views." His declaration for the Constitution was unqualified:

> It therefore astonishes me, sir, to find this system approaching so near to perfection as it does; and I think it will astonish our enemies, . . . Thus I consent, sir, to this Constitution because I expect no better, and because I am not sure that it is not the best. The opinions I have had of its errors, I sacrifice to the public good.

The doctor's speech, according to Dr. McHenry of Maryland, was "plain, insinuating, persuasive." And "in any event of the system," McHenry added waspishly, the speech "guarded the Doctor's fame."
Franklin finished with a direct plea to the dissidents.

> I cannot help expressing a wish that every member of the Convention who may still have objection to [the Constitution] would with me, on this occasion, doubt a little of his own infallibility—and to make manifest our unanimity, put his name to this instrument.

To secure those precious signatures, Gouverneur Morris had contrived a verbal sleight of hand. Rather than have the signers attest that they personally agreed with the Constitution, Morris drafted the following statement to appear above the signatures:

> Done in Convention, by the unanimous consent of the states [*not,* that is, of the *delegates*] present the 17th of September. In witness whereof we have hereunto subscribed our names.

In this way, the signers affirmed only that the states had voted for the Constitution, as indeed they had.

Morris's dodge, as presented by Franklin, was only partly successful. A North Carolina delegate who intended not to sign "was relieved by the form proposed" and agreed to sign it. But the principal targets of the dodge—Mason, Gerry, and Randolph—were unmoved. Gerry and Randolph announced they would not sign; Mason sat in angry silence; he did not sign.

Though the state delegations had approved the Constitution, a last drama remained. Gorham of Massachusetts rose on the matter of representation, the question that consumed the largest part of the Convention's time. The Constitution provided that each congressman should represent up to 40,000 citizens. Gorham proposed to lower the number to 30,000, which would produce more representatives with smaller districts. Nine days before, a North Carolina delegate had made the same motion, with support from Hamilton and Madison, but lost by one vote. In the interim, Madison and Hamilton had enlisted support from the heaviest artillery in the East Room.

General Washington rose. He had held his tongue through the sultry summer, never asserting his immense prestige on any dispute. Having preserved his influence by husbanding it, he applied it in a precise fashion.

Noting his silence until then, Washington said "he could not forebear expressing his wish that the alteration proposed might take place"; he warned that the "smallness of the proportion of representatives [was] an insufficient security for the rights and interests of the people."

Who would oppose the presumptive first president in his lone wish for the new government? The motion was adopted without a roll call.

The time to sign had arrived. As president of the Convention, Washington signed first, placing foremost on the paper the name that Americans most wanted to see. Moving by state delegation from North to South, as they had done everything that summer, the delegates filed to the front of the room to add their names.

Many of those names would recede to the back pages of history, beginning with John Langdon and Nicholas Gilman of New Hampshire and ending with William Few and Abraham Baldwin of Georgia. Hamilton signed though he belonged to no delegation. As Washington wrote that night, the document was executed by "11 states and Colonel Hamilton."

A few delegations signed in full force. All eight Pennsylvanians took their turns, led by Dr. Franklin. The proud James Wilson and peg-legged Morris brought up the rear of the delegation. Only four Delaware delegates were present, but one signed for John Dickinson, laid low by another migraine. Slim and proud, John Rutledge led the South Carolinians to the signing table.

Other state delegations were much reduced, including those leaders of the Revolution, Massachusetts and Virginia. Only Gorham and King signed for the New England state, while Madison and silent John Blair joined the General as the only Virginians to sign.

Many had misgivings. McHenry echoed Dr. Franklin: Though the Marylander did not much like the document, "I distrust my own judgment, especially as it is opposite to the opinion of a majority of gentlemen whose abilities and patriotism are of the first cast." He concluded that the Constitution, which could be amended, promised better than "the evils which we labor under." Gilman of New Hampshire wrote the next day that "it was done by bargain and compromise, yet notwithstanding its imperfections, on the adoption of it depends (in my feeble judgment) whether we shall become a respectable nation."

It fell to Dr. Franklin to provide the coda. A much-repeated anecdote turns on his conversation as southern delegates applied the final names to the document. Franklin pointed to the carving of a sun on the back of Washington's chair (which sits today in the same place in the same room). Madison captured the moment in his final entry of the summer. Franklin said he had often looked at the carving

> without being able to tell whether it was rising or setting. But now at length I have the happiness to know that it is a rising and not a setting sun.

The delegates lost no time in beginning the critical process of securing state ratification. Thomas Fitzsimons of Pennsylvania carried the Constitution upstairs and presented it to the Pennsylvania Assembly, which was then in session. Dr. Franklin would report formally to that body in the morning. Copies were sent to destinations throughout the nation. Fitzsimons sent one to Noah Webster, whom he had recruited to write a pamphlet supporting ratification. In three weeks, Webster produced *An Examination into the Leading Principles of the Federal Constitution,* which was widely distributed by proratification forces.

Before they scattered, the delegates gathered that afternoon for a last dinner at the City Tavern. On his way there, Washington stopped to buy a translation of *Don Quixote,* which the Spanish emissary Guardoqui had recommended. Finally, the General might have time and energy to do some reading.

In the high-ceilinged space of the City Tavern, the toasts and fellowship were heartfelt. After sweating through the summer, the delegates warmed themselves before fires on the coldest day of the

City Tavern, engraving, W. Birch & Son (1800)

Convention, the temperature not breaking 50 degrees. With wits like Hamilton and Gouverneur Morris, the assembly was high-spirited. It was an occasion for recalling misadventures that men share when they spend time together away from home.

Which delegate showed up one morning with mismatched shoes, or stained linen? Who had fallen asleep most often during debate, or had induced the most drowsiness in others? Who celebrated too hard one or more evenings, arriving the worse for wear the next day? Who gambled recklessly, or pursued female companionship most avidly, or most piteously longed to return to a distant wife? Those now absent were surely remembered without much respect, beginning with Luther Martin. Though the presence of the three dissidents must have damped down any true exultation, the long summer bred the rare camaraderie of being part of a great event.

When it came time for toasts, as it always did, the light manner would drop. Tributes to the General and the doctor would come early, but other delegates would be recognized. These men of the new United States would pay the most solemn honor to the Union and to its new Constitution.

The delegates did not linger at the tavern. Many were leaving in the morning. All knew the work was not over, but now would shift to the state ratifying conventions.

So they "took a cordial leave of each other," General Washington recorded. He retired to his room at the Morrises' home. There he received the papers of the Convention, confided to his safekeeping. There, also, he "meditate[d] on the momentous work which had been executed." Thirty-nine men around Philadelphia shared in that meditation, and wondered at what they had done.

Chapter Twenty

*Happiness, Perpetual
and Otherwise*

JULY 4, 1788

S CANNING A CROWD of 17,000 on the outskirts of Philadelphia, James Wilson felt a satisfaction he had not before imagined. Twenty-two years before that Fourth of July in 1788, he arrived from Scotland owning only talent, drive, and a few letters of introduction. The fears and excitement of those days were always with him.

This day proved how right Wilson had been to leave the narrow life Scotland offered him. What greater affirmation could this imposing immigrant receive? He was a principal drafter of the first charter of government adopted by "the people." Only three weeks after the Convention adjourned, he delivered the rejoinder to George Mason's critique of the Constitution. Wilson's "State-House Yard" speech was circulated widely through the land. He had fought to assure that Pennsylvania was the second state to ratify, on December 12, 1787, building force behind the ratification effort. Now Wilson was the featured orator for the nation's biggest celebration of the new Constitution.

Philadelphia's party was assembled on short notice, as ratification had happened only two weeks before when New Hampshire became the ninth state to approve the Constitution. Since then, Virginia also had ratified by a narrow margin, so the nation had ten states.

Others had fought in the war of words. Under the pseudonym "Publius," Hamilton and Madison (with minor help from John Jay) wrote dozens of powerful essays explaining the Constitution (later collected as *The Federalist*).

Some states ratified quickly and by overwhelming margins. Delaware was first and unanimous, and unanimity prevailed in New Jersey and Georgia, as well. Pro-Constitution forces in Connecticut and Maryland rolled over modest opposition. Massachusetts, though, was a donnybrook, stout resistance coming from the towns in the western part of the state, where the men of Daniel Shays still mistrusted all governments. Though Shaysite delegates opposed the Constitution by a 2–1 margin, Massachusetts ratified by a vote of 187 to 168.

With a comfortable win in South Carolina and a narrow one in New Hampshire, the ratification drive reached the minimum needed. Virginia's approval in June had rewarded ten days of inspired advocacy by Madison, who faced tough opposition from Mason and Patrick Henry. Madison had benefited from Randolph's further change of heart. After more agonizing, the governor had switched to support the Constitution. Hamilton browbeat New York into a sullen form of ratification in late July, though North Carolina did not follow until September of the next year. Reluctant Rhode Island entered the Union in May of 1790.

With the news of New Hampshire's vote, Philadelphia's planning for the Fourth of July moved to another level. Most of the 40,000 people in the nation's largest city staged a memorable blowout.

The party began at dawn, with the pealing of Christ Church's bells and a cannon blast from the *Rising Sun*, anchored in the Delaware River. Ten other ships stood in the harbor from north to south, each flying a white flag emblazoned with the name of a ratifying state. New Hampshire, fittingly, was off the Northern Liberties neighborhood, while Georgia's banner was opposite South Street. The celebration was so rife with symbolism that it has been called a "jubilee of allegory."

The Constitution proclaimed that it was written by "We, the people," so the organizers included all the people. The parade had the usual staples—bands and soldiers and dignitaries—but the featured marchers were workers from almost fifty different trades and crafts, from butchers to rope makers, from carpenters to clerks, from hatters to coopers. Philadelphia showed the world how a republic marks its birth.

For early July, the weather was favorable. A brisk south wind cooled the parade route, while clouds shielded the stone streets from the summer sun.

Five thousand Philadelphians began to assemble at 8 A.M., preparing to walk the three-mile route through the center of town and out to William Hamilton's Bush Hill estate. The procession featured five of Pennsylvania's delegates to the Convention; Franklin's grandson stood in for the good doctor.

James Wilson had the pride of place. The Scot marched arm in arm with nine other Philadelphians, the ten of them representing the ratifying states (allegory!). They walked behind a "lofty, ornamental car in the form of a large eagle" proclaiming the Constitution and "The People." Drawn by six horses, the "truly sublime" car was "raised above every other object." Wilson bore a flag with PENNSYLVANIA in gold letters.

Close behind Wilson rolled the "grand federal edifice," the metaphorical high point. Ten white horses pulled a stage carrying a domed building that sported thirteen columns (three of which were, allegorically, incomplete). Above the dome soared a cupola topped with a figure of Plenty. The federal edifice carried the message, IN UNION THE FABRIC STANDS FIRM, while ten gentlemen sat (allegorically) inside. Wilson delivered his afternoon oration from this new federal edifice.

Just behind, an entire ship rode on another carriage drawn by ten horses. Thirty-three feet long, the *Union* carried twenty cannon and a crew of twenty-five on a British barge that John Paul Jones had seized during the war.

One float bore a spinning machine and several women printing chintz fabric. A smithy operated on another, selling the nails and spikes it produced. Printers manned their own float, running off copies of an ode composed by the event chairman, Francis Hopkinson, which were tossed to the crowd. They also printed a second ode in German, tribute to the diversity of the population, which they also distributed to on-lookers.

But the day was about much more than remarkable floats and the numbers ten and thirteen. Above all, it honored the people and the dignity of their work. "Rank for a while forgot all its claims," Dr. Benjamin Rush wrote afterward. Eighty weavers marched, with 450 carpenters and 330 ship's carpenters, 300 rope makers, 250 tailors, 200 smiths, 70 tobacconists, 40 porters, and 40 night watchmen. Clerks processed proudly behind a man carrying "a large ledger." Bringing up the rear were (in order) members of Congress, local officials, the night watch-men, lawyers, clergy, and physicians.

Many trades wore unifying colors to sharpen the impression they left. Butchers and bakers wore "clean white dresses," while tin makers marched in green aprons, chandlers in blue ones, rope makers in white.

The marchers unabashedly promoted their products. The coach makers' banner proclaimed NO TAX ON AMERICAN CARRIAGES, while the hatters' flag announced WITH THE INDUSTRY OF THE BEAVER, WE SUP-PORT OUR RIGHTS. The bricklayers' motto was BOTH BUILDINGS AND RULERS ARE THE WORKS OF OUR HANDS, while the brewers' standard an-nounced BEER, ALE, PORTER—PROPER DRINK FOR AMERICANS. The bak-ers' flag reflected the hard times of recent years, entreating MAY THE FEDERAL GOVERNMENT RESTORE OUR TRADE.

Thousands of watchers crowded the route, women and children "on fences, scaffolds, and roofs of the houses." The most difficult ac-count to accept, though, is the parade chairman's assertion that the route was quiet:

> A solemn silence reigned both in the streets and at the windows of the houses. This might be ascribed to the sublimity of the sight, and the pleasure it excited in every mind, for sublime objects and intense pleasure never fail of producing silence.

Despite this picture of sober republican virtue for three uninterrupted miles, surely "huzzas" and hat-waving broke out at least a few times.

The marchers and most of the watchers poured onto the grounds of the Bush Hill estate, where a circle of tables under awnings held a "cold collation." The beverages were American beer and cider. The "grand federal edifice" was pulled to the center of the tables. Before the 17,000 were permitted to eat and drink, James Wilson mounted the edifice that he had, allegorically, done so much to erect.

Though many in the crowd stood too far away to hear him, they saw a tall, broad man with his head thrown back, his spectacle lenses glinting, his gestures forceful. Even some close to him struggled to discern the words that Wilson roared forth in his distinctive burr. He exulted in the prospect of

[a] people, free and enlightened, establishing and ratifying a system of government, which they have previously considered, examined, and approved! This is the spectacle which we are assembled to celebrate; and it is the most dignified one that has yet appeared on our globe.

Bush Hill Estate, site of July 4, 1788, celebration

He found the Constitution superior to the charters of Sparta, Athens, and Rome, where "the people were either unfit to be trusted, or their lawgivers were too ambitious to trust them."

Wilson warmed to the theme of the procession, "the arts of peace," which he listed as agriculture, manufactures, commerce, science, and "the virtues" of frugality, temperance, and industry. To achieve these, he insisted, "[a] good constitution is the greatest blessing which a society can enjoy." But the new government would only be as good as those serving in it, so Wilson urged each American to "consider the public happiness as depending on his single vote." His Elysian vision of the future was designed to fire the crowd's imagination:

> The rivers and lakes and seas are crowded with ships. Their shores are covered with cities. . . . The arts, . . . appear in beautiful variety, . . . With heart felt contentment, industry beholds his honest labors flourishing and secure. Peace walks serene and unalarmed . . . while liberty, virtue and religion go hand in hand harmoniously, protecting, enlivening and exalting all! HAPPY COUNTRY! MAY THY HAPPINESS BE PERPETUAL!

Then the toasts; unavoidably, there were ten, each announced by a trumpet call and followed by ten artillery shots that were answered by the *Rising Sun*. The crowd drank to "the people," to the Convention, to General Washington, to the French king, to the Netherlands, to other foreign allies, to agriculture and manufactures and commerce, to heroes who fell in the war, and that "reason, and not the sword, hereafter decide all national disputes." The final toast honored "the whole family of mankind."

The crowd dispersed by day's end. The federal edifice was pulled back to the State House grounds "with loud huzzas," the time for silence evidently having passed.

In the evening, the celebration became celestial. The heavens were "illuminated by a beautiful aurora borealis."

For many of the delegates, the future would be happy. General Washington, of course, soon would be president, while Madison also would serve two terms in that office. Madison's vice president in his second term was none other than Elbridge Gerry, who had refused to sign the Constitution and also was "against having any vice president." (Gerry's most lasting impact on American politics came in 1812 when, as governor of Massachusetts, he signed a law creating such distorted voting districts that they were compared to a salamander, or a "gerrymander.") Three delegates (General Pinckney, Rufus King, and Jared Ingersoll) were unsuccessful candidates for president or vice president.

Five delegates would become Supreme Court justices—Rutledge, Wilson, William Paterson, John Blair of Virginia, and Oliver Ellsworth. Sixteen would sit in the Senate, and thirteen in the House of Representatives (Jonathan Dayton of New Jersey rising to be Speaker of that body). Four would be cabinet secretaries.

Yet despite James Wilson's fervent plea for "perpetual happiness," a surprising number of delegates foundered on the reefs of America's future. Their mixed fates reflect the rugged life of a rambunctious new democracy at the end of the eighteenth century, as well as the random qualities of fate itself.

Two died in duels growing from political conflict. Alexander Hamilton's death at the hands of Aaron Burr is legendary, but few know that Richard Spaight of North Carolina met a similar end at the hands of a Federalist rival for a seat in the state legislature. Spaight's slaying may be the more noteworthy for the determined rancor of the dueling parties. Each missed his first three shots, and thus both elected on three occasions to reload and start over again, until Spaight was struck down.

Two others died under mysterious circumstances, presumed murdered. In 1806, George Wythe of Virginia was fed poison by a grand-nephew and heir. John Lansing of New York disappeared in 1829 after checking into a hotel room.

Two saw their public careers unravel in accusations of treason. William Blount was a senator from Tennessee in 1797 when evidence surfaced that he had conspired to enlist the British in the conquest of Florida and Louisiana. He was expelled from the Senate. Jonathan Dayton was indicted with Aaron Burr in 1806 for joining in a similar venture. After Burr was acquitted (thanks to his defense lawyers, former delegates Edmund Randolph and Luther Martin), the charges against Dayton were dropped.

Financial reverses brought down several delegates. The most stunning bankruptcy was that of "the Financier," Robert Morris of Philadelphia, who had shared his magnificent home with General Washington during the Convention. Even in 1787, Morris's financial empire was beginning to fray. In late June, Washington wrote in his diary that Morris's notes had been denied, which the General prissily found "a little mal-apropos." From 1798 to 1801, Morris languished in debtors' prison; Gouverneur Morris (no relation) arranged both his release and an annuity to see him through his final years. Less lurid bankruptcies were endured by Nathaniel Gorham of Massachusetts, Thomas Mifflin and Thomas Fitzsimons of Pennsylvania, and William Pierce of Georgia.

A lifetime of drink and casual financial management left Luther Martin destitute and silly in old age. For a time, the Maryland Assembly taxed each lawyer in the state for his benefit. When the subsidy expired, Aaron Burr, Martin's former client, took him in.

Gouverneur Morris served the new government as ambassador to France during that nation's Revolution, and also was a senator. The charming rake finally married in his fifty-eighth year and settled into domesticity. Politically, though, he was forced to the margins. He bitterly opposed the War of 1812, writing that upon reading Madison's second inaugural address in 1813, "I supposed him to be out of his senses." Morris blamed that war on the South's enhanced power under the three-fifths ratio: "If peace be not immediately made with England," he wrote, "the question on Negro votes must divide the union."

Morris's end, in 1816, was gruesome even by the standards of the time. Suffering a painful blockage of the urinary tract, he tried to open it himself with a piece of whalebone from his wife's undergarments. He was found dead of the attempt.

As tales worthy of the ancient Greeks, few stories rival those of John Rutledge and James Wilson, the men behind the large-state/slave-state alliance, fellow members of the Committee of Detail, and indisputably leading delegates. Washington appointed both men to the first Supreme Court, yet both ended their days in such ignominy that their reputations have never recovered.

Rutledge's decline had its roots in 1792, when his wife and his mother died unexpectedly within weeks of one another. The deaths plunged the South Carolinian into depression. He had resigned from the Supreme Court the year before to serve as chief justice of South Carolina's highest court. Though he continued to sit on the state bench, a friend reported that "his mind was frequently so much deranged as to be in a great measure deprived of his senses." Having lived off his capital through years of public service, Rutledge also was sliding into debt.

Rutledge's collapse combined both hubris and bathos. In June 1795, he learned that John Jay would retire as chief justice of the Supreme Court. Rutledge wrote to President Washington and asked to succeed Jay. The day after receiving that letter, the president replied to offer him a recess appointment to the post. While that correspondence was pending, Rutledge delivered a violent speech denouncing the treaty with Great Britain that Jay had negotiated on behalf of President Washington. Rutledge had bitten hard the hand that was attempting to feed him.

Through a painful autumn, while Rutledge acted as the new chief justice, opposition to his appointment grew. Opponents cited his Jay Treaty speech and his mental condition. On December 15, the Senate rejected his appointment—the first exercise of its power to do so.

On a morning just after Christmas, Rutledge left his Charleston home "by stealth" and walked to Gibbes's Bridge over the Ashley River. He walked into the river until the water was over his head. As described in a contemporary account, slave hands saved the defender of slavery:

> A Negro child was near, and struck with the uncommonness of the sight she called to some Negroes on the deck of a vessel. . . . The fellows had the presence of mind to run with a boat hook and catch hold of [Rutledge's] arm—he made violent opposition to them but they dragged him out and detained him by force, they calling out for assistance, while he cursed and abused them, and would drive them away.

Regaining some balance after the episode, Rutledge lived another five years in quiet private life.

History's tendency to overlook Rutledge's role at the Convention may be traced in part to his devotion to the interests of the South; also, unlike the posterity-conscious Virginians, he left behind little correspondence that grants an intimate view of his strategies, his hopes, and his judgments. More than those factors, though, the events of 1795 cost him an honored place in America's pantheon. As one of his neighbors predicted after his suicide attempt, "Mr. Rutledge has lost ground more by his behavior lately than his life time of services will regain."

James Wilson's suffering was equally self-inflicted and equally painful. Lauded as the most learned of the new Supreme Court justices, Wilson was not satisfied with high office and great honor. Deep within him lay a burning need to be rich. He dreamt of vast profits from frontier lands. As early as 1785, he had solicited investors for a "very lucrative" land deal. Wilson promised a Dutch official "rapid accumulation of the capital, beyond any rate of interest," adding that "the rapidity of this accumulation is often surprising to those whose ideas have been formed only on what happens in long settled countries."

By 1794, Wilson was staggering with debt from the development of a new town named Wilsonville on the shores of Lake Wallenpaupack in northeast Pennsylvania. Wilson planned to build sawmills, cotton mills and dye works, but costs swiftly overtook his resources. In 1797, he fled Philadelphia to avoid his creditors, taking refuge in Bethlehem. Forced to travel to New Jersey on court business, he was arrested and jailed for his debts.

After his son bailed him out, Wilson took to his heels again, this time landing in Edenton, North Carolina, close by the home of Supreme Court Justice James Iredell. He discovered in Edenton that one of his principal creditors was a former delegate, Major Butler of South Carolina, who held $200,000 of Wilson's notes. In May of 1798, Butler wrote his lawyer that he had "hitherto waited patiently" for payment, but was now "reluctantly forced to proceed against [Wilson]."

When Butler's agents seized Wilson in Edenton, the justice agreed to remain confined at the Hornblow Tavern if they would not jail him. In short order, Wilson contracted malaria, then suffered a fatal stroke. He remains the only Supreme Court justice to die on the run from the law. At his death, Wilson was a national embarrassment. His reputation, like Rutledge's, never rebounded from the obloquy earned in his final days.

Less calamitous, though still poignant, were the tortured relationships among the Virginians who had traveled to Philadelphia to lead the Convention—Madison, Randolph, Mason, and General Washington.

Mason, the eldest, died first, estranged from the others. Though his opposition to the Constitution was based on principle, not personality, it was not easy to keep the two separate. Randolph's last-minute switch to support the Constitution at Virginia's ratifying convention maddened the older man, who took to calling him "young A——d." Though comparison to Benedict Arnold has never been a positive, for the revolutionary generation it was the bitterest invective.

Mason's relations with Washington and Madison grew icy. A month after the Convention, Madison gleefully sent the General a copy of Mason's objections to the Constitution, gloating that "it is no small satisfaction to find him [Mason] reduced to such distress for a proper gloss" on his opposition. In 1791, Mason worried to Thomas Jefferson about the "coolness" between him and Madison, "one of the few men, whom from a pretty thorough acquaintance, I really esteem."

Even harder for Mason, though, was the loss of "the friendship which has long existed (indeed from our early youth) between General Washington and myself." When Mason was unable to assist a son's friend with a presidential appointment, he explained:

> You know I believe there are few men in whom [Washington] placed greater confidence; but it is possible my opposition to the new government, both as a member of the national and of the Virginia Convention, may have altered the case.

The new president's feelings about Mason were, indeed, much changed. Shortly after taking office, Washington wrote that he expected Mason "would mark his opposition to the new government with consistency." The president did not admire that consistency:

Pride on the one hand, and want of manly candor on the other, will not I am certain let [Mason] acknowledge an error in his opinions respecting [the Constitution] though conviction should flash on his mind as strongly as a ray of light.

Mason, still a homebody and pleading health problems, in 1790 declined appointment to the United States Senate by the Virginia Assembly. He had spent as much time in Philadelphia as he cared to. He had much public business to look back on with pride. His Fairfax Resolves in 1774 helped stir the Revolution; his Virginia Declaration of Rights was the first draft of the Declaration of Independence; his 1785 compact with Maryland had started the nation down the road to the Constitutional Convention; and he had begun the momentum toward the Bill of Rights. Yet Mason also could plausibly write, "[A]t my time of life, my only satisfaction and pleasure is in my children, and all my views are centered in their welfare and happiness."

Mason, little honored in his final years, has been largely forgotten since. In an aside a few months before Mason's death in December 1792, Washington called him "my neighbor and quondam [former] friend." Because General Washington would not forgive Mason, neither did the nation.

Edmund Randolph served in President Washington's cabinet, first as attorney general, then as secretary of state. His imprudent dealings with a French diplomat forced his resignation from the cabinet in 1795 and severed his relations with the president. His public career was over. By the time of his death in 1813, Randolph was on civil terms with Madison, but had been forced to sell his slaves to pay debts.

When Madison and Washington left Philadelphia in September 1787, their alliance was stronger than ever, but it would not last. They worked closely through the ratification process, and Washington relied on the slight Virginian in his first years as president. But he came to rely even more on Hamilton, his gifted treasury secretary, whose strengthening of the government repelled Madison and Secretary of State Thomas Jefferson.

When Jefferson resigned from the cabinet at the close of Washington's first term, the president offered the post to Madison, who de-

clined. Together, Jefferson and Madison withdrew to nurture a new political party that would sweep both of them into the presidency. Washington knew he had been abandoned. After retiring to Mount Vernon in
1797, the General "never again even mentioned Madison's name in his
letters or writing."

By the time Washington died in late 1799, he had lost or spurned
the friendship and support of each of the leading Virginians at the
Philadelphia Convention. For the austere Washington, preserving
friendships was more difficult—or less important—than preserving his
place in history.

Washington's role at the Convention illustrates both his remarkable
leadership and how difficult it is to convey it in words. His remarks con-
sume five sentences in Madison's notes, yet no other delegate was half
so important. His intangible qualities travel poorly across the centuries,
unlike the bons mots of literary lights or the careful intellectual work of
scholars. Yet in a time and place that was crowded with talented and
ambitious Americans, none imagined he was a rival to Washington.

The General was sixty-five when he retired to Mount Vernon,
weary of political sniping and of shouldering the cares of the nation.
Despite his lifetime of astonishing achievement, one more of America's
cares nagged at him—slavery. As general of the army, as president of the
Philadelphia Convention, and as the first president, he never challenged it. He thought the nation would not accept such a challenge. But
the crime of slavery was personal to him as a slave owner. At the end of
his days, he resolved to make a last gesture.

In the summer of 1799, Washington wrote his will. He directed that
his slaves be given their freedom. Because they were intermarried with
his wife's slaves, whom he could not release from bondage, he specified
that his slaves be released upon his wife's death. He directed his estate
to support freed slaves who were too old to work and to pay to educate
the others. Within two years of his death, all the slaves at Mount Vernon—his and his wife's—had their freedom. The nation would not follow his example for another sixty years.

Chapter Twenty-one

Making Amends

T HE STORY of the Constitution did not end on September 17, 1787, or on July 4, 1788. Among George Mason's incisive remarks, none was more telling than his insistence that amending the Constitution should be easy because "the plan now to be formed will certainly be defective." The first generation had no illusions as to the Constitution's perfection; they adopted twelve amendments during the first fifteen years, starting with the Bill of Rights.

The Twelfth Amendment rescued presidential elections from the mess the delegates created. The problem began to emerge with the first election, an event that would hardly be recognizable to a modern voter. Only five of the states allowed their citizens to vote for presidential electors; in three states, the legislature picked; New Jersey's governor and Executive Council chose that state's electors, while Massachusetts combined popular and legislative balloting. (North Carolina and Rhode Island did not vote since they had not ratified yet, while political stalemate prevented New York from participating.)

With General Washington's selection as president a foregone conclusion, John Adams of Massachusetts agreed to stand for vice president, providing regional balance. In early 1789, Hamilton worried in a letter to James Wilson that the election could be manipulated because each elector cast two votes for president. If a few electors "insidiously withheld" their votes from Washington, while all voted for Adams, the New Englander would become president. To avoid such a disturbing result, Hamilton encouraged a few electors to "throw away a few votes to . . . persons not otherwise thought of."

Hamilton's maneuver was chancy. All electors cast secret ballots in their home states on exactly the same date, so there was a risk of counterplotting, or that key electors would change their minds. For that first election, though, the maneuver worked. Adams finished a distant second to the General.

The flaw festered with the contested presidential election in 1796. Jefferson and Adams faced off at the head of fledgling political parties. Jefferson's supporters called themselves Republicans, while Adams led the Federalists. Hamilton again was manipulator in chief. Unhappy with the prospect of Adams as president, Hamilton hoped to leapfrog him with Federalist vice presidential candidate Thomas Pinckney (brother of General Pinckney).

Hamilton urged southern electors to withhold their second votes from Adams. But every move has a response. New England electors withheld *their* second votes from Pinckney, so Adams won the presidency but Jefferson eclipsed Pinckney and came in second. Thus Adams was saddled with his opponent as his vice president. The perversity of this outcome is highlighted by the question of presidential succession. Had Adams died in office, his opponent would have become president.

In the election of 1800, the flaw in the elector system twisted in a new direction. The rematch between Adams and Jefferson was so close that no Republican elector considered throwing away his second vote. The result? Jefferson and Aaron Burr tied at the top of the totals. The choice between them fell to the House of Representatives, with each state casting a single vote.

Though many at the Convention had expected the House to decide presidential contests, they did not appreciate the dangers of the process. In February 1801, lame-duck Federalists dominated the Congress yet had to choose between two Republicans. After thirty-five ballots over five grinding days, the House had elected no president. The constitutional crisis was real. What if Congress could not decide before it expired on March 3? Who would be president then? Who would choose the new president?

The lone congressman from tiny Delaware averted the crisis. Because each state cast only one vote, Representative James Bayard personally controlled Delaware's vote. His move toward Jefferson triggered a reshuffling of votes that made the Virginian president.

The electoral flaw had become unbearable. To spackle it over, Congress approved the Twelfth Amendment in 1803, which the states ratified in six months. Beginning with the 1804 election, each elector cast one vote for president and a second for vice president. There would be no more Hamiltonian manipulation, a lot less throwing away of votes on minor candidates, no more adversaries elected as vice president, and no more deadlocks between running mates.

Despite the essential repairs in the Twelfth Amendment, the Convention's perplexity over presidential elections is still reflected in the nation's disputed elections and minority presidencies. In four of the fifty presidential elections since 1803, the elector system has installed a president who won fewer votes than the "losing" candidate. (This is explained further in Appendix 1.)

Elections have not been the only problem with the presidency. Two twentieth-century amendments addressed the structure of the office. The Twenty-Second Amendment limited the president to two terms, while the Twenty-Fifth Amendment set out the method for transferring power from a disabled president.

Even greater consequences flowed from the delegates' compromises over slavery. Most obviously, preservation of the slave trade meant the continued importation of many thousands of Africans in chains. The Fugitive Slave Clause gave slave owners a critical tool for enforcing their dominion over the people they held in bondage.

Though less obvious in its impact, the three-fifths ratio rankled for decades. By granting additional representation based on slaves, that clause enhanced southern power, as reflected in many measures:

- Ten of the first fifteen presidents were slave owners.
- John Adams would have won a second term as president but for twelve electoral votes cast for Jefferson (and Burr) that represented southern slaves (counted at three-fifths of their real number).
- For twenty-seven of the nation's first thirty-five years, southerners sat as Speaker of the House of Representatives.
- Nineteen of the first thirty-four Supreme Court justices were slaveholders.

Because of the three-fifths ratio, Virginia in the 1790s had six more congressmen than did Pennsylvania even though both states had roughly the same number of free inhabitants. The three-fifths ratio gave slave states fourteen extra seats in the House in 1793, twenty-seven additional seats in 1812, and twenty-five added seats in 1833.

Those extra votes meant that when crises erupted over slavery in 1820, in 1850, and in 1856, slave owners in positions of power ensured that the political system did not challenge human bondage. House seats created by the three-fifths rule allowed Missouri to be admitted as a slave state in 1820, and ensured enactment of the 1840 gag rule that choked off antislavery petitions to Congress.

As pointed out in a recent work by Akhil Reed Amar, the three-fifths ratio also enhanced the power of slave owners within their states. The extra seats in the House of Representatives went to the slave-owning areas of Virginia and the Carolinas, not to western counties where slaves were few. When southern states adopted the ratio for their own legislatures, the slave-owning regions again were the winners, gaining power in those bodies.

Historians disagree over the terrible bargains that the Convention struck over slavery. Some insist that the delegates did the best they could under the circumstances. America was not ready for emancipation, they say. The delegates needed to form a new government. Concessions on slavery had to be made to hold the Union together. Some single out the Connecticut delegates for praise, finding statesmanship in the act of giving the slave states what they wanted, and then excluding the word "slavery" from the Constitution, keeping the document unsullied by the word while millions lived their lives in that condition.

Others counter that the northern delegates caved in too easily to implausible southern threats to abandon the Union. Georgia had the Creek Confederacy at its back and the Spanish next door. South Carolina was in dire economic distress, dependent on external markets for its rice and indigo. Those states could not have stood on their own any more than Delaware or Rhode Island could have. Perhaps outright abolition was not feasible, but why make the slave system even stronger by extending the slave trade and using the three-fifths ratio to increase the political power of slavery?

For all they have been celebrated, the delegates bear responsibility for having entrenched slavery ever deeper, for not even beginning to express disapproval of it. They created a government so entwined with slavery that in 1859 the abolitionist John Brown could write in his gallows statement that "the sins of this guilty land can only be purged with blood." Having gathered to form a government that would avoid rebellions like that of Captain Shays, their legacy included the indescribably greater horror of the Civil War.

The excuses and denunciations of historians, though, remain beside the point. The nature of the Convention ensured that slavery would be inscribed in the Constitution.

The delegates journeyed to Philadelphia to form a vigorous republican government. Each state delegation that showed up, and stayed through the summer, demonstrated its commitment to that paramount goal. An indispensable component of that mutual commitment was the understanding that each "faction" or "interest" could demand consideration of its most critical needs. Small states insisted on equal votes in the Senate. Though it violated democratic theory and infuriated the large states, it was adopted.

The southerners demanded security for their system of slavery and special limits on navigation laws. The nonslave states granted them the three-fifths ratio for representation, then balked when Rutledge's committee granted the South's entire wish list. The southerners had to yield on what mattered most to the North, the navigation laws, and accepted a twenty-year term on the slave trade. But because the southerners remained in the East Room of the State House—because, in Rutledge's words, they joined in laying the foundation for a great empire—they knew they were entitled to consideration for their slave system. And they got it.

After the Civil War, the nation approved the amendments that wiped the stain of slavery from the document, and began to clean it from the nation's life. The Thirteenth Amendment banned slavery; the Fourteenth guaranteed equal protection of the laws; the Fifteenth protected the right to vote. Twentieth-century amendments extended voting rights to women, allowed the people (not state legislatures) to elect senators, and barred the poll tax used by southerners to seal the ballot box against the descendants of slaves.

So far, Americans have amended the Constitution twenty-seven times. The most recent change bars any modification in congressional pay from taking effect until after the next biennial election. Remarkably, Congress approved that provision in 1789 but the states did not ratify it until 1992, more than two centuries later.

Several amendments approved by Congress still await ratification. The most startling of these is a measure adopted two days before Abraham Lincoln was sworn in as president in 1861, which would bar any federal government interference with slavery. Lincoln himself approved the provision. Only two states have ratified that one, which in any case has been superseded by the Thirteenth Amendment's ban on slavery.

Still, every session of Congress brings scores of suggestions for amendments. The most visible recent proposals would prohibit burning the flag and would bar same-sex marriages.

And so, as the delegates intended, the story of the Constitution continues. Born in secrecy, the child of lofty idealism and rough political bargains, the Constitution is a story that will continue as long as the nation does.

Appendix 1

THE ELECTOR SYSTEM

Even after the essential repair achieved by the Twelfth Amendment, the elector system still can defeat the popular will. Some analyses conclude that the system exaggerates the influence of large states, and through history it has favored the nomination of candidates from large states. Four of the first five presidents were from Virginia, the most populous state in the early republic. From 1840 to 1920, America elected seven presidents from Ohio, while New Yorkers and Californians won nine presidential elections in the twentieth century.

Yet, as a legacy of the small states' tenacity at the Convention, the elector system gives those states extra electoral votes. Because each state's electoral vote total is based on its number of representatives and senators, the system skews in favor of voters in smaller states.

In the 2004 election, for example, California received one electoral vote for each of its representatives and senators, or 55 electoral votes. With Californians casting over 12.4 million votes for president, each of California's electoral votes represented about 225,000 voters. Alaska had only three electoral votes that year (for one representative and two senators). With only 312,000 Alaskans voting, the state cast one electoral vote for every 104,000 Alaskans who voted. Each Alaskan's vote carried more than twice the weight of a Californian's.

This bias in the allocation of electoral votes is significant when small states disproportionately favor a candidate in a close race. The problem is exacerbated by the winner-take-all rules that virtually every state has adopted, granting all of its electoral votes to the candidate with the highest vote total. That means that narrow victories in many small states can create an electoral vote triumph over a candidate who wins the popular vote nationwide based on big margins in large states. This has happened three times.

- In 1876, Democrat Samuel Tilden won almost 52 percent of the popular vote but fell short of a majority of the electoral votes when fraud allegations prevented the recording of votes from three southern states. A commission created by Congress reviewed the fraud allegations. Voting on party lines (8–7), the commission awarded every disputed electoral vote to Rutherford Hayes, who won the final electoral count 185–184.
- In the 1888 election, Benjamin Harrison lost the popular election by 90,000 votes to his Democratic opponent, Grover Cleveland, but won handily in the electoral college, 233–168.
- In 2000, George W. Bush was defeated in the popular count by a half-million votes, but won in the electoral college, 271–266. The Supreme Court prevented Florida state courts from reviewing claims by Democrat Albert Gore that the votes were counted incorrectly, even though Bush won Florida by only 537 votes of 5.9 million votes cast.

Other problems have infected the elector system. In the four-candidate election of 1824, the House of Representatives chose John Quincy Adams even though his leading opponent, Andrew Jackson, attracted more than 30 percent more popular votes (151,271–113,122) and also more electoral votes (99–84).

On eight occasions, "faithless" electors have refused to vote for the candidate to whom they were pledged, while protest movements in two southern states in 1960 produced "unpledged" electors who hoped to trade their support for political advantage. In recent elections, campaigns have focused obsessively on battleground states, where the shift of a few thousand votes might tip the state's electoral votes one way or the other, completely ignoring many states. And the electors themselves are rarely the "assembly of wise men and learned elders" intended by the Convention delegates; one study has called them "a state-by-state collection of political hacks and fat cats."

The delegates adopted the elector system in 1787 because of the physical barriers to conducting a nationwide election for president. Fearing the voters would not have access to information about the candidates, they could not imagine the logistics of taking a national ballot. Two hundred and twenty years later, those reasons against popular election of the president no longer apply.

Appendix 2

THE CONSTITUTION

OF 1787

We the People of the United States, in Order to form a more perfect Union, establish Justice, insure domestic Tranquility, provide for the common defence, promote the general Welfare, and secure the Blessings of Liberty to ourselves and our Posterity, do ordain and establish this Constitution for the United States of America.

ARTICLE. I.

Section. 1.

All legislative Powers herein granted shall be vested in a Congress of the United States, which shall consist of a Senate and House of Representatives.

Section. 2.

Clause 1: The House of Representatives shall be composed of Members chosen every second Year by the People of the several States, and the Electors in each State shall have the Qualifications requisite for Electors of the most numerous Branch of the State Legislature.

Clause 2: No Person shall be a Representative who shall not have attained to the Age of twenty five Years, and been seven Years a Citizen of the United States, and who shall not, when elected, be an Inhabitant of that State in which he shall be chosen.

Clause 3: Representatives and direct Taxes shall be apportioned among the several States which may be included within this Union, according to their respective Numbers, which shall be determined by adding to the whole Number of free Persons, including those bound to Service for a Term of Years, and excluding Indians not taxed, three fifths of all other Persons. The actual Enumeration shall be made within three Years after the first Meeting of the Congress of the United States, and within every subsequent Term of ten Years, in such Manner as they shall by Law direct. The Number of Representatives shall not exceed one for every thirty Thousand, but each State shall have at Least one Representative; and until such enumeration shall be made, the State of New Hampshire shall be entitled to chuse three, Massachusetts eight, Rhode-Island and Providence Plantations one, Connecticut five, New-York six, New Jersey four, Pennsylvania eight, Delaware one, Maryland six, Virginia ten, North Carolina five, South Carolina five, and Georgia three.

Clause 4: When vacancies happen in the Representation from any State, the Executive Authority thereof shall issue Writs of Election to fill such Vacancies.

Clause 5: The House of Representatives shall chuse their Speaker and other Officers; and shall have the sole Power of Impeachment.

Section. 3.

Clause 1: The Senate of the United States shall be composed of two Senators from each State, chosen by the Legislature thereof, for six Years; and each Senator shall have one Vote.

Clause 2: Immediately after they shall be assembled in Consequence of the first Election, they shall be divided as equally as may be into three Classes. The Seats of the Senators of the first Class shall be vacated at the Expiration of the second Year, of the second Class at the Expiration of the fourth Year, and of the third Class at the Expiration of the sixth Year, so that one third may be chosen every second Year; and if Vacancies happen by Resignation, or otherwise, during the Recess of the Legislature of any State, the Executive thereof may make temporary Appointments until the next Meeting of the Legislature, which shall then fill such Vacancies.

Clause 3: No Person shall be a Senator who shall not have attained to the Age of thirty Years, and been nine Years a Citizen of the United States, and who shall not, when elected, be an Inhabitant of that State for which he shall be chosen.

Clause 4: The Vice President of the United States shall be President of the Senate, but shall have no Vote, unless they be equally divided.

Clause 5: The Senate shall chuse their other Officers, and also a President pro tempore, in the Absence of the Vice President, or when he shall exercise the Office of President of the United States.

Clause 6: The Senate shall have the sole Power to try all Impeachments. When sitting for that Purpose, they shall be on Oath or Affirmation. When the President of the United States is tried, the Chief Justice shall preside: And no Person shall be convicted without the Concurrence of two thirds of the Members present.

Clause 7: Judgment in Cases of Impeachment shall not extend further than to removal from Office, and disqualification to hold and enjoy any Office of honor, Trust or Profit under the United States: but the Party convicted shall nevertheless be liable and subject to Indictment, Trial, Judgment and Punishment, according to Law.

Section. 4.

Clause 1: The Times, Places and Manner of holding Elections for Senators and Representatives, shall be prescribed in each State by the Legislature thereof; but the Congress may at any time by Law make or alter such Regulations, except as to the Places of chusing Senators.

Clause 2: The Congress shall assemble at least once in every Year, and such Meeting shall be on the first Monday in December, unless they shall by Law appoint a different Day.

Section. 5.

Clause 1: Each House shall be the Judge of the Elections, Returns and Qualifications of its own Members, and a Majority of each shall constitute a Quorum to do Business; but a smaller Number may adjourn from day to day, and may be authorized to compel the Attendance of absent Members, in such Manner, and under such Penalties as each House may provide.

Clause 2: Each House may determine the Rules of its Proceedings, punish its Members for disorderly Behaviour, and, with the Concurrence of two thirds, expel a Member.

Clause 3: Each House shall keep a Journal of its Proceedings, and from time to time publish the same, excepting such Parts as may in their Judgment require Secrecy; and the Yeas and Nays of the Members of either House on any question shall, at the Desire of one fifth of those Present, be entered on the Journal.

Clause 4: Neither House, during the Session of Congress, shall, without the Consent of the other, adjourn for more than three days, nor to any other Place than that in which the two Houses shall be sitting.

Section. 6.

Clause 1: The Senators and Representatives shall receive a Compensation for their Services, to be ascertained by Law, and paid out of the Treasury of the United States. They shall in all Cases, except Treason, Felony and Breach of the Peace, be privileged from Arrest during their Attendance at the Session of their respective Houses, and in going to and returning from the same; and for any Speech or Debate in either House, they shall not be questioned in any other Place.

Clause 2: No Senator or Representative shall, during the Time for which he was elected, be appointed to any civil Office under the Authority of the United States, which shall have been created, or the Emoluments whereof shall have been encreased during such time; and no Person holding any Office under the United States, shall be a Member of either House during his Continuance in Office.

Section. 7.

Clause 1: All Bills for raising Revenue shall originate in the House of Representatives; but the Senate may propose or concur with Amendments as on other Bills.

Clause 2: Every Bill which shall have passed the House of Representatives and the Senate, shall, before it become a Law, be presented to the President of the United States; If he approve he shall sign it, but if not he shall return it, with his Objections to that House in which it shall have originated, who shall enter the Objections at large on their Journal, and proceed to reconsider it. If after such Reconsideration two thirds of that House shall agree to pass the Bill, it shall be sent, together with the Objections, to the other House, by which it shall likewise be reconsidered, and if approved by two thirds of that House, it shall become a Law. But in all such Cases the Votes of both Houses shall be determined by yeas and Nays, and the Names of the Persons voting for and against the Bill shall be entered on the Journal of each House respectively. If any Bill shall not be returned by the President within ten Days (Sundays excepted) after it shall have been presented to him, the Same shall be a Law, in like Manner as if he had signed it, unless the Congress by their Adjournment prevent its Return, in which Case it shall not be a Law.

Clause 3: Every Order, Resolution, or Vote to which the Concurrence of the Senate and House of Representatives may be necessary (except on a question of Adjournment) shall be presented to the President of the United States; and before the Same shall take Effect, shall be approved by him, or being disapproved by him, shall be repassed by two thirds of the Senate and House of Representatives, according to the Rules and Limitations prescribed in the Case of a Bill.

Section. 8.

Clause 1: The Congress shall have Power To lay and collect Taxes, Duties, Imposts and Excises, to pay the Debts and provide for the common Defence and general Welfare of the United States; but all Duties, Imposts and Excises shall be uniform throughout the United States;

Clause 2: To borrow Money on the credit of the United States;

Clause 3: To regulate Commerce with foreign Nations, and among the several States, and with the Indian Tribes;

Clause 4: To establish an uniform Rule of Naturalization, and uniform Laws on the subject of Bankruptcies throughout the United States;

Clause 5: To coin Money, regulate the Value thereof, and of foreign Coin, and fix the Standard of Weights and Measures;

Clause 6: To provide for the Punishment of counterfeiting the Securities and current Coin of the United States;

Clause 7: To establish Post Offices and post Roads;

Clause 8: To promote the Progress of Science and useful Arts, by securing for limited Times to Authors and Inventors the exclusive Right to their respective Writings and Discoveries;

Clause 9: To constitute Tribunals inferior to the supreme Court;

Clause 10: To define and punish Piracies and Felonies committed on the high Seas, and Offences against the Law of Nations;

Clause 11: To declare War, grant Letters of Marque and Reprisal, and make Rules concerning Captures on Land and Water;

Clause 12: To raise and support Armies, but no Appropriation of Money to that Use shall be for a longer Term than two Years;

Clause 13: To provide and maintain a Navy;

Clause 14: To make Rules for the Government and Regulation of the land and naval Forces;

Clause 15: To provide for calling forth the Militia to execute the Laws of the Union, suppress Insurrections and repel Invasions;

Clause 16: To provide for organizing, arming, and disciplining, the Militia, and for governing such Part of them as may be employed in the Service of the United States, reserving to the States respectively, the Appointment of the Officers, and the Authority of training the Militia according to the discipline prescribed by Congress;

Clause 17: To exercise exclusive Legislation in all Cases whatsoever, over such District (not exceeding ten Miles square) as may, by Cession of particular States, and the Acceptance of Congress, become the Seat of the Government of the United States, and to exercise like Authority over all Places purchased by the Consent of the Legislature of the State in which the Same shall be, for the Erection of Forts, Magazines, Arsenals, dock-Yards, and other needful Buildings;—And

Clause 18: To make all Laws which shall be necessary and proper for carrying into Execution the foregoing Powers, and all other Powers vested by this Constitution in the Government of the United States, or in any Department or Officer thereof.

Section. 9.

Clause 1: The Migration or Importation of such Persons as any of the States now existing shall think proper to admit, shall not be prohibited by the Congress prior to the Year one thousand eight hundred and eight, but a Tax or duty may be imposed on such Importation, not exceeding ten dollars for each Person.

Clause 2: The Privilege of the Writ of Habeas Corpus shall not be suspended, unless when in Cases of Rebellion or Invasion the public Safety may require it.

Clause 3: No Bill of Attainder or ex post facto Law shall be passed.

Clause 4: No Capitation, or other direct, Tax shall be laid, unless in Proportion to the Census or Enumeration herein before directed to be taken.

Clause 5: No Tax or Duty shall be laid on Articles exported from any State.

Clause 6: No Preference shall be given by any Regulation of Commerce or Revenue to the Ports of one State over those of another: nor shall Vessels bound to, or from, one State, be obliged to enter, clear, or pay Duties in another.

Clause 7: No Money shall be drawn from the Treasury, but in Consequence of Appropriations made by Law; and a regular Statement and Account of the Receipts and Expenditures of all public Money shall be published from time to time.

Clause 8: No Title of Nobility shall be granted by the United States: And no Person holding any Office of Profit or Trust under them, shall, without the Consent of the Congress, accept of any present, Emolument, Office, or Title, of any kind whatever, from any King, Prince, or foreign State.

Section. 10.

Clause 1: No State shall enter into any Treaty, Alliance, or Confederation; grant Letters of Marque and Reprisal; coin Money; emit Bills of Credit; make any Thing but gold and silver Coin a Tender in Payment of Debts; pass any Bill of Attainder, ex post facto Law, or Law impairing the Obligation of Contracts, or grant any Title of Nobility.

Clause 2: No State shall, without the Consent of the Congress, lay any Imposts or Duties on Imports or Exports, except what may be absolutely necessary for executing its inspection Laws: and the net Produce of all Duties and Imposts, laid by any State on Imports or Exports, shall be for the Use of the Treasury of the United States; and all such Laws shall be subject to the Revision and Control of the Congress.

Clause 3: No State shall, without the Consent of Congress, lay any Duty of Tonnage, keep Troops, or Ships of War in time of Peace, enter into any Agreement or Compact with another State, or with a foreign Power, or engage in War, unless actually invaded, or in such imminent Danger as will not admit of delay.

ARTICLE. II.

Section. 1.

Clause 1: The executive Power shall be vested in a President of the United States of America. He shall hold his Office during the Term of four Years, and, together with the Vice President, chosen for the same Term, be elected, as follows.

Clause 2: Each State shall appoint, in such Manner as the Legislature thereof may direct, a Number of Electors, equal to the whole Number of Senators and Representatives to which the State may be entitled in the Congress: but no Senator or Representative, or Person holding an Office of Trust or Profit under the United States, shall be appointed an Elector.

Clause 3: The Electors shall meet in their respective States, and vote by Ballot for two Persons, of whom one at least shall not be an Inhabitant of the same State with themselves. And they shall make a List of all the Persons voted for, and of the Number of Votes for each; which List they shall sign and certify, and transmit sealed to the Seat of the Government of the United States, directed to the President of the Senate. The President of the Senate shall, in the Presence of the Senate and House of Representatives, open all the Certificates, and the Votes shall then be counted. The Person having the greatest Number of Votes shall be the President, if such Number be a Majority of the whole Number of Electors appointed; and if there be more than one who have such Majority, and have an equal Number of Votes, then the House of Representatives shall immediately chuse by Ballot one of them for President; and if no Person have a Majority, then from the five highest on the List the said House shall in like Manner chuse the President. But in chusing the President, the Votes shall be taken by States, the Representation from each State having one Vote; A quorum for this Purpose shall consist of a Member or Members from two thirds of the States, and a Majority of all the States shall be necessary to a Choice. In every Case, after the Choice of the President, the Person having the greatest Number of Votes of the Electors shall be the Vice President. But if there should remain two or more who have equal Votes, the Senate shall chuse from them by Ballot the Vice President.

Clause 4: The Congress may determine the Time of chusing the Electors, and the Day on which they shall give their Votes; which Day shall be the same throughout the United States.

Clause 5: No Person except a natural born Citizen, or a Citizen of the United States, at the time of the Adoption of this Constitution, shall be eligible to the Office of President; neither shall any Person be eligible to that Office who shall not have attained to the Age of thirty five Years, and been fourteen Years a Resident within the United States.

Clause 6: In Case of the Removal of the President from Office, or of his Death, Resignation, or Inability to discharge the Powers and Duties of the said Office, the Same shall devolve on the Vice President, and the Congress may by Law provide for the Case of Removal, Death, Resignation or Inability, both of the President and Vice President, declaring what Officer shall then act as President, and such Officer shall act accordingly, until the Disability be removed, or a President shall be elected.

Clause 7: The President shall, at stated Times, receive for his Services, a Compensation, which shall neither be encreased nor diminished during the Period for which he shall have been elected, and he shall not receive within that Period any other Emolument from the United States, or any of them.

Clause 8: Before he enter on the Execution of his Office, he shall take the following Oath or Affirmation:—"I do solemnly swear (or affirm) that I will faithfully execute the Office of President of the United

States, and will to the best of my Ability, preserve, protect and defend the Constitution of the United States."

Section. 2.

Clause 1: The President shall be Commander in Chief of the Army and Navy of the United States, and of the Militia of the several States, when called into the actual Service of the United States; he may require the Opinion, in writing, of the principal Officer in each of the executive Departments, upon any Subject relating to the Duties of their respective Offices, and he shall have Power to grant Reprieves and Pardons for Offences against the United States, except in Cases of Impeachment.

Clause 2: He shall have Power, by and with the Advice and Consent of the Senate, to make Treaties, provided two thirds of the Senators present concur; and he shall nominate, and by and with the Advice and Consent of the Senate, shall appoint Ambassadors, other public Ministers and Consuls, Judges of the supreme Court, and all other Officers of the United States, whose Appointments are not herein otherwise provided for, and which shall be established by Law: but the Congress may by Law vest the Appointment of such inferior Officers, as they think proper, in the President alone, in the Courts of Law, or in the Heads of Departments.

Clause 3: The President shall have Power to fill up all Vacancies that may happen during the Recess of the Senate, by granting Commissions which shall expire at the End of their next Session.

Section. 3.

He shall from time to time give to the Congress Information of the State of the Union, and recommend to their Consideration such Measures as he shall judge necessary and expedient; he may, on extraordinary Occasions, convene both Houses, or either of them, and in Case of Disagreement between them, with Respect to the Time of Adjournment, he may adjourn them to such Time as he shall think proper; he shall receive Ambassadors and other public Ministers; he shall take Care that the Laws be faithfully executed, and shall Commission all the Officers of the United States.

Section. 4.

The President, Vice President and all civil Officers of the United States, shall be removed from Office on Impeachment for, and Conviction of, Treason, Bribery, or other high Crimes and Misdemeanors.

Article. III.

Section. 1.

The judicial Power of the United States, shall be vested in one supreme Court, and in such inferior Courts as the Congress may from time to time ordain and establish. The Judges, both of the supreme and inferior Courts, shall hold their Offices during good Behaviour, and shall, at stated Times, receive for their Services, a Compensation, which shall not be diminished during their Continuance in Office.

Section. 2.

Clause 1: The judicial Power shall extend to all Cases, in Law and Equity, arising under this Constitution, the Laws of the United States, and Treaties made, or which shall be made, under their Authority;—to all Cases affecting Ambassadors, other public Ministers and Consuls;—to all Cases of admiralty and maritime Jurisdiction;—to Controversies to which the United States shall be a Party;—to Controversies between two or more States;—between a State and Citizens of another State;—between Citizens of different States,—between Citizens of the same State claiming Lands under Grants of different States, and between a State, or the Citizens thereof, and foreign States, Citizens or Subjects.

Clause 2: In all Cases affecting Ambassadors, other public Ministers and Consuls, and those in which a State shall be Party, the supreme Court shall have original Jurisdiction. In all the other Cases before mentioned, the supreme Court shall have appellate Jurisdiction, both as to Law and Fact, with such Exceptions, and under such Regulations as the Congress shall make.

Clause 3: The Trial of all Crimes, except in Cases of Impeachment, shall be by Jury; and such Trial shall be held in the State where the said Crimes shall have been committed; but when not committed within any

State, the Trial shall be at such Place or Places as the Congress may by Law have directed.

Section. 3.

Clause 1: Treason against the United States, shall consist only in levying War against them, or in adhering to their Enemies, giving them Aid and Comfort. No Person shall be convicted of Treason unless on the Testimony of two Witnesses to the same overt Act, or on Confession in open Court.

Clause 2: The Congress shall have Power to declare the Punishment of Treason, but no Attainder of Treason shall work Corruption of Blood, or Forfeiture except during the Life of the Person attainted.

ARTICLE. IV.

Section. 1.

Full Faith and Credit shall be given in each State to the public Acts, Records, and judicial Proceedings of every other State. And the Congress may by general Laws prescribe the Manner in which such Acts, Records and Proceedings shall be proved, and the Effect thereof.

Section. 2.

Clause 1: The Citizens of each State shall be entitled to all Privileges and Immunities of Citizens in the several States.

Clause 2: A Person charged in any State with Treason, Felony, or other Crime, who shall flee from Justice, and be found in another State, shall on Demand of the executive Authority of the State from which he fled, be delivered up, to be removed to the State having Jurisdiction of the Crime.

Clause 3: No Person held to Service or Labour in one State, under the Laws thereof, escaping into another, shall, in Consequence of any Law or Regulation therein, be discharged from such Service or Labour, but shall be delivered up on Claim of the Party to whom such Service or Labour may be due.

Section. 3.

Clause 1: New States may be admitted by the Congress into this Union; but no new State shall be formed or erected within the Jurisdiction of any other State; nor any State be formed by the Junction of two or more States, or Parts of States, without the Consent of the Legislatures of the States concerned as well as of the Congress.

Clause 2: The Congress shall have Power to dispose of and make all needful Rules and Regulations respecting the Territory or other Property belonging to the United States; and nothing in this Constitution shall be so construed as to Prejudice any Claims of the United States, or of any particular State.

Section. 4.

The United States shall guarantee to every State in this Union a Republican Form of Government, and shall protect each of them against Invasion; and on Application of the Legislature, or of the Executive (when the Legislature cannot be convened) against domestic Violence.

ARTICLE. V.

The Congress, whenever two thirds of both Houses shall deem it necessary, shall propose Amendments to this Constitution, or, on the Application of the Legislatures of two thirds of the several States, shall call a Convention for proposing Amendments, which, in either Case, shall be valid to all Intents and Purposes, as Part of this Constitution, when ratified by the Legislatures of three fourths of the several States, or by Conventions in three fourths thereof, as the one or the other Mode of Ratification may be proposed by the Congress; Provided that no Amendment which may be made prior to the Year One thousand eight hundred and eight shall in any Manner affect the first and fourth Clauses in the Ninth Section of the first Article; and that no State, without its Consent, shall be deprived of its equal Suffrage in the Senate.

ARTICLE. VI.

Clause 1: All Debts contracted and Engagements entered into, before the Adoption of this Constitution, shall be as valid against the United States under this Constitution, as under the Confederation.

Clause 2: This Constitution, and the Laws of the United States which shall be made in Pursuance thereof; and all Treaties made, or which shall be made, under the Authority of the United States, shall be the supreme Law of the Land; and the Judges in every State shall be bound thereby, any Thing in the Constitution or Laws of any State to the Contrary notwithstanding.

Clause 3: The Senators and Representatives before mentioned, and the Members of the several State Legislatures, and all executive and judicial Officers, both of the United States and of the several States, shall be bound by Oath or Affirmation, to support this Constitution; but no religious Test shall ever be required as a Qualification to any Office or public Trust under the United States.

ARTICLE. VII.

The Ratification of the Conventions of nine States, shall be sufficient for the Establishment of this Constitution between the States so ratifying the Same.

Done in Convention by the Unanimous Consent of the States present the Seventeenth Day of September in the Year of our Lord one thousand seven hundred and Eighty seven and of the Independence of the United States of America the Twelfth In witness whereof We have hereunto subscribed our Names,

GEO WASHINGTON—Presidt. and deputy from Virginia

[Signed also by the deputies of twelve States.]

New Hampshire

John Langdon
Nicholas Gilman

Massachusetts

Nathaniel Gorham

Rufus King

Connecticut

Wm: Saml. Johnson

Roger Sherman

New York

Alexander Hamilton

New Jersey

Wil: Livingston

David Brearley

Wm. Paterson

Jona: Dayton

Pennsylvania

B. Franklin

Thomas Mifflin

Robt. Morris

Geo. Clymer

Thos. FitzSimons

Jared Ingersoll

James Wilson

Gouv Morris

Delaware

Geo: Read

Gunning Bedford jun

John Dickinson

Richard Bassett

Jaco: Broom

Maryland

James McHenry
Dan of St Thos. Jenifer
DanL Carroll

Virginia

John Blair
James Madison Jr.

North Carolina

Wm. Blount
Richd. Dobbs Spaight
Hu Williamson

South Carolina

J. Rutledge
Charles Cotesworth Pinckney
Charles Pinckney
Pierce Butler

Georgia

William Few
Abr Baldwin

NOTES

For quotations, I have modernized spellings and used more current punctuations. Also, although the delegates most often referred to the two houses of the proposed new legislature as the "first branch" (the future House of Representatives) and the "second branch" (the future Senate), the text uses their final titles to reduce confusion for modern readers.

A great deal of original material about the Constitutional Convention and the delegates has been gathered in convenient form, or made available online. I relied heavily on materials assembled in the following sources, and have cited them as indicated below:

- Max Farrand, ed., *The Records of the Federal Convention of 1787* (New Haven: Yale University Press, 1966; originally 1911), Vols. I–III (cited as Farrand).
- James Hutson, ed., *Supplement to Max Farrand's The Records of the Federal Convention of 1787* (New Haven: Yale University Press, 1987) (cited as Hutson).
- Journals of the Continental Congress, made available by the Library of Congress at http://memory.loc.gov/ammem/amlaw/lawhome.html (cited as JCC).
- Letters of Delegates to Congress, made available by the Library of Congress at http://memory.loc.gov/ammem/amlaw/lawhome.html (cited as LDC).
- Correspondence of George Washington, James Madison, and Thomas Jefferson, made available by the Library of Congress at http://memory.loc.gov/ammem/browse/ListSome.php?category=Presidents (cited, respectively, as Washington Papers, Madison Papers, and Jefferson Papers).
- Diary of John Adams, made available by the Massachusetts Historical Society at http://www.masshist.org/digitaladams/aea/diary/ (cited as Adams Diary).
- Debates of the state ratifying conventions, gathered in Elliot's Debates, made available by the Library of Congress at http://memory.loc.gov/ammem/amlaw/lwed.html (cited as ED).

CHAPTER 1. IT STARTED AT MOUNT VERNON: MARCH 1785

PAGE

1   *Together they had hunted:* Kate Mason Rowland, *The Life and Correspondence of George Mason, 1725–1792* (New York: Russell & Russell, 1964; reprint of 1892 volume), vol. I, 120–22; Helen Hill, *George Mason Constitutionalist* (Cambridge: Harvard University Press, 1938), 28–29.

2   *Both were local leaders:* Peter Henriques, "An Uneven Friendship: The Relationship Between George Washington and George Mason," *Virginia Magazine of History and Biography* 97 (April 1989): 185.

2   *In 1774, Washington had presided:* Stephen A. Schwartz, "Forgotten Founder," *Smithsonian Magazine,* May 2000.

2   *"the privileges of a free people":* Willard Sterne Randall, *George Washington: A Life* (New York: Henry Holt & Co., 1997), 265–67.

2   *At fifty-three, he retained:* Gordon S. Wood, "The Greatness of George Washington," *Virginia Quarterly Review* 68 (Spring 1992): 191.

2   *"addicted to gambling":* Forrest McDonald, *Novus Ordo Seculum: The Intellectual Origins of the Constitution* (Lawrence: University Press of Kansas, 1985), 193.

2   *"passions almost too mighty":* Joseph Ellis, *His Excellency* (New York: Alfred A. Knopf, 2004), 472 [large-print] (quoting Gouverneur Morris's eulogy). Ellis's discussion of the conflicting elements of Washington's nature is persuasive.

2   *"would look like a valet de chambre":* James Thomas Flexner, *Washington: The Indispensable Man* (Boston: Little, Brown & Co., 1969), 69.

2   *"clear gray eyes":* The description came from a young woman who met Mason at Mount Vernon, a Miss Lewis of Fredericksburg. Rowland, vol. II, 67.

3   *When Thomas Jefferson assembled:* The resemblances between the two documents are too close not to conclude that Jefferson began with Mason's Declaration before him and revised it for his purposes. Thus, the Virginia Declaration of Rights begins:

> That all men are by nature equally free and independent, and have certain inherent rights, of which, when they enter into a state of society, they cannot, by any compact, deprive or divest their posterity; namely, the enjoyment of life and liberty, with the means of acquiring and possessing property, and pursuing and obtaining happiness and safety. That all power is vested in, and consequently derived from, the people; that magistrates are their trustees and servants, and at all times amenable to them.
>
> That government is, or ought to be, instituted for the common benefit, protection, and security of the people, nation or community;

of all the various modes and forms of government that is best, which is capable of producing the greatest degree of happiness and safety and is most effectually secured against the danger of maladministration; and that, whenever any government shall be found inadequate or contrary to these purposes, a majority of the community hath an indubitable, unalienable, and indefeasible right to reform, alter or abolish it, in such manner as shall be judged most conducive to the public weal.

Jefferson smoothed and condensed this opening passage, while retaining its essential content.

We hold these truths to be self-evident, that all men are created equal, that they are endowed by their Creator with certain unalienable Rights, that among these are Life, Liberty and the pursuit of Happiness. That to secure these rights, Governments are instituted among Men, deriving their just powers from the consent of the governed,— That whenever any Form of Government becomes destructive of these ends, it is the Right of the People to alter or to abolish it, and to institute new Government, laying its foundation on such principles and organizing its powers in such form, as to them shall seem most likely to effect their Safety and Happiness.

3   *Subject to painful gout:* Rowland, vol. I, 273 (Jefferson letter); vol. I, 178 (Edmund Randolph letter).
3   *"Where are our men of abilities?":* Washington to Mason, March 27, 1779, in Washington Papers.
4   *When snarls developed:* Washington to Mason, May 10, 1776, in Robert Rutland, *The Papers of George Mason, 1725–1792* (Chapel Hill: University of North Carolina Press, 1970), vol. I, 269.
4   *Only four months before:* Washington to Mason, December 13, 1784, in Rutland, vol. II, 808.
4   *The letter said the meeting:* Rutland, vol. II, 813n.
4   *Mason surmised that Virginia:* Randolph to Madison, July 17, 1785, in Madison Papers.
4   *Mason was certain they would not:* Ibid.
4   *That document defined Maryland:* That conflict reached into the twenty-first century, when the Supreme Court had to decide whether Virginia was entitled to draw water from the river. *Virginia v. Maryland,* 540 U.S. 56 (2003).
5   *The document shed no light:* Resolutions Authorizing an Interstate Compact on Navigation and Jurisdiction of the Potomac, December 28, 1784, enclosed in Madison to Washington, January 9, 1785, in Madison Papers.

5   *Pursuing this vision:* Joel Achenbach, *The Grand Idea* (New York: Simon & Schuster, 2004).

5   *By January 1785, he had persuaded:* Douglas Southall Freeman, *George Washington, Patriot and President* (New York: Chas. Scribner's Sons, 1954), vol. VI, 28.

5   *They had to decide what to do:* Washington Diary, March 20–28, 1785, in Washington Papers.

5   *"brought with them the most amicable dispositions":* Mason to Madison, August 9, 1785, in Rowland, vol. II, 85.

5   *"activity and urgency":* Randolph to Madison, July 17, 1785, in Madison Papers.

6   *"sen[d] the bottle about pretty freely":* Achenbach, 129, quoting Robert Hunter, Jr., "Quebec to Carolina in 1785–1786: Being the Travel Diary and Observations of Robert Hunter, Jr., a Young Merchant of London," ed. Louis B. Wright and Marion Timlin (San Marino, Calif.: Huntington Library, 1943), 193.

6   *Though five unscheduled guests:* Mary V. Thompson, "The Hospitable Mansion: Hospitality at George Washington's Mount Vernon," Mount Vernon Ladies' Association, November 7, 2004.

7   *"a half-starved, limping Government":* Washington to Benjamin Harrison, January 18, 1784, in Washington Papers.

7   *Their agreement:* VA Code Ann. § 7.1–7.

7   *He recommended that the conference:* Rowland, vol. II, 379–80.

7   *Maryland expanded on Mason's proposal:* Votes and Proceedings of the House of Delegates of the State of Maryland, November Session, 1785, 11 (November 22, 1785); Madison to Washington, December 9, 1785, in James Madison, *Writings* (New York: Library of America, 1999).

8   *Madison first worked with General Washington:* Stuart Leibiger, *Founding Friendship* (Charlottesville: University Press of Virginia, 1999), 11–12, 33–58.

8   *Ironically, Madison also sponsored:* Ibid., 160, 169.

8   *For the rest of his life:* Ralph Ketcham, *James Madison: A Biography* (Charlottesville: University of Virginia Press, 1990), 51–52.

8   *By late 1785, Madison recognized:* Madison to Monroe, August 7, 1785, in Madison, *Writings*.

8   *When three New England states:* Christopher Collier and James Lincoln Collier, *Decision in Philadelphia: The Constitutional Convention of 1787* (New York: Ballantine Books, 1986), 225.

9   *"Every liberal good man":* Robert A. Feer, "Shays's Rebellion and the Constitution: A Study in Causation," *New England Quarterly* 42 (1969), 388, 390.

9   *One idea in circulation:* The earliest suggestion of this course seems to have been in a letter from Alexander Hamilton in 1780. Ron

Chernow, *Alexander Hamilton* (New York: Penguin Press, 2004), 138–39.

9   *The legislatures in New York and Massachusetts:* Hubert Irving Beatty, *Why Form a More Perfect Union?: A Study of the Origin of the Constitutional Convention of 1787* (Ph.D. dissertation, Stanford University, 1962), 116.

9   *Visiting Mount Vernon:* Irving Brant, *James Madison: the Nationalist, 1780–1787* (Indianapolis: Bobbs-Merrill Co., 1941), 376; Washington Diary, October 12–14, 1787.

9   *"We are either a united people":* Washington to Madison, November 30, 1785, in Washington Papers.

9   *"the requisite augmentation":* Madison to Washington, December 9, 1785, in Madison, *Writings.*

9   *The Virginia Assembly:* Chernow, 223; Brant, 381. In retirement, Madison recalled that the resolution in the Virginia General Assembly was brought forward by John Tyler, "who having never served in Congress, had more the ear of the House than those [like Madison] whose services there exposed them to an imputable bias." Farrand, vol. III, 544. That John Tyler was the grandfather of President John Tyler.

9   *Arriving eight months later:* Richard B. Morris, *Witnesses at the Creation* (New York: Holt, Rinehart & Winston, 1985), 165.

9   *"can bear a worse aspect":* Brant, 383, quoting Madison to Ambrose Madison, September 8, 1786.

9   *None came from New England:* Rhode Island, which boycotted the Constitutional Convention, sent two delegates to Annapolis because that conference was to address only commercial matters, which were important to the state. By the time the Rhode Island delegates reached Philadelphia, however, they learned that the Annapolis conference was over, so they turned around and went home. Patrick T. Conley, "First in War, Last in Peace: Rhode Island and the Constitution, 1786–1790" (Rhode Island Bicentennial Foundation, 1987), 12.

10   *Hamilton drafted a fiery call:* Garry Wills, *Explaining America: The Federalist* (New York: Penguin, 1982), 11–12; Brant, 386.

CHAPTER 2. BLOOD ON THE SNOW: WINTER 1787

PAGE

11   *They groaned under "ancient debts":* George Richards Minot, *History of the Insurrections in Massachusetts in 1786 and of the Rebellion Consequent Thereon* (New York: Da Capo Press, 1971; original dated 1788), 14.

12   *As many as two-thirds of them:* David P. Szatmary, *Shays' Rebellion: The Making of an Agrarian Insurrection* (Amherst: University of Massachusetts Press, 1980), 66.

12   *As they trudged:* Minot, 89.

12   *The rebels had cut off the roads:* Szatmary, 100–101. The description of Shays' Rebellion draws from the excellent account in Leonard L. Richards, *Shays's Rebellion* (Philadelphia: University of Pennsylvania Press, 2002).

12   *In a chilling ultimatum:* Szatmary, 101.

12   *To avoid spreading alarm:* October 20, 1786, JCC.

12   *The thirteen states refused to pay:* Szatmary, 84–85.

13   *"I have lost eight years":* Shepard to Henry Knox, December 20, 1786, Connecticut Valley Historical Museum.

13   *He enlisted as a private:* Walter A. Dyer, "Embattled Farmers," *New England Quarterly* 4 (1931): 460, 465.

13   *"a brave and good soldier":* "Park Holland's Account of His Family History," February 28, 1832, in Massachusetts Historical Society.

13   *He and his wife, Abigail:* Dyer, 466.

13   *"it was always against my inclination":* Manuscript, Army Intelligence Report, December 10, 1786, Library of Congress Manuscript Division ("A Spy's Relation—the Vermont Manuscript").

13   *General Shepard sent messengers:* Shepard to Governor Bowdoin, January 26, 1787, reprinted in "Documents Relating to the Shays Rebellion," *American Historical Review* 2 (1896): 693, 694; depositions of William Lyman (February 6, 1786) and Samuel Buffington (February 1, 1786), both in the Caleb Strong Papers at Forbes Memorial Library, Northampton, Mass. The battle description also benefits from the studies of Richard Colton, historian for the National Park Service at the Springfield Armory.

13   *"dropped prostrate":* Diary of Daniel Stebbins, Forbes Memorial Library, Northampton, Mass.

14   *"at waistband height":* Szatmary, 102; Minot, 111.

14   *A ball ripped both arms:* Stebbins Diary.

14   *Shays tried to stop:* Letter of Elnathan Haskell (DSM 02-03-06), in Connecticut Valley Historical Museum; Minot, 111.

14   *"There was not a single musket fired":* Shepard to Gov. Bowdoin, January 26, 1787.

14   *"half leg high":* Quoted in Szatmary, 105.

14   *"in whirls and eddies":* Ibid.

15   *"a peaceable entrance":* Park Holland History.

15   *"throng[ed] into a back road":* Minot, 132–34.

15   *The rebellion died:* Szatmary, 111–13.

15   *He made his way:* Marion L. Starkey, *A Little Rebellion* (New York: Alfred A. Knopf, 1955), 250–51; Robert A. Gross, "The Uninvited Guest: Daniel Shays and the Constitution," in Gross, ed., *In Debt to Shays: The Bicen-*

tennial of an Agrarian Revolution (Charlottesville: University Press of Virginia, 1993), 2.

15　*The rebels raged at a state government:* Massachusetts Constitution of 1780, chap. I, § II, Art. 1; Richards, 72–73; E. James Ferguson, *The Power of the Purse* (Chapel Hill: University of North Carolina Press, 1961), 245.

15　*"wrought prodigious changes":* Knox to Washington, December 21, 1786, quoted in Szatmary, 127.

15　*"I am mortified beyond expression":* Washington to Harry Lee, October 31, 1786, Washington Papers.

16　*"Without some alteration":* Washington to Madison, November 5, 1786, Washington Papers.

16　*"the most intricate":* Chernow, 224, quoting Jacob E. Cooke, *Alexander Hamilton: A Profile* (New York: Hill and Wang, 1967), xviii.

CHAPTER 3. "A HOUSE ON FIRE": SPRING 1787

PAGE

17　*Even before Daniel Shays:* Virginia, New Jersey, Pennsylvania, and North Carolina.

17　*In March, Madison reported:* Madison to Jefferson, March 19, 1787, in Madison, *Writings*, 63.

17　*"a rheumatic complaint":* Washington to Randolph, March 28, 1787, Washington Papers.

18　*Indeed, his prestige:* James Thomas Flexner, *George Washington and the New Nation (1783–1793)* (Boston: Little, Brown & Co., 1969), 85–111.

18　*"God forbid":* Jefferson to William Smith, November 13, 1787, in Jefferson Papers.

18　*"What stronger evidence":* Washington to Madison, November 5, 1786, in Washington Papers.

18　*"tended to draw together":* Allan Nevins, *The American States During and After the Revolution, 1775–1789* (New York: Augustus M. Kelley, 1969; originally 1924), 549.

18　*Each state tailored its tax system:* David Brian Robertson, *The Constitution and America's Destiny* (Cambridge: Cambridge University Press, 2005), 32–33.

19　*A southerner wrote resentfully:* William Blount to Richard Caswell, January 28, 1787, LDC.

19　*"the great extent of territory":* Farrand, vol. III, 103 (Pierce Butler to Weedon Butler, October 8, 1787).

19　*Congressional delegates from:* Nevins, 603–4.

19　*"Certain it is":* Monroe to Patrick Henry, August 12, 1786, LDC. Monroe made a similar report to Madison in a letter dated September 3, 1786, LDC.

19 *"rope of sand"*: Timothy Bloodworth to Richard Caswell, September 4, 1786, LDC.

19 *"a partition of the Union"*: Madison to Edmund Pendleton, February 24, 1787, LDC.

19 *"[t]hirteen sovereignties"*: Washington to Madison, November 5, 1786, Washington Papers.

19 *The state systems:* Knox to Rufus King, July 15, 1787, in Charles R. King, ed., *Life and Correspondence of Rufus King* (New York: G. P. Putnam's Sons, 1894), vol. I, 228.

20 *"the primary cause of all our disorders"*: Farrand, vol. III, 51 (Washington to David Stuart, July 1, 1787).

20 *By July of 1779, a Continental dollar:* Beatty, *Why Form a More Perfect Union?*, 194; R. V. Harlow, "Aspects of Revolutionary Finance," *American Historical Review* 35 (1929): 46, 61.

20 *In 1780, a sheep could be purchased:* Marquis de Chastellux, *Travels in North America in the Years 1780–1781–1782* (New York: Augustus M. Kelley, 1970), 153.

20 *When Madison in 1786:* Madison to Jefferson, August 12, 1786, in Madison, *Writings*, 54.

20 *In Virginia, it held:* Achenbach, 11–12.

20 *To establish an American currency:* Chernow, 201.

20 *The New England states and Virginia:* Forrest McDonald, *We the People: The Economic Origins of the Constitution* (Chicago: University of Chicago Press, 1992; originally 1958), 385.

20 *Transactions also might be:* John Fiske, *The Critical Period of American History, 1783–1789* (Boston: Houghton Mifflin & Co., 1876), 171–76.

20 *"the lead in this folly"*: Madison to Jefferson, August 12, 1786, in Madison, *Writings*, 53.

21 *Monetary anarchy:* Farrand, vol. III, 15 (E. Gerry to J. Monroe, June 11, 1787). Ben Franklin was not alarmed by depreciated paper money, which he called a "wonderful machine." In his view, "It performs its office when we issue it; it pays and clothes troops and provides victuals and ammunition; and when we are obliged to issue a quantity excessive, it pays itself off by depreciation." Franklin to Samuel Cooper, April 22, 1779, in Albert Henry Smyth, ed., *The Writings of Benjamin Franklin*, vol. VII, 292–94.

21 *With different currencies of doubtful value:* Nevins, 570.

21 *The British, not deigning:* Morris, *Witnesses at the Creation*, 148; Szatmary, 19–26.

21 *Martial law prevailed:* Catherine Drinker Bowen, *Miracle at Philadelphia* (Boston: Little, Brown & Co., 1966), 31.

21   *Virginia separately ratified:* Robertson, 32.

21   *More serious, Spain allowed:* Brant, 403–5; Morris, 150–51.

21   *For a year, the Confederation:* Morris, 150–57.

21   *British troops still manned:* Rufus King to Elbridge Gerry, May 14, 1786, LDC.

21   *Despite a treaty:* Madison to Jefferson, March 19, 1787, in Madison, *Writings,* 67.

21   *The Confederation Congress fared:* Richards, *Shays' Rebellion,* 15–16, 23–25.

21   *From Massachusetts to South Carolina:* Nevins, 659.

22   *Western settlers proclaimed:* Morris, 124.

22   *Vermont functioned as a sort of free state:* William Grayson to James Madison, November 22, 1786, LDC; Richards, 120–24.

22   *The state lost the land claim:* Nevins, 586.

22   *In recompense, Connecticut was granted:* Robertson, 41–42; Charles Page Smith, *James Wilson, 1742–1798* (Chapel Hill: University of North Carolina Press, 1956), 199–201.

22   *"a patient bleeding at both arms":* Farrand, vol. III, 542 (unpublished preface to Debates in the Convention of 1787).

22   *To retaliate, New Jersey:* Ibid.; Walter Isaacson, *Benjamin Franklin: An American Life* (New York: Simon & Schuster, 2003), 444; Nathaniel Gorham to Caleb Davis, March 1, 1786, LDC.

22   *No state could contest:* Nathaniel Gorham to Caleb Davis, June 15, 1786, LDC.

22   *Congress could not protect:* Rufus King to John Adams, May 5, 1786; Rufus King to Elbridge Gerry, May 14, 1786, LDC.

22   *"[o]ur commerce is almost ruined":* Rufus King to John Adams, May 5, 1786, LDC.

22   *Its requisitions met with very mixed results:* One scholar has estimated that the states' compliance with requisitions during the life of the Confederacy ranged from a high of 67 percent for New York to 3 percent for North Carolina and zero for Georgia. Roger H. Brown, *Redeeming the Republic: Federalists, Taxation, and the Origins of the Constitution* (Baltimore: Johns Hopkins University Press, 1993), 14.

22   *"afforded a most melancholy aspect":* Address of Rufus King, October 11, 1786, LDC; Rufus King, Memorandum of September 13, 1786, LDC.

23   *Many decided to let tax collections slide:* Brown, 108–19.

23   *"[N]o respect is paid":* Madison to Edmund Pendleton, February 24, 1787, in Madison, *Writings,* 62.

23   *Princeton, little more than a hamlet:* June 21, 1783, JCC. Alexander Hamilton's report to Congress of this episode makes gripping reading. Ibid., July 1, 1783.

23   *After a spell in Annapolis:* E.g., ibid., August 13, 1784 (moving official pa-

pers from Annapolis to Philadelphia, in anticipation of move to Trenton); November 1, 1784 (convening in Trenton).

23 *In throwing off the British yoke:* Merrill Jensen, *The Articles of Confederation* (Madison: University of Wisconsin Press, 1966), 239.

24 *"a mere diplomatic body":* Farrand, vol. I, 256 (June 16, 1787).

24 *As a final guarantee:* April 17, 1783; March 28, 1785, JCC.

24 *"deranged condition":* Rufus King to Elbridge Gerry, May 14, 1786, LDC.

24 *"[t]he present phantom":* Hutson, 14 (Nathaniel Gorham to Caleb Davis, May 22, 1787).

24 *At Madison's prodding:* Brant, 394–95; Madison to Washington, November 8, 1786, Madison Papers; Journal of the Virginia House of Delegates, November 9, 1786.

25 *"scandalous conduct":* Farrand, vol. III, 51 (Washington to David Stuart, July 1, 1787).

25 *The absence of states' rights advocates:* Forrest McDonald, *E Pluribus Unum* (Boston: Houghton Mifflin Co., 1965), 155.

25 *"It really is an assembly of demigods":* Jefferson to Adams, August 30, 1787, in Jefferson Papers.

25 *"The present system":* Madison to Edmund Pendleton, February 24, 1787, in Madison, *Writings*, 62.

25 *"like a house on fire":* Washington to Henry Knox, February 3, 1787, Washington Papers.

CHAPTER 4. DEMIGODS AND COXCOMBS ASSEMBLE: MAY 1787

PAGE

28 *Here, at the same moment: Pennsylvania Herald,* May 16, 1787, 3.

28 *Madison had lodged:* William Peters, *A More Perfect Union* (New York: Crown Publishers, 1987), 12–13.

28 *"His ordinary manner":* Recollections of Edward Coles, quoted in Leibiger, *Founding Friendship,* 7.

28 *"an air of reflection":* Fisher Ames to George Minot, May 29, 1789, quoted in Irving Brant, *James Madison: Father of the Constitution, 1787–1800* (Indianapolis: Bobbs-Merrill Co., 1950), 261.

29 *The first was an examination of republics:* Madison, "Of Ancient and Modern Confederacies," in Gaillard Hunt, ed., *Writings of James Madison,* vol. II, 369–90.

29 *The vices numbered eleven:* Madison, *Writings,* 69–80.

29 *"All civilized societies":* Ibid., 76, 79.

29 *Had other servants or slaves:* Brant, *James Madison: Father of the Constitution,* 16–17.

29 *The contrast with Madison's quiet entry:* Although not mentioned by

Washington's biographers, he certainly was attended by slaves from Mount Vernon. Only eleven days after his arrival, the general recorded in his diary that he summoned a doctor because one of his "Postilion boys (Paris)" was sick. Paris is listed as a stable boy in Washington's 1786 listing of "all my Negroes," Washington Papers, diary entry for February 18, 1786, and Paris later attended Washington in Philadelphia during his first term as president. Edward Lawler, Jr., "Recognize those who served George Washington in Philly as distinct individuals," *Philadelphia Inquirer* (August 28, 2002). Washington probably also brought Giles and Austin, the slaves who ordinarily managed his carriage. Washington Diary, February 18, 1786, in Washington Papers.

30 *An artillery company:* Pennsylvania Herald, May 16, 1787, 3.

30 *Washington did not tarry there:* Washington Diary, May 13, 1787, in Washington Papers; Flexner, *George Washington and the New Nation,* 112–13; John Dos Passos, *The Men Who Made the Nation* (New York: Doubleday & Co., 1957), 123.

31 *The presentation was on American trade:* Michael Vinson, "The Society for Political Inquiries: The Limits of Republican Discourse in Philadelphia on the Eve of the Constitutional Convention," *Pennsylvania Magazine of History and Biography* 113 (1989): 203.

31 *He was later unanimously added:* Max Mintz, *Gouverneur Morris and the American Revolution* (Norman: University of Oklahoma Press, 1970), 176; Smith, 217–18.

32 *The title dated from:* Isaacson, *Benjamin Franklin,* 198.

33 *His gifts and achievements defied summary:* It is a major chore to keep up with the flood of Franklin scholarship. E.g., Page Talbott, ed., *Benjamin Franklin: In Search of a Better World* (New Haven: Yale University Press, 2005); Isaacson; H. W. Brands, *The First American: The Life and Times of Benjamin Franklin* (New York: Doubleday & Co., 2000); Stacy Schiff, *The Great Improvisation: Franklin, France, and the Birth of America* (New York: Henry Holt & Co., 2005); Gordon S. Wood, *The Americanization of Ben Franklin* (New York: Penguin Books, 2004); Edmund Morgan, *Benjamin Franklin* (New Haven: Yale University Press, 2002).

34 *"I am ashamed":* Letters of James Wilson, Historical Society of Pennsylvania, Allison Landes to Wilson, March 9, 1785.

34 *He won Pennsylvania's land dispute:* Smith, *James Wilson,* 146–58.

34 *As a member of the Confederation Congress:* Feer, "Shays' Rebellion," 400.

34 *Tall, well-dressed, and solidly built:* Smith, 202.

34 *"not by the charm of his eloquence":* Farrand, vol. III, 92 (Pierce). William Pierce of Georgia, a 47-year-old businessman, recorded his thumbnail impressions of the other delegates. Though he had little im-

pact on the Constitution, his descriptions of the delegates were deft and insightful.

34 *"powerful, though not melodious"*: Mark David Hall, *The Political and Legal Philosophy of James Wilson* (Columbia: University of Missouri Press, 1997), 128–29; Remarks of William Rawle, recorded in Lucien Alexander, "James Wilson, Nation-Builder," in *Green Bag* 19 (1907): 268, 269.

34 *"were far from disagreeable"*: Quoted in Alexander.

34 *The lingering effects of that controversy*: Geoffrey Seed, *James Wilson* (Millwood, N.Y.: KTO Press, 1978), 186–87.

35 *From what became known as "Fort Wilson"*: Smith, 133–36. Something about Wilson seemed to incite politically motivated violence. On the evening after Pennsylvania ratified the Constitution in December 1787, he was attacked by a group of "anti-Federalists" who knocked him to the ground and beat him with clubs. He was saved from serious injury when a Revolutionary War veteran flung himself on top of Wilson to protect him from the blows. Wayne L. Trotta, "James Wilson, Forgotten Founding Father," *Pennsylvania Heritage* 18 (1992): 19.

35 *Called "Tall Boy" by some*: Howard Swiggett, *The Extraordinary Mr. Morris* (Garden City: Country Life Press, 1952), 75.

35 *"kept us in a continual smile"*: Richard Brookhiser, *Gentleman Revolutionary: Gouverneur Morris, the Rake who Wrote the Constitution* (New York: Free Press, 2003), 65.

35 *"to possess the most spirit and nerve"*: Quoted in Mintz, 146 (remarks of Prince de Broglie).

35 *Seven years earlier*: William Howard Adams, *Gouverneur Morris* (New Haven: Yale University Press, 2003), 126.

35 *Owing to his rakish reputation*: Ibid., 127. In 1779, John Jay referred to Morris as making "daily oblations to Venus." Quoted in Swiggett, 66.

35 *Morris duly administered*: Farrand, vol. III, 85 (undated anecdote).

35 *"throws around him such a glare"*: Farrand, vol. III, 92 (Pierce).

37 *"to form a proper correspondence"*: Farrand, vol. III, 23, 28 (Mason to George Mason, Jr., May 20 and May 27, 1787).

37 *"it occurred to [the Virginia delegates]"*: Farrand, vol. III, 549 (Madison's unpublished "Preface to Debates in the Convention").

37 *"the principal states"*: Farrand, vol. III, 23 (Mason to George Mason, Jr., May 20, 1787).

37 *With the benefit of Madison's preparation*: The Virginians' consultations certainly started with Madison's outline and ended up very close to that plan. As presented at the beginning of the Convention, the Virginia Plan resembled the ideas sketched by Madison in a letter to Randolph in early April, a month before he arrived in Philadelphia. Madison to Randolph, April 8, 1787, LDC.

38 *"Men of learning":* Madison to Jefferson, June 6, 1787, in Madison, *Writings,* 96–97.

38 *John Rutledge of Charleston:* Richard Barry, *Mr. Rutledge of South Carolina* (New York: Duell, Sloan & Pearce, 1942), 315–16. Barry's biography includes some assertions that later historians have not been able to confirm. The assertion that Rutledge lodged temporarily with Wilson is consistent with the close working relationship between the two through the Convention.

38 *The two remaining delegation members: Pennsylvania Packet,* May 28, 1787.

38 *The sister of General Pinckney's wife:* Malcolm Bell, Jr., *Major Butler's Legacy: Five Generations of a Slaveholding Family* (Athens: University of Georgia Press, 1989), 19–20. The South Carolinians had some remarkable female relatives. The mother of Charles Cotesworth Pinckney— Eliza Lucas Pinckney—introduced to South Carolina the cultivation of indigo. As the daughter of the governor of Antigua, where indigo was grown, she concluded that South Carolina's conditions would favor the crop, and proved to be right. Christopher E. Gadsden, *A Sermon on the Occasion of the Decease of Gen. Charles Cotesworth Pinckney* (Charleston: A. E. Miller, 1825). Through his wife, Elizabeth Grimké, John Rutledge was uncle to Angelina and Sara Grimké, who became leading southern abolitionists.

39 *"possibly the most successful lawyer":* McDonald, *We the People,* 79.

39 *Some complained:* Barry, 23.

39 *"too rapid in his public speaking":* Farrand, vol. III, 96 (Pierce).

39 *"no keenness in his eye":* Adams Diary, September 1, 3; October 10, 1774.

39 *"an air of reserve":* Adams Diary, September 3, 1774.

39 *"Hang them":* David Ramsay, *Ramsay's History of South Carolina* (Newberry, S.C.: W. J. Duffie, 1858), vol. II, 270.

39 *As South Carolina's governor:* Robert W. Barnwell, Jr., "Rutledge, the Dictator," *Journal of Southern History* 7 (1941): 215.

39 *"court, jury and audience quailed before him":* Henry Flanders, *The Lives and Times of the Chief Justices of the Supreme Court of the United States* (Philadelphia: Lippincott, Grambo & Co., 1855), 601.

39 *Rutledge's remarks at the Convention:* Collier and Collier, *Decision in Philadelphia,* 197.

40 *"the cleverest being alive":* Hutson, 255 (E. Gerry to Ann Gerry, September 1, 1787).

40 *Sometimes sharp-elbowed:* Collier and Collier, 92.

40 *While in the Confederation Congress:* JCC (August 7, 1786).

40 *"only true and radical remedy":* Speech to New Jersey Legislature, March 16, 1786; "Account of a Deputation of Congress to the Assembly of New Jersey," *American Museum* 2 (1787): 153–60.

40   *Young Charles arrived:* Andrew Bethea, *The Contribution of Charles Pinckney to the Formation of the American Union* (Richmond: Garrett & Massie, 1937), 35–36; Marty D. Matthews, *Charles Pinckney: A Forgotten Founder* (Ph.D. dissertation, University of South Carolina, 2001), 87.

40   *Charles showed his draft:* Jacob Broom of Delaware reported several days before the Convention began that Pinckney had a plan of government that was "a compound, abstracted from the several [state] constitutions and the Articles of Confederation." Hutson, 16 (Jacob Broom to Thomas Collins, May 23, 1787). Another Delaware delegate, George Read, who was lodging at Mrs. House's, reported reviewing a plan of government that had to be Pinckney's. Farrand, vol. III, 25 (George Read to John Dickinson, May 21, 1787).

40   *"a sponger and a plagiarist":* Brant, *James Madison: Father of the Constitution,* 28.

40   *Charles's* post hoc *glory-seeking:* The most lasting stain on Charles's reputation derives from the document he sent to the nation's archives in 1819 as his initial plan for the Constitution. The 1819 document diverged on central points from the version Charles himself had published in the fall of 1787, shortly after the Convention. The injury to Charles's standing was compounded when he unwisely predeceased Madison, which allowed the aged Virginian to deliver additional and unanswered critiques of the South Carolinian's efforts in Philadelphia.

41   *More than any other:* Bell, 77; e.g., Farrand, vol. I, 168 ("vehement"); Farrand, vol. II, 541 ("strenuous").

41   *Nine, like Madison:* According to a review of the records of credentials presented at Congress, these included Rufus King of Massachusetts, William Samuel Johnson of Connecticut, Charles Pinckney of South Carolina, William Few and William Pierce of Georgia, Madison, William Blount of North Carolina, and Gunning Bedford of Delaware.

41   *"The streets and alleys reeked of garbage":* Sam Bass Warner, Jr., *The Private City* (Philadelphia: University of Pennsylvania Press, 1968), 16.

41   *"dead dogs, cats, fowls":* Charles S. Olton, "Philadelphia's First Environmental Crisis," *Pennsylvania Magazine of History and Biography* 98 (April 1974): 99.

41   *Pigs running free:* J. P. Brissot de Warville, *New Travels in the United States of America, 1788,* trans. Mara Soceanu Vamos and Durand Echeverria; ed. Durand Echeverria (Cambridge, Mass.: Belknap Press, 1964; originally 1792), 201.

41   *On Wednesday, May 23:* Hutson, 16 (Washington Diary).

41   *Yellow fever had struck:* J. H. Powell, *Bring Out Your Dead: The Great Plague of Yellow Fever in Philadelphia in 1793* (Philadelphia: University of Pennsylvania Press, 1949), xiii.

41 *"Having never had the small pox":* Hutson, 3 (Erastus Woolcott to the Governor and General Assembly of Connecticut, May 15, 1787).

42 *"very sickly":* Hutson, 216 (Elbridge Gerry to Ann Gerry, August 10, 1787).

42 *"[T]here is nothing but streets all alike":* Johann D. Schoepf, *Travels in the Confederation [1783–84]*, trans. and ed. Alfred J. Morrison (New York: Bergman Publishers, 1968), vol. I, 58.

42 *Still, visitors admired:* Brissot, 254.

42 *To fight crime:* Schoepf, vol. I, 59.

42 *"with Billingsgate language":* Ibid., 263.

42 *In March of 1787, eighteen inmates: A Daybook for 1787,* Bicentennial of the Constitution of the United States (Independence National Historical Park), citing *Pennsylvania Herald* of March 1, 1787 (hereafter *Daybook*).

42 *On May 12: Pennsylvania Herald,* May 16, 1787; Thompson Westcott, *History of Philadelphia, 1609–1884* (Philadelphia: L. H. Everts & Co., 1884), 445.

42 *"nest of footpads": Pennsylvania Journal and General Advertiser,* June 20, 1787.

42 *"[a]t Philadelphia there is always something":* Schoepf, vol. I, 68.

42 *"Everything is adjusted in perfect order":* William Parker Cutler and Julia Perkins Cutler, *Life, Journals, and Correspondence of Rev. Manasseh Cutler, LL.D.* (Cincinnati: Robert Clarke & Co., 1888), vol. I, 271.

42 *"Even meat":* Brissot, 199.

42 *The offerings included raccoon:* Schoepf, vol. I, 112.

42 *"One would think it is a market of brothers":* Brissot, 199.

43 *In 1774, Philadelphia:* Warner, 19.

43 *The better inns were full:* Bowen, *Miracle in Philadelphia,* 50.

43 *"very crowded":* Farrand, vol. III, 25 (George Read to John Dickinson, May 21, 1787).

43 *"old tormenters, the bugs":* John D. R. Platt, "The City Tavern," Denver Service Center, Historic Preservation Team, National Park Service, U.S. Department of the Interior, Denver, April 1973, 51.

43 *The servant produced two London magazines:* Cutler and Cutler, vol. I, 254; Platt, 49 n. 90.

43 *Although the enthusiastic drinking habits:* Clinton Rossiter, *1787: The Grand Convention* (New York: Macmillan Co., 1966), 115–16.

43 *When the Philadelphia City Troop: Daybook,* September 15, 1787. Comparable volumes were consumed at a dinner of the St. Andrew's Society in the following year. Peter John Thompson, *A Social History of Philadelphia's Taverns, 1683–1800* (Ph.D. Dissertation, University of Pennsylvania, 1989), 514.

43 *William Samuel Johnson:* Platt, 205.

43 *A Delaware delegate wrote: Daybook,* June 30, 1787.

43 *For July 2, Pennsylvania's chief justice:* Ibid., July 1, 1787.

44 *Of the thirty-eight delegates:* Ibid., June 24, 1787.

44 *The daughter of William Samuel Johnson:* Ibid., May 29, 1787.

44 *More than half of those came from:* Farrand, vol. III, 587–90.

44 *"Upon the event of this great council":* Pennsylvania Journal and Weekly Advertiser, May 12, 1787.

44 *"only means to avoid flagitious evils":* Hutson, 13 (Knox to Governor John Sullivan of New Hampshire, May 21, 1787).

44 *[T]he influence which the [government]:* Farrand, vol. III, 33 (Mason to George Mason, Jr., June 1, 1787).

45 *"the choicest talents and the noblest hearts":* Alexis de Tocqueville, *Democracy in America* (New York: Vintage Books, 1990), vol. I, 114.

45 *You may have been taught:* Hutson, 295 (Williamson to John Gray Blount, June 3, 1788).

CHAPTER 5. VIRGINIA LEADS: MAY 25–JUNE 1

PAGE

47 *"lament[ing] his want of better qualifications":* Farrand, vol. I, 3–4 (May 25, 1787).

47 *By seconding the motion:* Farrand, vol. I, 3 (May 25, 1787).

48 *"a seat in front of the presiding member":* Farrand, vol. III, 550 (unpublished "Preface to Debates in the Convention of 1787").

48 *For several decades after the Convention:* James H. Hutson, "Riddles of the Federal Constitutional Convention," *William and Mary Quarterly* 44 (1987): 411, 412–15.

49 *More disturbing:* Ibid., 412. The route by which Yates's notes found their way into publication is highly improbable. In 1808, Governor George Clinton of New York was challenging Madison for the Republican Party nomination for president. One of Clinton's partisans was his son-in-law, Edmond Genêt, the notorious "Citizen Genêt" of the 1790s who had stirred great political unrest while representing the revolutionary French regime. Resolving not to risk the guillotine by returning to France in 1793, Genêt married Clinton's daughter and settled near Albany, New York, which also was home to Yates. In 1808, Genêt acquired from Yates's widow the notes her husband had taken during the Convention, intending to use them against Madison politically. The notes were not actually published until 1821, by which time Genêt had edited them. The evidence of Genêt's edits comes from comparing the published version with two pages of a copy made by John Lansing (another New York delegate); though many of Genêt's edits seem innocuous in that small sample, others may have altered the nuance of statements, or more.

James H. Hutson, "Robert Yates's Notes on the Constitutional Convention of 1787: *Citizen Genêt's Edition,*" *Quarterly Journal of the Library of Congress* 35 (1978): 173.

50 *Geography also dictated:* The seating followed by the delegates is not known to a certainty, and may have fluctuated during the course of the Convention. The accepted facts are (1) that Congress followed the north-to-south table arrangement on at least one recorded occasion in 1782 (Charles Thompson announcement, in E. C. Burnett, *Letters of Members of the Continental Congress* [Gloucester, Mass.: P. Smith, 1963], vol. VI, 348–50), (2) that such seating was recommended in a committee report that was not adopted in 1781, and (3) that both Congress and the Convention recorded state votes from north to south. From these materials, the historians and curators at Independence National Historical Park have reached the "interpretation" of the seating arrangements that this volume presents.

50 *Figure to yourself:* Hutson, 201 (John Langdon to Joshua Bracket, August 1, 1787).

51 *New York required:* Farrand, vol. III, 560–86 (authorizations adopted by the twelve states that sent delegates to the Convention).

51 *"discountenanced and stifled":* Farrand, vol. I, 8, 10–11 (May 28, 1787).

51 *"against licentious publications":* Ibid., 13 (May 28, 1787).

51 *"nothing spoken in the House":* Ibid., 17 (May 29, 1787).

51 *To enforce the rule:* Ibid., vol. III, 59 (Manasseh Cutler, Journal, July 13, 1787); Paul S. Clarkson and R. Samuel Jett, *Luther Martin of Maryland* (Baltimore: Johns Hopkins Press, 1970), 80.

52 *"So great is":* Farrand, vol. III, 60 (*Pennsylvania Packet and General Advertiser,* July 19, 1787).

52 *"necessary precaution":* Ibid., 33 (Mason to George Mason, Jr., June 1, 1787).

53 *The delegates expected an initial proposal:* Ibid., 25 (George Read to John Dickinson, May 21, 1787).

53 *"anarchy from the laxity of government":* Ibid., vol. I, 25–27 (May 29, 1787).

54 *Moreover, the version of his plan:* Ibid., vol. II, 134–37.

54 *The German rejected Gorham's overture:* Szatmary, 82; Richard Krauel, "Prince Henry and the Regency of the United States," *American Historical Review* 17 (October 1911): 44–51.

55 *"presume[d] from the silence of the house":* Farrand, vol. I, 41 (McHenry notes, May 30, 1787).

55 *"unnecessary":* Ibid., 39 (May 30, 1787).

56 *"on the shyness of the gentlemen":* Ibid., 65 (June 1, 1787).

56 *"general silence":* Hutson, 62 (Gunning Bedford Notes).

CHAPTER 6. WILSON'S BARGAIN: MAY 31–JUNE 10

PAGE

59 *"rais[e] the federal pyramid":* Farrand, vol. I, 49 (May 31, 1787).

61 *"like every other day":* de Chastellux, *Travels in North America,* 97.

61 *The delegates dwelt in close quarters:* An exception was Daniel Carroll of Maryland. Fearing Philadelphia's reputation for pestilential diseases, Carroll lodged in Germantown, some miles away. William G. Carr, *The Oldest Delegate: Franklin in the Constitutional Convention* (Newark: University of Delaware Press, 1990), 24.

61 *"walked together, they talked together":* Max Farrand, "If James Madison Had a Sense of Humor," *Pennsylvania Magazine of History and Biography* 62: 136 (1938).

61 *By June 8, Pierce Butler:* Papers of Pierce Butler, Library of Congress Manuscript Collection (June 8, 1787).

62 *"it might become their duty":* Farrand, vol. I, 37 (May 30, 1787).

63 *Having led the colonists:* James H. Hutson, "John Dickinson and the Federal Constitutional Convention," *William and Mary Quarterly* 40: 256, 257 (1983).

63 *On the last day of May:* Farrand, vol. I, 48 (May 31, 1787).

63 *Though of humble origins himself:* After the Convention was over, the 67-year-old Sherman would have to take some cases on the Connecticut court circuit in order to repair his finances. Christopher Collier, *Roger Sherman's Connecticut: Yankee Politics and the American Revolution* (Middletown, Conn.: Wesleyan University Press, 1971), 173.

63 *"should have as little to do":* Farrand, vol. I, 48 (May 31, 1787).

63 *"attend to the rights of every class":* Ibid., 49 (May 31, 1787).

64 *"even the diseases":* Ibid., 142 (June 6, 1787).

64 *"turbulence and follies":* Ibid., 51 (May 31, 1787).

64 *Others, however, thought state legislatures:* Ibid., vol. II, 291 (August 14, 1787); Ibid., vol. I, 150 (June 7, 1787); Robertson, 210–11.

64 *"a chasm":* Farrand, vol. I, 52 (May 31, 1787).

64 *"We have seen the mere distinction":* Ibid., 135 (June 6, 1787).

64 *John Dickinson moved:* Ibid., 156 (June 7, 1787).

65 *"compared the proposed national system":* Ibid., 153 (June 7, 1787).

65 *"will continually fly":* Ibid., 165 (June 8, 1787).

65 *"will never confederate":* Ibid., 177–79 (June 9, 1787).

65 *Never short on truculence:* Ibid., 180 (June 9, 1787).

66 *Shall New Jersey:* Ibid., 183 (June 9, 1787).

66 *That the Articles had adopted:* Ibid., 179 (June 9, 1787).

67 *Moreover, many southerners:* Ibid., 491 (June 30, 1787, Bedford); 561 (July 9, 1787, G. Morris).

67 *Though Wilson made the deal:* Paul Finkelman, "Slavery and the Consti-

tutional Convention: Making a Covenant with Death," in Richard Beeman, Stephen Botein, and Edward C. Carter II, eds., *Beyond Confederation: Origins of the Constitution and American National Identity* (Chapel Hill: University of North Carolina Press, 1987).

68 *After all, at least a third:* McDonald, *We the People,* 68–85. The documented slaveholders included Wilson, four Maryland delegates, all seven Virginians, four South Carolinians, and three North Carolina delegates.

68 *Twelve states adopted resolutions:* Farrand, vol. II, 559–86 (Appendix B).

68 *"very pure, perspicuous":* Fisher Ames correspondence, quoted in Brant, *James Madison, Father of the Constitution,* at 249.

68 *"the warmest excitement":* Hugh Blair Grigsby, *The History of the Virginia Federal Convention of 1787* (New York: Da Capo Press, reissued 1969), vol. I, 96.

69 *I . . . cannot think of punishing:* James Madison, Jr., to James Madison, Sr., September 8, 1783, Madison Papers.

69 *"to depend as little as possible":* James Madison, *The Writings of James Madison, Comprising His Public Papers, and His Private Correspondence, Including Numerous Letters and Documents Now for the First Time Printed* (New York: G. P. Putnam's Sons, 1908–10), vol. II, 154.

70 *"there is not a man living":* Washington to Robert Morris, April 12, 1786, Washington Papers.

70 *George Wythe freed his slaves:* Joyce Blackburn, *George Wythe of Williamsburg* (New York: Harper & Row, 1975), 123.

70 *"I should emancipate":* Randolph to Madison, June 30, 1789, in Madison Papers.

70 *Every gentleman here:* Quoted in Schwartz, "Forgotten Founder," 143.

70 *"submit to every imposition":* W. W. Abbott et al., eds., *Papers of George Washington,* Colonial Series, vol. 10, Washington to Bryan Fairfax (August 24, 1774).

70 *Others struck that clause:* Blackburn, 97; Joseph Ellis, *American Sphinx: The Character of Thomas Jefferson* (New York: Alfred A. Knopf, 1997), 51–52.

70 *Wythe, Mason, and Jefferson:* Autobiography Draft, February 7, 1821, in Jefferson Papers.

70 *In 1787 only Massachusetts: Commonwealth v. Jennison* (unreported) (1787), reprinted in Paul Finkelman, *The Law of Freedom and Bondage: A Casebook* (New York: Oceana Publications, 1986), 36–37.

71 *Four other states:* Rossiter, 32; Paul Finkelman, *Slavery and the Founders* (Armonk, N.Y.: M. E. Sharpe, 2nd ed., 2001), 41; Pennsylvania Acts, 1780 ("An Act for the Gradual Abolition of Slavery"); Rhode Island Laws, 1784 ("An Act Concerning Indian, Mulatto, and Negro Servants and Slaves"); Connecticut Laws, 1784.

71   *New York adopted:* Arthur Zilversmit, *The First Emancipation: The Abolition of Slavery in the North* (Chicago: University of Chicago Press, 1967), 16–17, 121–24, 150, 180–82, 193–94.

71   *Under those statutes, slaves were held:* Ira Berlin, *Many Thousands Gone* (Cambridge, Mass.: Belknap Press, 1998), 232–33.

71   *In 1802, Virginia enacted:* Drew R. McCoy, *The Last of the Fathers: James Madison and the Republican Legacy* (Cambridge: Cambridge University Press, 1989), 283.

71   *Shortly before the Convention began:* Brands, 701–4.

71   *Southerners surely were unsettled: Pennsylvania Journal and General Advertiser* (May 23, 1787).

71   *Wilson, the transplanted Scot:* Hall, *Politics and Legal Philosophy of James Wilson,* 30; Smith, *James Wilson,* 367.

71   *Gouverneur Morris's family:* Mintz, *Gouverneur Morris,* 7, 14–15.

71   *Having pressed for an abolition clause:* Adams, *Gouverneur Morris,* 4–9, 81–88.

71   *He formed an "Ethiopian Regiment":* Henry Wiencek, *An Imperfect God: George Washington, His Slaves, and the Creation of America* (New York: Farrar, Straus & Giroux, 2003), 203; Berlin, 257.

72   *"would leave us, if they believed":* W. W. Abbot, ed., *The Papers of George Washington: Revolutionary War Series* (Charlottesville: University Press of Virginia, 1985–91), vol. II, 479–80.

72   *Washington reclaimed:* John C. Fitzpatrick, ed., *The Writings of George Washington, 1745–1799,* vol. XXII, 14 (Washington, D.C.: Government Printing Office, 1931–44) (note to letter from Washington to Lund Washington, April 30, 1781) (available through online project of the University of Virginia Library, http://etext.virginia.edu/washington/fitzpatrick/); Wiencek, 251.

72   *The slave population in Georgia:* Berlin, 263, 304; James McMillin, *The Final Victims: Foreign Slave Trade to North America, 1783–1810* (Columbia: University of South Carolina Press, 2004), 8.

72   *at their work:* Quoted in Fritz Hirschfeld, *George Washington and Slavery: A Documentary Portrayal* (Columbia: University of Missouri Press, 1997), 30.

72   *"If the Negroes":* Ibid., 36.

72   *After 1783 the Deep South states:* Donald Robinson, *Slavery in the Structure of American Politics* (New York: W. W. Norton & Co., 1971), 298.

72   *John Rutledge, General Pinckney:* James Haw, *John and Edward Rutledge of South Carolina* (Athens: University of Georgia Press, 1997), 168; Bell, 40; Marvin R. Zahniser, *Charles Cotesworth Pinckney, Founding Father* (Chapel Hill: University of North Carolina Press, 1967), 73, 76.

73 *Allen left that nondenominational group:* The founding of the African Methodist Episcopal Church grew from a dispute over segregated seating at St. George's.

73 *"In vain will be":* Hutson, 44.

73 *"being informed that": Daybook,* note to August 17, 1787.

CHAPTER 7. THREE-FIFTHS OF A HUMAN BEING: JUNE 11

PAGE

76 *The "justice" of that approach:* Farrand, vol. I, 196 (June 11, 1787).

77 *King also warned:* Ibid., 36 (May 30, 1787).

77 *After reviewing the arithmetic:* Ibid., 197–200 (June 11, 1787). When he "threw his ideas" together, Franklin evidently remembered his remarks during the debates on the Articles of Confederation, when he made a similar reference to the merger of England and Scotland. August 1, 1776, JCC.

77 *So endorsed, Wilson's resolution was adopted:* Farrand, vol. I, 200 (June 11, 1787). The poor attendance of the five Maryland delegates meant that the state's delegation was often divided between one delegate supporting a stronger central government (Daniel of St. Thomas Jenifer), and one highly protective of state powers (Luther Martin). Through many weeks, those two deadlocked on key votes, though the arrival of another Marylander could break the logjam.

78 *The wealthy delegate from Marblehead:* George Athan Billias, *Elbridge Gerry: Founding Father and Republican Statesman* (New York: McGraw-Hill, 1976), 7; James T. Austin, *The Life of Elbridge Gerry, Vol. II* (New York: Da Capo Press, 1970), 158, 308.

78 *"hesitating and laborious speaker":* Farrand, vol. III, 88 (Pierce).

78 *A corresponding member:* Richard S. Newman, *The Transformation of American Abolitionism: Fighting Slavery in the Early Republic* (Chapel Hill: University of North Carolina Press, 2002), 21–22.

78 *While Wilson sat:* March 18, 1783, JCC.

79 *The committee toyed with counting slaves:* March 28, 1783; February 11, 1783; February 17, 1783; March 18, 1783, JCC. The issue also had been debated in the Continental Congress in 1776. Adams Diary, July 30–31, 1776.

79 *The ratio never took effect:* Finkelman, *Slavery and the Founders*, 13; Bowen, 95.

79 *Indeed, in one of those stinging ironies:* Robinson, 156–59; Farrand, vol. I, 587 (July 11, 1787).

79 *In all its perversity:* Madison made precisely this argument in *The Federalist*, No. 54, contending that the Constitution properly viewed them "in

the mixt character of persons and of property, [which] is in fact their true character." He concluded, "Let the compromising expedient of the constitution be mutually adopted, which regards them as inhabitants, but as debased by servitude below the equal level of free inhabitants, which regards the *slave* as divested of two fifths of the *man.*" (Emphasis in original.)

80   *"The smaller states would never":* Farrand, vol. I, 201 (June 11, 1787).

80   *He proposed that the Senate:* The opportunistic quality of this last step of the day is reflected in Hamilton's participation. There is little evidence of Wilson and Hamilton cooperating at any point during the Convention.

80   *Nevertheless, versions of his actual plan:* This impressive bit of historical detective work is described in Farrand, vol. III, 604–5, and in John Jameson, *Studies in the History of the Federal Convention of 1787* (Washington, D.C.: Government Printing Office, 1903), 117–32. This evidence is reinforced by a May 21 letter from George Read, a Delaware delegate who lodged with Mrs. House, where James Madison and young Charles also resided. Howard A. Ohline, "Republicanism and Slavery: Origins of the Three-Fifths Clause in the United States Constitution," *William & Mary Quarterly* 38 (1971): 563, 568. Read wrote that he had a copy of "a Federal system intended to be proposed," Farrand, vol. III, 25 (Read to Dickinson, May 21, 1787), and described the plan as including a "house of delegates . . . chosen by the Legislature of each state, in proportion to its number of white inhabitants, *and three-fifths of all others.*" Read certainly wrote of Pinckney's plan; the Virginians were still working on their own outline at the time, while Pinckney was showing his plan to anyone who would look at it. Another Delaware delegate, Jacob Broom, reported reviewing Pinckney's plan before the Convention began. Hutson, 17 (Jacob Broom to Thomas Collins, May 23, 1787). Moreover, a number of elements in Read's description match only Pinckney's plan, including the selection of a Senate on the basis of "four great districts, into which the United States are to be divided." The principal evidence against Pinckney's paternity of the three-fifths clause comes from the South Carolinian's attempts to rewrite history. Pinckney plainly was chagrined to see his plan totally eclipsed by the Virginia Plan. His proposal was not even recorded in the official Journal of the Convention. More than thirty years later, Pinckney provided a supposed version of his plan to be preserved with the records of the Convention. That 1819 version states that the legislature shall be selected on the basis of "the number of inhabitants" in each state, a phrase that would include both slaves and free inhabitants and would deny Pinckney credit for the three-fifths rule. Farrand, vol. III, 535–36 (Madison to W. A. Duer, June 5, 1835). But the 1819 version of his plan was likely a fraud. Madison denied that it was the one presented in Philadelphia, and detailed several instances in the 1819 version where "Mr. Pinckney interwove . . . passages" from the final Constitution, in-

cluding the requirement of popular election of the House of Representatives. Madison also pointed out inconsistencies between Pinckney's 1819 version and a pamphlet Pinckney published in October 1787 that purported to describe his plan. That 1787 pamphlet omits any mention of the three-fifths ratio, leaving the records drawn from Wilson's papers and George Read's letter as the principal ties between Pinckney and the ratio.

81 *"quite overcome" by it:* Hutson, 94 (Gorham to Theophilus Parsons, June 18, 1787).

81 *"could not support the excessive heat":* Hutson, 141 (Mary Butler to Thomas Butler, July 4, 1787).

81 *"the warmest place";* Hutson, 163 (William Paterson to Euphemia Paterson, July 11, 1787).

81 *The sketchy diary of William Samuel Johnson:* Farrand, vol. III, 552–54.

82 *"in general terms Philadelphia":* Hutson, appendix.

82 *"the heat renders walking":* de Chastellux, 155.

82 *"not less than 30 sudden deaths":* Schoepf, vol. I, 61.

82 *"it is no uncommon thing":* de Chastellux, 155.

82 *"fatal effects":* Pennsylvania Journal and Weekly Advertiser, July 7, 1787.

82 *Through the summer:* Hutson, 72 (June 12 diary entry); Platt, "The City Tavern," 217.

83 *On a Tuesday in mid-July:* Hutson, 172 (July 17 diary entry).

83 *He enjoyed stopping at farms:* Ibid., 179 (July 22 diary entry).

83 *Washington wrote of dining:* Ibid., 12 (May 21 diary entry).

83 *In a menu touch: Daybook* (June 6, 1787).

83 *"heartily tired":* Farrand, vol. III, 28 (Mason to George Mason, Jr., May 27, 1787).

84 *"I mix with company":* Hutson, 121 (Ellsworth to Abigail Ellsworth, June 26, 1787).

84 *"rouged up to the ears":* Phyllis Lee Levin, *Abigail Adams* (New York: St. Martin's Press, 1987), 374.

84 *"almost as varied":* Brissot, *New Travels*, 256.

84 *"whatever their origins":* Wendy Anne Nicholson, *Sober Frugality and Siren Luxury: The Transformation of Elite Culture in Philadelphia, 1750–1800* (Ph.D. dissertation, University of California at Berkeley, 1994), 203–4.

84 *"truly barbarous":* de Chastellux, 89–90.

84 *"promoted a heavy consumption":* Peter Thompson, *Rum Punch and Revolution: Taverngoing and Public Life in Eighteenth Century Philadelphia* (Philadelphia: University of Pennsylvania Press, 1999), 193.

84 *"the male guests invariably":* Ibid.

CHAPTER 8. *FESTINA LENTE:* JUNE 12–19

PAGE

87 "Festina lente": Farrand, vol. III, 32 (Mason to George Mason, Jr., June 1, 1787).

87 *"the 140 miles":* Rutland, *The Papers of George Mason,* cxxi.

88 *"indifference for distinction":* Rowland, vol. II, 129.

88 *"a man of talents":* John Jay to William Livingston (August 27, 1787), in *Daybook,* August 27.

88 *Mr. Mason is a gentleman:* Farrand, vol. III, 94 (Pierce).

89 *"Was a combination to be apprehended":* Farrand, vol. I, 447–48 (June 28, 1787).

89 *Could a central government:* Although the comparison is imperfect, echoes of the Framers' concerns can be heard in the contemporary debate in Europe over the evolving European Union, which some hope will become a "United States of Europe."

89 *"of a very low stature":* Farrand, vol. III, 90 (Pierce).

91 *"with more coolness":* Ibid., vol. I, 151 (June 7, 1787).

91 *"will certainly be defective":* Ibid., 202–3 (June 11, 1787).

91 *"a hesitation in his speech":* Ibid., vol. III, 90 (Pierce).

92 *under the Virginia Plan:* Ibid., vol. I, 252 (June 16, 1787).

92 *As for himself:* Ibid., 261 (June 15, 1787).

92 *"the bastard brat":* Quoted in Chernow, 522.

93 *"Without numbers":* Jefferson to Madison, September 21, 1795, in Jefferson Papers.

94 *"the three greatest men":* James Thomas Flexner, *The Young Hamilton: A Biography* (New York: Fordham University Press, 1997), 449.

94 *"flagrant errors":* Chernow, 235.

94 *"The voice of the people":* Farrand, vol. I, 299 (June 18, 1787).

95 *"if it eventuates":* Ibid., 298 (June 18, 1787).

95 *Senators, too:* Ibid., 289–90 (June 18, 1787). After the Convention, Hamilton was unfairly singled out for the label of monarchist. When the full Convention debated the presidency in mid-July, Dr. McClurg of Virginia moved that the presidential term be for "good behavior," exactly as Hamilton had. Though George Mason denounced the proposal, Madison offered a baffling variety of equivocal arguments on the motion, neither opposing nor supporting it. Though Madison faithfully reported his own doublespeak, he asserted in a footnote that he was trying to "parry the animadversions likely to fall on the motion of Dr. McClurg, for whom J.M. had a particular regard." Farrand, vol. II, at 34n. Madison's embarrassment over the episode was acute: a Virginia delegation including Washington and Madison actually voted in favor of Dr. McClurg's protomonarchist motion. Three other states did, as well, prompting Madi-

son to drop another footnote, this time asserting that those votes should not "be considered as any certain index of opinion," but as an attempt "to alarm those attached to a dependence of the Executive on the Legislature, and thereby facilitate some final arrangement of a contrary tendency." He adds that no more than "three or four" delegates truly supported a presidential term of good behavior. If revealed during his lifetime, Madison's vote for a lifelong presidential term would have required considerable explanation.

95   *"pork still"*: Farrand, vol. I, 301 (June 18, 1787).

95   *"has been praised"*: Ibid., 363 (June 21, 1787).

96   *Moreover, Hamilton started backtracking:* Ibid., 323 (June 19, 1787).

96   *His side had the votes:* Ibid., 321 (June 19, 1787).

96   *He was tall:* Collier, *Roger Sherman's Connecticut,* 10.

96   *"Sherman's air"*: Quoted in Julian Boyd, "Roger Sherman: Portrait of a Cordwainer Statesman," *New England Quarterly* 5 (1932): 221, 226 (September 15, 1775 entry).

97   *"the oddest shaped character"*: Farrand, vol. III, 88 (Pierce).

97   *"[Sherman] is as cunning"*: Ibid., 34 (Jeremiah Wadsworth to King, June 3, 1787).

98   *"no man has a better heart"*: Ibid., 89 (Pierce).

98   *"never said a foolish thing"*: Boyd, 221.

98   *"When you are in a minority"*: Clarkson and Jett, *Luther Martin,* 87.

98   *"We move slowly"*: Hutson, 97 (William R. Davie to Richard Caswell, June 19, 1787).

98   *"the living is cheap"*: Farrand, vol. III, 24 (Mason to George Mason, Jr., May 20, 1787).

98   *delegates from New Jersey and North Carolina:* Hutson, 34 (Richard Dobbs Spaight to John Gray Blount, May 30, 1787); Hutson, 40 (David Brearley, William Houston, William Paterson to the Council and General Assembly of New Jersey, June 1, 1787).

98   *By July, the Virginians:* Farrand, vol. III, 57 (Edmund Randolph to Beverley Randolph, July 12, 1787).

98   *a Massachusetts delegate urgently:* Hutson, 199 (Caleb Strong to Alexander Hodgden, July 30, 1787).

98   *William Samuel Johnson: Daybook,* July 18.

98   *"[w]hen I left Charleston"*: Rutledge to John F. Grimké, July 18, 1787, South Caroliniana Library, University of South Carolina.

98   *Two weeks before the Convention finished:* Hutson, 256 (Spaight to John Gray Blount, September 2, 1787).

CHAPTER 9. TO THE BRINK: JUNE 21–JULY 10

PAGE

102   *the rollicking witty:* Henry Adams, *John Randolph* (Boston: Houghton Mifflin, 1893), 141.

102   *"as coarse and unseemly":* Clarkson and Jett, 311 (reprinting from *Memoir of Roger Brooke Taney, L.L.D.*)

102   *He labors hard:* Joseph Story to Samuel P. Fay (February 16, 1808), in William Wetmore Story, ed., *Life and Letters of Joseph Story* (Boston: C. C. Little & J. Brown, 1851), 162.

102   *He kept at the job:* Farrand, vol. I, 437–38 (June 27, 1787).

102   *"diffuse, and in many instances desultory":* Ibid., 438–39 (June 27, 1787).

102   *"two months":* Ibid., vol. III, 271 ("The Landholder," February 29, 1788). Decrying Martin's "eternal volubility," Ellsworth wrote that the delegates "prepared to slumber when [Martin] rose to speak."

103   *In any event, another chimed in:* Farrand, vol. I, 452 (June 28, 1787).

103   *"Look to the votes":* Ibid., 476 (June 29, 1787).

104   *[R]epresent[ation] in one branch:* Ibid., 486–87 (June 30, 1787).

104   *As the summer wore on:* Ibid., 605 (July 13, 1787).

105   *"The affairs of the United States":* Ibid., vol. III, 94 (Pierce).

105   *"of seventy-one":* McDonald, *Novus Ordu Seculum,* 208–9; quoted in David Brian Robertson, "Madison's Opponents and Constitutional Design," *American Political Science Review* 99 (2005): 225.

105   *"the offspring of a single brain":* Farrand, vol. III, 533 (Madison to William Cogswell, March 10, 1834).

105   *A joiner:* Ibid., vol. I, 499 (June 30, 1787).

106   *"an amphibious monster":* Ibid., 490 (June 30, 1787).

106   *"the most intemperate speech":* John P. Nields, *Gunning Bedford, Jr.* (Wilmington, 1907), 12.

106   *"I do not, gentlemen, trust you":* Farrand, vol. I, 500 (June 30, 1787).

106   *"take a foreign power":* Ibid., 502 (June 30, 1787).

107   *"[T]wo or three days":* Farrand, vol. III, 50 (Mason to Beverley Randolph, June 30, 1787).

108   *"would go home":* Ibid., 188 ("Genuine Information" provided to Maryland Assembly on November 29, 1787).

108   *According to a report:* Ibid., 467 (William Steele to Jonathan D. Steele, September 1825).

109   *Baldwin and Oliver Ellsworth boarded:* William R. Casto, *Oliver Ellsworth and the Creation of the Federal Republic* (New York: Second Circuit Committee on History and Commemorative Events, 1997), 47.

109   *Later in July, Baldwin:* Hutson, 193 (Baldwin to Joel Barlow, July 26, 1787).

109   *Noah Webster: The Autobiographies of Noah Webster,* ed. Richard M.

Rollins (Columbia: University of South Carolina Press, 1989), 243 (July 4, 1787), 246 (September 11, 1787).

109 *That Connecticut connection:* E. Merton Coulter, *Abraham Baldwin: Patriot, Educator, and Founding Father* (Arlington, Va.: Vandamere Press, 1987), 97.

109 *"That he was too illiterate":* Adams to Benjamin Rush, March 19, 1812, in Gordon S. Wood, *Revolutionary Characters: What Made the Founders Different* (New York: Penguin Press, 2005), 33.

109 *"neither copiousness of ideas":* Jefferson to Walter Jones, January 2, 1814, in Jefferson Papers.

110 *He refused to allow:* Farrand, vol. III, 188 (Martin's "Genuine Information"). In 1785, Washington had hosted Jenifer during the Mount Vernon Conference. At roughly the same time, the General engaged in a complex transaction with Jenifer in the latter's capacity as intendant of the revenue of Maryland (the state's chief fiscal officer). The General wished to cash out certain loan certificates that had been purchased on his behalf in 1779, and there was some wrangling over both the interest rate and the conversion of the certificates from dollars to pounds sterling. Jenifer to Washington, February 28, 1785, and Washington to Jenifer, April 12, 1785, in Washington Papers.

110 *With the tide turning:* Farrand, vol. I, 511–16 (July 2, 1787).

110 *Washington dined that evening:* Hutson, 143 (Washington Diary, July 2, 1787).

110 *"so serious as to threaten":* Farrand, vol. III, 264.

111 *"scarce held together":* Ibid., 190.

111 *He proposed an arrangement:* Madison attributed the motion in the Committee to Dr. Franklin, Farrand, vol. I, 526 (July 5, 1786), as did Luther Martin, ibid., vol. III, 190 ("Genuine Information," November 29, 1787).

111 *"far more comfortable":* Isaacson, *Benjamin Franklin,* 447.

112 *"daily a spectacle":* Farrand, vol. III, 33 (Rush to Richard Price, June 2, 1787).

112 *"exercise of going and returning":* Ibid., 98 (Franklin to Jane Mecom, September 20, 1787).

112 *Throughout the summer:* E.g., ibid., 21 (Franklin to Thomas Jordan, May 18, 1787); ibid., 59 (Manasseh Cutler diary entry for July 13, 1787); Hutson, 268 (Washington Diary, September 12, 1787).

112 *"a short, fat, trunched old man":* Cutler and Cutler, vol. I, 267.

112 *His first major address:* Farrand, vol. I, 81–85 (June 2, 1787).

112 *"It is certain":* Ibid., vol. III, 91 (Pierce).

112 *"ablest of the profession":* Ibid., vol. I, 120 (June 5, 1787).

112 *"tells a story":* Ibid., vol. III, 91 (Pierce).

113 *"a system of government": Pennsylvania Herald,* July 7, 1787.

113   *General Washington visited:* Hutson, 145 (Washington Diary, July 4, 1787); Carr, *The Oldest Delegate,* 23.

113   *Pennsylvania militia officers: Pennsylvania Packet,* July 6, 1787.

113   *"Is the science of government":* Charles Warren, *The Making of the Constitution* (Boston: Little, Brown & Co., 1928), 269.

114   *"have only assented conditionally":* Farrand, vol. I, 527 (July 5, 1787).

114   *"as a representative of the whole human race":* Ibid., 530 (July 5, 1787).

114   *"serious thoughts of adjourning":* Ibid., vol. III, 423 (Autobiography of William Few).

114   *"a profusion of those hems":* Billias, *Elbridge Gerry,* 7; Farrand, vol. III, 271 ("The Landholder" essay of February 29, 1788 by Oliver Ellsworth, with his trademark thumping sarcasm).

115   *It could not be more inconvenient:* Farrand, vol. I, 533 (July 5, 1787).

115   *"diverse and almost opposite":* Ibid., vol. III, 55 (Hugh Williamson to James Iredell, July 8, 1787).

115   *"progressed a single step":* Hutson, 163 (King to Knox, July 11, 1787).

115   *"we have not made":* Hutson, 167 (Jonathan Dayton to William Livingston, July 13, 1787).

116   *With two state delegations deadlocked:* Farrand, vol. I, 50–51 (July 7, 1787).

116   *"little more than a guess":* Ibid., 559 (July 9, 1787).

116   *He could regard:* Ibid., 561 (July 9, 1787).

117   *The simple ability of wives:* Joan Hoff, *Law, Gender and Injustice: A Legal History of U.S. Women* (New York: New York University Press, 1991), 98–103; Marlene Stein Wortman, *Women in American Law* (New York: Holmes & Meier Publishers, 1985), vol. I, 13–15, 62. Women's suffrage was eliminated in New Jersey as part of purported "reforms" adopted after a notably fraudulent election in Essex County.

118   *"men who oppose a strong and energetic government":* Farrand, vol. III, 56–57 (Washington to Hamilton, July 10, 1787).

118   *For five of the next six nights:* Hutson, 162–71.

CHAPTER 10. THE SMALL STATES WIN: JULY 11–17

PAGE

119   *"eloquent appeals":* Farrand, vol. III, 500 (Madison to Jared Sparks, April 8, 1831).

119   *[Davie] saw:* Ibid., vol. I, 593 (July 12, 1787).

120   *The episode is sufficiently puzzling:* Suspicions about the record of the exchange on July 12 derive in part from the notation that Madison "corrected" his notes for this day on three occasions (two corrections made years later, and one "contemporary"), ibid., 593, but we know nothing

concrete to explain either the North Carolinian's outburst or the powerful impact it had.

120   *"It has been said"*: Ibid., 593 (July 12, 1787).

121   *"[P]roperty in slaves"*: Ibid., 594 (July 12, 1787).

122   *"every thing was to be apprehended"*: Ibid., 597 (July 12, 1787).

122   *"The security the southern states want"*: Ibid., 605 (July 13, 1787).

123   *"What hopes will our constituents"*: Ibid., vol. II, 4 (July 14, 1787).

124   *"In all cases where"*: Ibid., 8–9 (July 14, 1787).

124   *The positive votes came from:* The margin of victory for the compromise
was a whisker. The shift of a single Massachusetts delegate would have
moved that state to a no vote and defeated the compromise. Equally,
the margin of victory consisted of North Carolina, which had not supported per-state voting in earlier ballots. That shift remains unexplained.
McDonald, *Novus Ordo Seculum,* 237 and n. 42.

124   *[Rutledge] could see no chance:* Farrand, vol. II, 19 (July 16, 1787).

125   *Thunderstorms moved through:* Hutson, 332 (weather records).

125   *"had the Convention separated"*: Farrand, vol. III, 249 (January 16,
1788).

125   *"the Convention must have dissolved"*: Ibid., 333 (June 20, 1788).

125   *"my admiration can only be equaled"*: Ibid., 102 ("Address to a Meeting of
the Citizens of Philadelphia on October 6, 1787") (the "State House
yard" speech).

126   *"reconciling the larger states"*: Farrand, vol. III, 483 (Madison to James
Hillhouse, May 1830).

CHAPTER 11. THE TOUCH OF A FEATHER: JULY 9–14

PAGE

127   *Also, one strategy for paying off:* William Pierce to William Short, July
25, 1787, LDC.

127   *Leading citizens formed companies:* Brant, *James Madison: The Nationalist,* 90.

129   *At least nine of the delegates:* Other delegate-speculators included
Gorham and Gerry of Massachusetts, Dayton of New Jersey (for whom
Dayton, Ohio, was named), Williamson and Blount of North Carolina,
Mason of Virginia, and Wilson and Fitzsimons of Pennsylvania. McDon-
ald, *We the People,* 41–77. Rutledge of South Carolina acquired over
70,000 acres of land in his state. Haw, 177–78. At various times, Robert
Morris owned virtually all of western New York State; in 1795 he held
more than 6 million acres of land (the equivalent of the state of Maryland)
in Kentucky, western Pennsylvania, North Carolina, South Carolina, and
Georgia. Ellis P. Oberholtzer, *Robert Morris: Patriot and Financier* (New
York: Chelsea House, 1983; originally 1903), 301–4, 312–13.

129   *Many settlers were simple squatters:* Washington's trip out West in 1784 was undertaken in part to eject squatters from his land in western Pennsylvania, a legal battle that consumed many months. Achenbach, *The Grand Idea,* 6–7, 85.

129   *Rufus King in 1786 worried:* King to Elbridge Gerry, June 4, 1786, LDC.

129   *"interests will be opposed":* James Monroe to Thomas Jefferson, January 19, 1786, LDC.

129   *I need not pose to you:* Washington to Benjamin Harrison, October 10, 1784, in Washington Papers.

130   *"a formidable and dangerous neighbor":* Washington to Henry Knox, December 5, 1784, in Washington Papers.

130   *Future President Andrew Jackson:* Arthur Preston Whitaker, *The Spanish-American Frontier, 1783–1795* (Lincoln: University of Nebraska Press, 1969; originally 1927), 111–12.

130   *Kentucky settlers held two conventions:* Richard B. Morris, *The Forging of the Union, 1781–1789* (New York: Harper & Row, 1987), 225.

130   *Purporting to represent Kentucky:* Robert V. Remini, "The Northwest Ordinance of 1787: Bulwark of the Republic," *Indiana Magazine of History* 84 (March 1988): 19–21.

130   *The congressman said that in return:* Whitaker, 80.

130   *Southerners hotly denounced:* Morris, *Witnesses at the Creation,* 151–59.

131   *During Madison's boyhood:* Ketcham, 14–16.

131   *Some Georgia and North Carolina delegates:* Abraham Baldwin and William Few of Georgia; Alexander Martin and Hugh Williamson of North Carolina (though Williamson was born in Pennsylvania and had lived in North Carolina for only seven years).

131   *When Luther Martin of Maryland:* Erwin Neal Southard, *Reprobate Genius: Luther Martin, Attorney-at-Law* (Ph.D. dissertation, Ohio State University, 1941), 27, 74–76; Henry P. Goddard, *Luther Martin: The "Federal Bull-Dog"* (Baltimore: Maryland Historical Society, 1887), 12.

131   *was just a tunnel:* Achenbach, 59, 61.

131   *"The Indians are generally hated":* Schoepf, vol. I, 277–78.

131   *"about as wicked":* Achenbach, 91, quoting William Winans from Thomas P. Slaughter, *The Whisky Rebellion* (New York: Oxford University Press, 1986), 64.

132   *Some were on the run from the law:* Schoepf, vol. I, 261; Brissot, 264.

132   *"the cutthroat knave":* Archer Butler Herbert, *The Ohio River: A Course of Empire* (New York: G. P. Putnam's Sons, 1966), 88.

132   *"are often in a perfect state of war":* J. Hector St. John de Crevecoeur, *Letters from an American Farmer* (New York: A. & C. Boni, 1925; originally 1782), 42–43.

132   *"passion for migration":* Brissot, 269.

132 *In 1787, more than 900 flatboats:* Bowen, 171.

132 *The 1790 census:* Census of 1790; Rossiter, 28.

132 *Six states asserted overlapping claims:* The claim to lands as far as the South Sea, based on Virginia's colonial charter, was asserted in debates in the Continental Congress as early as 1776. August 2, 1776, JCC.

132 *By assuming the Iroquois' claim:* Jack N. Rakove, "Ambiguous Achievement: The Northwest Ordinance," in Frederick D. Williams, *Northwest Ordinance: Essays on Its Formulation, Provisions, and Legacy* (East Lansing: Michigan State University Press, 1988).

132 *Satisfied, Maryland ratified:* Jensen, *The Articles of Confederation,* 235–38.

133 *Each could join the Confederation:* March 1, 1784, JCC.

133 *Jefferson's legislation had lost:* September 19, 1786, JCC.

133 *The quorum that turned to the bill:* Samuel Holten and Nathan Dane (Massachusetts); Melancton Smith, John Haring, and Abraham Yates (New York); Abraham Clark and James Schureman (New Jersey); Dyre Kearny and Nathaniel Mitchell (Delaware); William Grayson, Richard Henry Lee, and Edward Carrington (Virginia); William Blount and Benjamin Hawkins (North Carolina); John Kean and Daniel Huger (South Carolina); and William Few and William Pierce (Georgia).

133 *"increasing infirmity":* Schoepf, vol. I, at 387.

133 *On July 6, Rufus King:* Farrand, vol. I, 541 (July 6, 1787).

134 *"out-vote the Atlantic":* Ibid., 560 (July 9, 1787).

134 *"keep a majority of votes":* Ibid., 571 (July 10, 1787).

134 *Ought we to sacrifice:* Ibid., 578–79 (July 11, 1787).

134 *The busy haunts of men:* Ibid., 583 (July 11, 1787).

134 *"determined the human character":* Ibid., 584 (July 11, 1787).

135 *The new states would join the union:* July 11, 1787, JCC.

135 *"The majority of people":* Farrand, vol. I, 604–5 (July 13, 1787).

136 *By a hair, the thirteen states:* Ibid., vol. II, 3 (July 14, 1787).

136 *On this issue, Mason:* Gordon T. Stewart, "The Northwest Ordinance and the Balance of Power in North America," in Williams, *Northwest Ordinance.*

CHAPTER 12. THE IPSWICH MIRACLE: JULY 13

PAGE

138 *He read law:* Cutler led his portion of Ipswich in seceding from the rest of the town in the early 1790s. It was renamed "Hamilton" after the then secretary of the treasury, whom Rev. Cutler admired greatly.

138 *At the end of the war:* Cutler and Cutler, *Life, Journals, and Correspondence of Rev. Manasseh Cutler,* vol. I, 159–60.

139 *The Ohio Company aimed to buy:* Marietta, a contraction of Marie An-

toinette, was chosen out of gratitude for French aid during the Revolution.

139   *A tall man of generous proportions:* Eliza Poole Wheeler, "Memories of our Grandparents," at Hamilton Historical Society.

139   *his hometown representative:* Dane appears as a schoolmaster in Ipswich in Cutler's diary for 1777. Cutler and Cutler, vol. I, 159–60.

139   *"an open, frank, honest New Englander":* Ibid., 302.

139   *A family member recalled him:* Wheeler.

139   *In early May, congressional committees:* May 9, 1787, JCC.

140   *"Hypocrisy":* Cutler and Cutler, vol. I, 230–37.

140   *As luck would have it:* Richard Henry Lee to Francis Lightfoot Lee, July 14, 1787, n. 2, LDC; Francis S. Philbrick, *The Rise of the West* (New York: Harper & Row, 1965), 124–25. Duer's company never actually purchased or settled any land in Ohio, and ultimately stranded five hundred French settlers in Ohio. The Ohio Company provided land for those deceived immigrants.

140   *"was acting for associates":* Cutler and Cutler, vol. I, 343–44. Staughton Lynd, *Class, Conflict, Slavery, and the United States Constitution* (Indianapolis: Bobbs-Merrill Co., 1967), 198–99.

141   *Gerry left his family's lodgings:* Cutler and Cutler, vol. I, 254–55.

141   *"I fancied myself":* Ibid., 257.

142   *Sadly, someone present:* Ibid., 268.

142   *"like the collection at the last day":* Ibid., 271–72.

142   *One hypothesis is that:* Bowen, 281–84, offers this explanation.

144   *In the first week of July:* William Blount of North Carolina and William Pierce and William Few of Georgia.

144   *Or maybe the news:* Alfred W. Blumrosen and Ruth G. Blumrosen, *Slave Nation: How Slavery United the Colonies and Sparked the American Revolution* (Naperville, Ill.: Sourcebooks, 2005), 189–225.

144   *As a concession to slave owners:* An early version of this fugitive slave provision had been proposed in April 1785. April 5, 1785, JCC.

145   *When I drew the ordinance:* Dane to Rufus King, July 16, 1787, LDC.

146   *"principally for New England settlers":* Nathan Dane to Daniel Webster, March 26, 1830, in Lynd, 193–94.

146   *"no doubt be settled chiefly":* Dane to Rufus King, July 16, 1787, LDC.

146   *Southerners in Congress:* Blumrosen and Blumrosen, 218–19.

146   *To suffer the continuance:* King, ed., *Life and Correspondence of Rufus King*, vol. I, 285 (March 6, 1785).

146   *"for the purpose of preventing tobacco":* Grayson to Monroe, August 8, 1787, LDC.

147   *By accepting abolition:* Lynd, at 194–98.

147   *"creat[ed] the great unanimity":* Lynd, 189, quoting Edward Coles, *History of the Ordinance of 1787* (Philadelphia, 1856), 28–29.

148   *"matters went on much better":* Cutler and Cutler, vol. I, 301; Morris, *The Forging of the Union,* 228–29.

148   *In order to get at:* Cutler and Cutler, vol. I, 297, 303.

CHAPTER 13. THE PRESIDENTIAL MUDDLE: JULY 17–26

PAGE

152   *With one more state represented:* Hutson, 193 (Abraham Baldwin to Joel Barlow, July 26, 1787).

152   *When Hamilton presented:* Farrand, vol. III, 64 (Hamilton to John Auldjo, July 26, 1787); Chernow, 238.

152   *Every delegate, and most Americans:* Hutson, 263 (Hamilton to Duche, September 8, 1787); Hutson, 250 (Benjamin Rush to Timothy Pickering, August 30, 1787).

153   *"deliver their sentiments":* Farrand, vol. I, 65 (June 1, 1787).

153   *"distinguished characters":* Ibid., vol. II, 32 (July 17, 1787).

153   *many of the members cast their eyes:* Ibid., vol. III, 302 (Butler to Weedon Butler, May 5, 1788).

154   *The delegates viewed with disgust:* E.g., Nathaniel Gorham to James Warren, March 6, 1786, LDC.

154   *In many states, the legislature:* Legislatures chose the governors of South Carolina, Maryland, North Carolina, Delaware, New Jersey, and Virginia. Popular elections prevailed in Massachusetts, New York, and Georgia.

154   *"tedious and reiterated":* Farrand, vol. III, 132 (Madison to Jefferson, October 24, 1787).

154   *"were perplexed":* Ibid., 166 (remarks in Pennsylvania Convention, December 11, 1787).

154   *Mason and Dr. Franklin successfully argued:* Ibid., vol. II, 65 (July 20, 1787).

155   *"refer[ring] a trial of colors":* Ibid., 31 (July 17, 1787).

155   *"the guardian of the people":* Ibid., 53 (July 19, 1787).

155   *The people could vote for "electors":* Ibid., vol. I, 80 (June 2, 1787).

155   *Those states would suffer:* Ibid., vol. II, 57 (July 19, 1787).

156   *On the next day, July 20:* Ibid., 64 (July 20, 1787).

156   *A North Carolinian proposed to divide:* Ibid., 100–101 (July 24, 1787).

157   *"the cringing dependent":* Ibid., vol. III, 346 (William Davie in North Carolina ratifying convention, July 26, 1788).

157   *Why not select a small number:* Ibid., vol. II, 103 (July 24, 1787).

158   *Gerry denounced the approach:* Ibid., 108–9 (July 25, 1787).

158   *"the best informed man":* Ibid., vol. III, 94 (Pierce).

158   *Another observer called Madison "cool":* Brant, *James Madison. Father of*

the Constitution, at 261–62 (Fisher Ames to George Minot, May 18, 1789).

158   *Elbridge Gerry erupted again:* Farrand, vol. II, 114 (July 25, 1787).

159   *There were about eighty newspapers:* Rossiter, *1787,* 35.

159   *As Jefferson observed:* Rowland, vol. I, 273.

160   *With little discussion, the delegates:* Farrand, vol. II, 118–21 (July 26, 1787).

CHAPTER 14. RUTLEDGE HIJACKS THE CONSTITUTION: JULY 27–AUGUST 6

PAGE

163   *"foundations, cornerstones":* Farrand, vol. III, 193 (Abraham Baldwin to Joel Barlow, July 26, 1787).

163   *"on the principles and outlines":* Ibid., 61 (Hugh Williamson to James Iredell, July 22, 1787).

164   *When he was governor of South Carolina:* Haw, *John and Edward Rutledge,* 107–10, 118.

164   *"the proudest and most imperious":* Ibid., 276–77 (quoting contemporary accounts).

165   *Ellsworth and Randolph served:* William Garrott Brown, "A Continental Congressman: Oliver Ellsworth, 1777–1783," *American Historical Review* 10 (1905): 769, 773–73.

166   *"in the grip of":* Jack N. Rakove, "The Great Compromise: Ideas, Interests, and the Politics of Constitution Making," *William and Mary Quarterly* 44 (1987): 435.

167   *"can trace the causes and effects":* Farrand, vol. III, 92 (Pierce).

167   *[Wilson's] manner was rather imposing:* The quote is attributed to an 1824 speech by William Rawle, a Pennsylvania lawyer, in Alexander, *James Wilson, Nation-Builder,* 269.

167   *Though dubbed "endless Ellsworth":* William Garrott Brown, *The Life of Oliver Ellsworth* (New York: Macmillan Co., 1905), 224–25.

167   *In debate and publication:* Casto, *Oliver Ellsworth and the Creation of the Federal Republic,* 14.

167   *"truly venomous":* Ibid., 55.

167   *Ellsworth referred to one Convention delegate:* Ibid., 55; Ronald John Lettieri, *Connecticut's Young Man of the Revolution: Oliver Ellsworth* (Hartford: American Revolution Bicentennial Commission of Connecticut, 1978), 79.

168   *"[t]he flesh which I tried":* Hutson, 177 (Oliver Ellsworth to Abigail Ellsworth, July 21, 1787).

168   *"uncanny talent":* John J. Reardon, *Edmund Randolph: A Biography* (New York: Macmillan Co., 1974), 189.

168   *"the chameleon on the aspen":* William Cabell Bruce, *John Randolph of Roanoke* (New York: Octagon Books, 1970; originally 1922), vol. II, 202.

168   *"by nature timid":* Quoted in Rowland, vol. II, 210.

168   *"No one was sure":* McDonald, *E Pluribus Unum,* 158.

168   *"lusty" fellow:* Farrand, vol. III, 88 (Pierce).

168   *"greatly overrated":* James Monroe to Thomas Jefferson, July 16, 1786, LDC.

169   *The outline began:* Farrand, vol. II, 137.

169   *In this first try:* Ibid., 163.

169   *More ambitious was the committee's decision:* Ibid., 169.

169   *The committee designated the president:* Ibid., 186.

170   *The committee reversed the Convention's decision:* Ibid., 180.

170   *Ellsworth later led the effort:* Ibid., 290 (August 14, 1787).

170   *In the Convention's early days:* Ibid., vol. I, 53 (May 31, 1787).

170   *Edmund Randolph responded in late May:* Ibid., 60 (May 31, 1787). This is one of those awkward points at which different note takers do not quite agree. Madison records Randolph as disclaiming any intention to give the national government "indefinite powers," while William Pierce of Georgia records Randolph as stating that a full listing of powers was impossible. Those versions may be reconciled, however, if Randolph's statement was that the national government should have a limited, though not specific, grant of powers. Such a statement—more politically supple than intellectually coherent—would be consistent with Randolph's performance at the Convention.

171   *In mid-July, Rutledge again demanded:* Ibid., vol. II, 17 (July 16, 1787).

171   *in all cases for the general interests:* Ibid., 21 (July 17, 1787).

171   *"not worth a farthing":* ED, vol. IV, at 312 (Rutledge's statement in South Carolina House of Representatives, January 18, 1788).

171   *The committee did not waste time:* Hutson, 282 (Rufus King and Nathaniel Gorham, "Response to Elbridge Gerry's Objections," November 3, 1787); Farrand, vol. III, 268 (statement of Rufus King in Massachusetts ratifying convention, January 24, 1788).

172   *Though he retained the enumeration:* Farrand, vol. II, 168.

172   *Two years before:* James Wilson, "Considerations on the Bank of North America," in Bird Wilson, ed., *The Works of the Honourable James Wilson, L.L.D.* (Philadelphia, 1804), vol. III, 406–7; Hall, 18.

172   *In a second revision:* Farrand, vol. II, 169.

172   *By eliminating that loophole:* Ibid., 169.

173   *"a monument to Southern craft":* Robinson, *Slavery in the Structure of American Politics,* 218; another prominent historian describes the Rutledge Committee report as an attempt to secure full counting of slaves for representation purposes, despite the Convention's previous rejection

of that approach. Don E. Fehrenbacher, *The Slaveholding Republic* (Oxford: Oxford University Press, 2001), 61.

173   *southerners had suffered:* Collier and Collier, 223–24.

173   *Those acts also were synonymous:* Oliver M. Dickerson, *The Navigation Acts and the American Revolution* (New York: A. S. Barnes & Co., 1963).

173   *[He] reminded the Convention:* Farrand, vol. II, 95 (July 23, 1787).

174   *Gorham of Massachusetts:* Ibid., vol. I, 580, 587 (July 11, 1787).

174   *"mild and conciliating":* "Dr. Thomas Welsh's Eulogy to the Memory of the Hon. Nathaniel Gorham, Esq.," June 19, 1796, in Massachusetts Historical Society, 12.

175   *Their first fishing day:* Hutson, 199–200 (Washington Diary).

175   *Many delegates fled:* Collier, *Roger Sherman's Connecticut*, 234n.*

175   *General Pinckney took his new wife: Extracts from the Diary of Jacob Hiltzheimer of Philadelphia*, ed. Jacob Cox Parsons (Philadelphia: William F. Fell & Co., 1893), 129.

CHAPTER 15. BACK TO WORK: AUGUST 6

PAGE

177   *With some delegates:* Farrand, vol. III, 276 (Luther Martin's Reply to the Landowner, March 3, 1788).

177   *Only eight states:* Ibid., vol. II, 176 (August 6, 1787).

178   *The suggestion was defeated handily:* Ibid., 189 (August 6, 1787).

178   *After all, in mid-July:* Rutledge to John F. Grimké (July 18, 1787), South Caroliniana Library, University of South Carolina.

178   *"complained much of the tediousness":* Farrand, vol. II, 301 (August 15, 1787).

178   *He proposed to add an hour:* Ibid., 328 (August 18, 1787).

179   *The Convention reverted to its former hours:* Ibid., 406 (August 24, 1787).

179   *A North Carolinian blithely:* Ibid., vol. III, 67–68 (W. R. Davie to James Iredell, August 6, 1787).

179   *Several expressed:* E.g., ibid., 68 (R. D. Spaight to James Iredell, August 12, 1787).

179   *The diligent Madison:* Ibid., 69 (Madison to James Madison, Sr., August 12, 1787).

179   *If no good came from the deliberations:* Ibid., 70 (Washington to Knox, August 19, 1787).

180   *Under the rules of the Convention:* David Bernstein, "The Constitutional Convention: Facts and Figures," *History Teacher* 21 (1987): 11, 12. Though the Virginia delegation started out with seven members, James McClurg and George Wythe did not attend in August or September.

180   *Luther Martin of Maryland was left off:* Farrand, vol. III, 273 ("The Landholder," February 29, 1788).

181 *Of the first five delegates selected:* Philip A. Crowl, "Anti-Federalism in Maryland, 1787–1788," *William and Mary Quarterly* 4 (1947): 454; Bernard C. Steiner, *The Life and Correspondence of James McHenry* (Cleveland: Burrows Brothers Co., 1907), 97.

181 *That political struggle delayed:* Bernard C. Steiner, "Maryland's Adoption of the Federal Constitution," *American Historical Review* 5 (1899): 22, 25.

182 *[McHenry] is a man of specious talents:* Farrand, vol. III, 93 (Pierce).

182 *They convened at Carroll's lodgings:* Carr, *Oldest Delegate*, 24.

182 *McHenry wanted the delegation:* Farrand, vol. II, 190 (August 6, 1787).

182 *With Jenifer supporting a strong government:* Ibid., vol. I, 461 (June 29, 1787), 313 (June 19, 1787).

182 *"so extremely prolix":* Ibid., vol. III, 93 (Pierce notes).

184 *Reacting positively:* Ibid., vol. II, 209 (August 7, 1787).

184 *They greatly feared:* Ibid., 481 (Daniel Carroll, August 31, 1787).

184 *Franklin's compromise:* Though Mercer left Philadelphia for good on August 17, having participated in only ten Convention sessions, he managed to make an impression. His first statement during debate came on August 8, when he announced that he disliked "the whole plan" of the draft charter, which he predicted "could never succeed." Ibid., 215 (August 8, 1787). For his remaining seven days in Philadelphia, Mercer was an active and not always negative participant in the debates. Nevertheless, his departure surely was a relief to those who had made it through the summer without taking instruction from this twenty-eight-year-old aristocrat.

185 *"Then I advise you":* Steiner, *Life and Correspondence of James McHenry*, 106.

185 *Rutledge brought the discussion:* Farrand, vol. II, 202–6 (August 7, 1787).

186 *South Carolina's motion:* Ibid., 249 (August 10, 1787).

186 *All but one state:* Ibid., 216 (August 8, 1787).

186 *Accordingly, a nine-year requirement:* Ibid., 235–39 (August 9, 1787).

187 *He made no headway:* Ibid., 268–69 (August 13, 1787).

187 *"would damn and ought to damn":* Ibid., 390–91 (August 23, 1787).

187 *By giving federal courts:* Ibid., 430 (August 27, 1787).

187 *State courts already applied:* Thornton Anderson, *Creating the Constitution: The Convention of 1787 and the First Congress* (University Park: Pennsylvania State University Press, 1993), 149–50. During his brief time at the Convention, Mercer of Maryland objected to judicial review by the new national courts, and John Dickinson of Delaware agreed with his statement. Farrand, vol. II, 298–99 (August 15, 1787). There was, however, no further discussion of the subject.

187 *"would be as alarming":* Farrand, vol. II, 309–10 (August 16, 1787).

188 *"crush paper money":* Ibid., 439 (August 28, 1787).

188 *Ninety-seven years later: Juilliard v. Greenman,* 110 U.S. 421 (1884) ("The Legal Tender Cases").

188 *"a source of injurious altercations":* Farrand, vol. II, 224 (August 8, 1787).

189 *"Experience must be our only guide":* A pithier version of the insight comes to most law students from Oliver Wendell Holmes, Jr.'s statement that "The life of the law has not been logic; it has been experience." See O. W. Holmes, Jr., *The Common Law* (New York: Little, Brown & Co., 1984; originally 1880), 1.

189 *Notably, Virginia now supported:* Farrand, vol. II, 273–80 (August 13, 1787).

CHAPTER 16. THE CURSE OF HEAVEN: AUGUST 8–29

PAGE

191 *"a most grating circumstance":* Farrand, vol. II, 220 (August 8, 1787).

191 *"something peculiarly strong and rich":* Ibid., vol. III, 87 (Pierce notes).

192 *"that at least a time":* Ibid., vol. II, 220 (August 8, 1787).

192 *"the barren wastes of Virginia":* European travelers made the same observation. A German wrote that upon entering Virginia from the North, "it was a matter of no little astonishment to see so much waste or new-cleared land, having just come from the very well settled and cultivated regions of Pennsylvania and Maryland." He described Virginians as "very easy and negligent husbandmen" and their buildings as having the "structure and solidity of a house of cards." Schoepf, vol. 2, 31–33.

194 *Only New Jersey voted yes:* Farrand, vol. II, 221–24 (August 8, 1787).

194 *The brutality of the passage:* McMillin, *The Final Victims,* 103–8; David Brion Davis, *The Problem of Slavery in the Age of Revolution, 1770–1823* (Ithaca: Cornell University Press, 1975), 47; Richards, *The Slave Power,* 34; Hugh Thomas, *The Slave Trade* (New York: Simon & Schuster, 1997), 311, 414–15, 425–27.

194 *The rolling sea: American Museum,* June 1787, 432.

195 *Just three weeks before: Pennsylvania Evening Chronicle,* May 1, 1787.

195 *When indigo prices fell:* McMillin, 79.

195 *Largely to repair:* Haw, 192.

195 *[W]hile there remained one acre:* ED, vol. IV, at 285 (January 17, 1788).

196 *The five slave states:* Farrand, vol. II, 359–63 (August 21, 1787).

197 *If left "at liberty":* Ibid., 364–65 (August 21, 1787).

197 *As nations cannot be rewarded:* Ibid., 370 (August 22, 1787).

199 *"frank, manly, and liberal":* Alexander Garden, *Eulogy for General Charles Cotesworth Pinckney* (Charleston, S.C.: A. E. Miller, 1825), 29.

200 *After the day's intense exchanges:* Hutson, 232 (John Fitch to William Samuel Johnson, August 21, 1787).

200 *"looking for the coats of arms"*: Hutson, 231 (Nathaniel Gorham to Nathan Dane, August 20, 1787).

200 *For steamboats, Dr. Franklin*: Andrea Sutcliffe, *Steam: The Untold Story of America's First Great Invention* (New York: Palgrave Macmillan, 2004), 30, 40–42.

201 *"Governor Randolph with several"*: Quoted in Sutcliffe, 103–4; Hutson, 232–33 (Fitch to William Samuel Johnson, August 21, 1787). Sutcliffe relates Fitch's sisyphean labors in developing his steamboat.

201 *In 1790, Fitch ran*: Sutcliffe, 94.

201 *Livingston had joined*: Chernow, 216.

201 *"is utterly inconsistent with the principles"*: Carl E. Prince, *William Livingston: New Jersey's First Governor* (Trenton: New Jersey Historical Commission, 1975), 20; Theodore Sedgwick, *A Memoir of the Life of William Livingston* (New York: J & J Harper, 1833), 400.

201 *[T]he eastern states*: Farrand, vol. III, 210–11 ("Genuine Information," November 29, 1787).

202 *"Show some period"*: ED, vol. IV, 285–86 (January 17, 1788).

202 *Finally, no two-thirds majority requirement*: Farrand, vol. II, 400 (August 24, 1787).

203 *The Convention postponed*: Ibid., 415–17 (August 25, 1787).

203 *The delegates greeted*: Ibid., 443 (August 28, 1787).

203 *He had himself*: Ibid., 449 (August 29, 1787).

204 *Major Butler renewed*: Ibid., 449–54 (August 29, 1787).

204 *It was the only provision*: Somewhat comparable is the provision in Article V that no state may be denied equal suffrage in the Senate without its consent.

204 *[W]e have secured*: ED, vol. IV, 286 (January 17, 1788). In a joint letter to the governor of their state, the North Carolina delegates were equally positive about the proslavery provisions in the Constitution. Farrand, vol. III, 83 (Letter to Governor Caswell, September 18, 1787).

204 *"lay the foundation for banishing slavery"*: Farrand, vol. III, 161 (Pennsylvania Ratifying Convention, December 4, 1787).

205 *"preponderance which it has given"*: Ibid., 399–400 (Rufus King to Col. Pickering, November 4, 1803).

205 *But the national government*: Ibid., 428–30 (Rufus King in the Senate, March 1819).

205 *"Great as the evil is"*: Ibid., 325 (Virginia Ratifying Convention, June 17, 1788).

205 *McHenry made the same point*: Ibid., 144–50 (James McHenry, before the Maryland House of Delegates, November 29, 1787).

205 *a view that Madison echoed*: Ibid., 436 (Madison to Robert Walsh, November 27, 1819).

205 *South Carolina imported 75,000*: McMillin, 48, 86.

205 *In 1819, the retired Madison:* Madison to Robert J. Evans, June 15, 1819, in Madison, *Writings.*

206 *In 1833, when he was eighty:* McCoy, *The Last of the Fathers,* 301.

206 *Eight years earlier, then-Senator King:* Annals of Congress, 1824–25, February 18, 1825, 623; see Joseph L. Arbena, "Politics or Principle? Rufus King and the Opposition to Slavery, 1785–1825," *Essex Institute Historical Collections* 101 (1965): 56.

206 *"We the children of the third":* Diary of Charles Francis Adams, April 18, 1861, reel 76, quoted in Doris Kearns Goodwin, *Team of Rivals: The Political Genius of Abraham Lincoln* (New York: Simon & Schuster, 2005), 352.

CHAPTER 17. DAVID BREARLEY'S PRESIDENCY: AUGUST 24–SEPTEMBER 7

PAGE

207 *"[e]very article is again argued":* Farrand, vol. III, 73 (Brearley to William Paterson, August 21, 1787).

208 *Despairing of forward motion:* Ibid., vol. II, 402–4 (August 25, 1787).

208 *"Although hardly a brilliant figure":* Ibid., vol. III, 90 (Pierce); Richard P. McCormick, *Experiment in Independence* (New Brunswick, N.J.: Rutgers University Press, 1950), 156–57.

208 *"perspicuity of argument":* New Jersey Journal, December 26, 1787, in Merrill Jensen, ed., *The Documentary History of the Ratification of the Constitution* (Madison: State Historical Society of Wisconsin, 1978), vol. III, 94.

208 *"as an orator he has little":* Farrand, vol. III, 90 (Pierce).

209 *Brearley's longest address:* Ibid., vol. I, 177 (June 9, 1787).

209 *He lived to see his sons:* Donald Scarinci, *David Brearley and the Making of the United States Constitution* (Trenton: New Jersey Heritage Press, 2005), 35–41.

210 *The decision marked the first time:* Ibid., at 103–115, discussing *Holmes v. Walton;* Austin Scott, "Holmes vs. Walton: The New Jersey Precedent: A Chapter in the History of Judicial Power and Unconstitutional Legislation," *American Historical Review* 4 (1899): 456.

210 *They had to keep moving:* Farrand, vol. II, 427 (August 27, 1787).

210 *"long wished for another Convention":* Ibid., 479 (August 31, 1787).

211 *in the East Room on Tuesday:* Ibid., 493 (September 4, 1787).

211 *John Dickinson left:* Hutson, 300–301 (Dickinson to George Logan, January 16, 1802). We have only two direct records from the committee other than its own report. George Mason delivered to several committee members a list of constitutional provisions to be inserted, but only one dealt with the president: that he should not be eligible for a second term

in office. Hutson, 251–52. Major Butler retained notes that record possible qualifications for presidential candidates, but they did not relate to the major issues in contention. Hutson, 252–53.

212 *On the morning of Monday:* Dickinson describes the committee members as adjourning as he arrived, with their report complete. Having been constituted on Friday, August 31, it is unlikely that the committee had a completed report by the next day (Saturday, September 1) or that it had a morning meeting on a Sunday. Placing the event on Monday the third would allow the committee time to reach the consensus that Dickinson reports, and also would allow time for the change of direction described by Dickinson before Brearley presented his report on Tuesday the fourth.

212 *He is a shadow:* Adams Diary, August 31, 1774.

214 *"[N]ineteen times in twenty":* Farrand, vol. II, 500, 501 (September 4, 1787).

214 *[t]he President will not be the man:* Ibid., 522–23 (September 6, 1787).

215 *Worn down, the delegates embraced:* Ibid., 527 (September 6, 1787). The proposal derived in part from Hugh Williamson, a native Pennsylvanian who received his medical degree in the Netherlands but abandoned medical practice upon his return to Philadelphia in 1771. After exploring scientific inquiries that led him, naturally enough, to Dr. Franklin, Williamson put his medical training to the service of the Revolution. North Carolina appointed him surgeon general to its troops. After the war he stood for office in his adopted state, serving in the Confederation Congress before he was selected for the Philadelphia Convention.

215 *"the most insignificant office":* John Adams to Abigail Adams, December 19, 1793, made available by the Massachusetts Historical Society at http://www.masshist.org/digitaladams/aea/cfm/doc.cfm?id=L17931219ja.

215 *The delegates agreed, adopting:* Farrand, vol. II, 550 (September 8, 1787).

215 *"a bad edition of a Polish king":* David McCullough, *John Adams* (New York: Simon & Schuster, 2001), 380 (quoting letter from Jefferson to John Adams, November 13, 1787).

215 *"in the latter stage of the session":* Farrand, vol. III, 458 (Madison to George Hay, August 23, 1823).

CHAPTER 18. THE LOYAL OPPOSITION: AUGUST 31

PAGE

217 *"unless hurried into it":* Farrand, vol. II, 478 (August 31, 1787).

218 *"to abolish and annihilate":* Ibid., vol. III, 195 (Martin, "Genuine Information," November 29, 1787).

219 *"undoubtedly one of the best":* Ibid., 94 (Pierce).

219   *This dissident caucus:* Ibid., 282 (Martin, "Reply to the Landholder," from the *Maryland Journal,* March 18, 1788).

219   *"at liberty to be governed":* Ibid., 135 (Madison to Jefferson, October 24, 1787).

219   *"covering all his options":* Reardon, *Edmund Randolph,* 119.

220   *To the Convention's last day:* McDonald, *Novus Ordo Seculum,* 202 and n. 21; Collier and Collier, 340.

220   *We ha[ve] numerous and monstrous difficulties:* Farrand, vol. II, 278–79 (August 13, 1787).

220   *there were features:* Ibid., 452 (August 29, 1787).

220   *"men of indigence":* Ibid., vol. I, 132 (June 6, 1787).

221   *At the beginning of the war:* Ibid., 393 (June 23, 1787).

221   *"is as complete an aristocracy":* Ibid., vol. II, 286 (August 14, 1787).

222   *"letting loose the myrmidons":* Ibid., 317 (August 17, 1787).

222   *"an excellent assurance":* Collier and Collier, 324, citing Samuel E. Morison, *The Oxford History of the American People* (New York: Oxford University Press, 1965), 308–9.

222   *"Few old bachelors":* Cutler and Cutler, vol. I, 255.

222   *"no foreign enemy should invade":* Hutson, 229 (anecdote).

222   *"entre nous, I do not expect":* Ibid., 234 (Gerry to Ann Gerry, August 21, 1787).

222   *"a system of despotism":* Farrand, vol. II, 385 (August 23, 1787).

222   *Let us at once destroy:* Ibid., 388 (August 23, 1787).

222   *"I am exceedingly distressed":* Hutson, 241 (Gerry to Ann Gerry, August 26, 1787).

222   *"I have been a spectator":* Ibid., 247 (Gerry to Ann Gerry, August 29, 1787).

223   *"to prevent my colleagues":* Ibid., 254 (Gerry to Ann Gerry, September 1, 1787).

223   *An aristocratic body:* Farrand, vol. II, 224 (August 8, 1787).

223   *Is it to be expected:* Ibid., 251 (August 29, 1787).

224   *The alliance between New England:* Ibid., vol. III, 367 ("George Mason's Account of Certain Proceedings in Convention"; notes in Jefferson's hand, dated September 30, 1792, Gunston Hall).

224   *"made a bold stroke for monarchy":* Farrand, vol. II, 513 (September 5, 1787).

224   *"prefer the Government of Prussia":* Ibid., 515 (September 5, 1787).

224   *Mason and Gerry objected:* Ibid., 510 (September 5, 1787).

224   *"high crimes and misdemeanors":* Ibid., 551 (September 8, 1787), 588–89 (September 12, 1787).

224   *The Convention now added:* Ibid., 558 (September 10, 1787).

225   *"in an exceeding ill humor indeed":* Ibid., vol. III, 135 (Madison to Jefferson, October 24, 1787).

225 *He wished the plan:* Ibid., vol. II, 587–88 (September 12, 1787).

225 *They knew a bill of rights:* Ibid., vol. III, 290 ("Luther Martin's Reply to the Landholder," March 29, 1788).

226 *"will be presumed to be purposely omitted":* Ibid., 143 (Pennsylvania Ratifying Convention, November 28, 1787).

226 *And if a bill of rights was superfluous:* Marc W. Kruman, *Between Authority and Law: State Constitution Making in Revolutionary America* (Chapel Hill: University of North Carolina Press, 1997), 37.

226 *Mason could not stomach:* Gerry gave his reasons in a speech on September 15, Farrand, vol. II, 632–33, and in a letter dated October 18, 1787, to the President of the Massachusetts Senate and the Speaker of the Massachusetts House, ibid., vol. III, 128. Randolph enumerated his reasons in a speech on September 10, ibid., vol. II, 563–64. Mason wrote out sixteen objections, which he circulated in published form after the Convention and which were influential in the ratification debates in the states, ibid., 637–40.

226 *"The sovereignty or liberty of the states":* Ibid., vol. II, 635 (September 15, 1787).

226 *"would end in tyranny":* Ibid., 564 (September 10, 1787).

226 *This government will set out:* Ibid., 640 (Mason's written objections).

227 *You have a Bill of Rights:* ED, vol. III, 446 (June 16, 1788).

227 *"what no just government should refuse":* Jefferson to Madison, December 20, 1787, Jefferson Papers.

227 *"Now, we should make that declaration":* Farrand, vol. III, 290 (March 19, 1788).

227 *Ten of them took effect:* The first proposed amendment that was not ratified would have allocated one member of the House of Representatives for every 30,000 people until there were 100 representatives. The last amendment proposed in 1789 actually was ratified in 1992, and is now the Twenty-Seventh Amendment, providing that changes in the compensation of congressional representatives may not take effect until after the next biennial election. Akhil Reed Amar, *America's Constitution* (New York: Random House, 2005), 82, 453.

CHAPTER 19. WITH ALL ITS FAULTS: SEPTEMBER 8–17

PAGE

230 *"no man's ideas were more remote":* Farrand, vol. II, 644–45 (September 17, 1787).

230 *"to revise the style of":* Ibid., 553, 554 (September 8, 1787).

230 *Randolph, Gerry, and Dayton:* Ibid., vol. III, 76 (Edmund Randolph to Beverley Randolph, September 2, 1787); Hutson, 264 (Elbridge Gerry to

Ann Gerry, September 9, 1787); Farrand, vol. III, 80 (Jonathan Dayton to Elias Dayton, September 9, 1787).

230 *"I am quite homesick"*: Hutson, 265 (Washington to George Augustine Washington, September 9, 1787).

231 *"will be obliged to buy"*: Ibid., 258 (Nicholas Gilman to John Sullivan, September 3, 1787).

231 *"mountains will bring forth"*: Ibid., 259 (Livingston to John Jay, September 4, 1787). Few New Jersey officeholders of the present day could match Livingston's reference to the "monster ghastly great" of Book 4 of Virgil's *Aeneid*.

231 *"clouded by reason"*: Ibid., 267 (Livingston to John Jay, September 11, 1787).

231 *Old Roger Sherman spent an afternoon: Daybook*, September 6, 1787.

231 *He visited Dr. Franklin:* Hutson, 256, 258 (September 2 and September 3 diary entries).

231 *"the first day which has been free"*: Farrand, vol. III, 77 (Madison to Jefferson, September 6, 1787).

232 *The punctuality with which: Pennsylvania Journal and Weekly Advertiser,* August 25, 1787.

232 *"was written by the fingers"*: Farrand, vol. III, 420 (Morris to Timothy Pickering, December 22, 1814).

232 *"with the ready concurrence"*: Ibid., 499 (Madison to Jared Sparks, April 8, 1831). Delegate Abraham Baldwin of Georgia also reported later that Morris had "the chief hand in the last arrangement and composition" of the Constitution." Ibid., 170 (from the Diary of Ezra Stiles, reporting on conversation with Baldwin).

233 *"The correctness of [Morris's] language"*: Ibid., 551 (Madison's draft "Preface to Debates in the Convention of 1787").

233 *"brilliance of his genius"*: Ibid., 500 (Madison to Jared Sparks, April 8, 1831).

234 *Morris placed it in one section:* compare ibid., vol. II, 566, 571 (from Committee of Detail draft) with ibid., 590–91 (consolidated revision reported by the Committee of Style).

235 *"A better choice"*: Ibid., vol. III, 499 (Madison to Jared Sparks, April 8, 1831).

235 *Morris inserted a clause:* Ibid., vol. II, 439–40 (August 28, 1787), 597 (new clause).

235 *"chosen in each state"*: Ibid., 608 (September 13, 1787).

236 *Each state [was] less rigid:* Ibid., 584 (September 12, 1787).

236 *"I not only took it"*: Brookhiser, *Gentleman Revolutionary,* 92 (quoting from Morris's papers).

236 *Eager to silence the Virginian:* Farrand, vol. II, 606–7 (September 13, 1787).

236 *"number of members":* Ibid., 608 (September 13, 1787).

237 *"the power of Congress":* Ibid., 618 (September 14, 1787).

237 *"these declarations from members":* Ibid., 631 (September 15, 1787).

237 *[T]hat Dr. Franklin's electrical rod:* McCullough, 420 (quoting letter from Adams to Benjamin Rush).

238 *As a North Carolina delegate wrote:* Hutson, 60 (W. R. Davie to James Iredell, July 17, 1787).

238 *When George Mason pleaded:* Farrand, vol. II, 542 (September 7, 1787).

239 *It therefore astonishes me:* Ibid., 642–43 (September 17, 1787).

239 *"plain, insinuating":* Ibid., 649 (September 17, 1787).

239 *I cannot help expressing:* Ibid., 643 (September 17, 1787).

240 *In this way:* Ibid.

240 *Gerry and Randolph announced:* Ibid., 646–47 (September 17, 1787).

240 *The motion was adopted:* Ibid., 643–44 (September 17, 1787).

241 *"11 states and Colonel Hamilton":* Ibid., vol. III, 81 (Washington Diary, September 17, 1787).

241 *Only four Delaware delegates:* Ibid., 81 (Dickinson to George Read, September 15, 1787).

241 *"I distrust my own judgment":* Ibid., vol. II, 649 (September 17, 1787).

241 *"it was done by bargain and compromise":* Ibid., 82 (Nicholas Gilman to Joseph Gilman, September 18, 1787).

241 *without being able to tell:* Ibid., 648 (September 17, 1787).

241 *Thomas Fitzsimons of Pennsylvania:* Jensen, *Documentary History,* vol. II, 58–60.

242 *Dr. Franklin would report:* Rollins, ed., *The Autobiographies of Noah Webster,* 246 (diary entry for September 18, 1787).

242 *Fitzsimons sent one to Noah Webster:* Ibid. (entry for September 15, 1787).

242 *On his way there:* John H. Rhodehamel, "The Renowned Don Quixote," 1983 Annual Report, The Mount Vernon Ladies' Association of the Union, 13–15.

243 *"meditate[d] on the momentous work":* Farrand, vol. III, 81 (September 17 diary entry).

CHAPTER 20. HAPPINESS, PERPETUAL AND OTHERWISE: JULY 4, 1788

PAGE

245 *Only three weeks after:* Ibid., 101–2 (James Wilson, Address to a Meeting of the Citizens of Philadelphia, October 6, 1787).

245 *Wilson's "State-House Yard" speech:* Bowen, 275.

246 *Though Shaysite delegates opposed:* Szatmary, 133; Richards, 150; Richard D. Brown, "Shays's Rebellion and the Ratification of the Federal Constitution in Massachusetts," in Richard Beeman, Stephen Botein,

and Edward C. Carter II, eds., *Beyond Confederation: Origins of the Constitution and American National Identity* (Chapel Hill: University of North Carolina Press, 1987).

246 *New Hampshire, fittingly:* The following description of the day is drawn from the July 1788 edition of the *American Museum or Repository of Ancient and Modern Fugitive Pieces, Prose and Poetical,* a prominent Philadelphia magazine of the time. That edition included a full description of the celebration by Francis Hopkinson, chairman of the Committee of Arrangements for the day, a copy of Wilson's oration, and further commentary by Dr. Benjamin Rush.

246 *"jubilee of allegory":* Susan G. Davis, *Parades and Power: Street Theatre in Nineteenth Century Philadelphia* (Philadelphia: Temple University Press, 1986), 117.

247 *"truly sublime":* American Museum, 76 (Dr. Rush's letter).

250 *The federal edifice was pulled:* Laura Rigal, " 'Raising the Roof': Authors, Spectators, and Artisans in the Grand Federal Procession of 1788," *Theatre Journal* 48 (1996): 253.

251 *"against having any vice president":* Farrand, vol. II, 537 (September 7, 1787).

251 *Each missed his first three shots:* John H. Wheeler, *Sketch of the Life of Richard Dobbs Spaight of North Carolina* (Baltimore: William K. Boyle, Printer, 1880); http://www.army.mil/cmh-pg/books/RevWar/ss/spaight.htm.

251 *William Blount was a senator:* Buckner F. Melton, Jr., *The First Impeachment* (Macon, Ga.: Mercer University Press, 1998).

252 *"a little mal-apropos":* Hutson, 126 (Washington Diary, June 28, 1787).

252 *When the subsidy expired:* Clarkson and Jett, *Luther Martin,* 303.

252 *"I supposed him":* Mintz, *Gouverneur Morris,* 238.

252 *"If peace be not immediately made":* Adams, *Gouverneur Morris,* 292.

252 *He was found dead:* Alan Pell Crawford, *Unwise Passions* (New York: Simon & Schuster, 2000), 196–98.

253 *The deaths plunged the South Carolinian:* Haw, 229.

253 *"his mind was frequently so much deranged":* Ralph Izard to J. Read, November 17, 1795, in Maeva Marcus and James R. Perry, eds., *Documentary History of the Supreme Court* (New York: Columbia University Press, 1985), vol. I, 807.

253 *A Negro child was near:* William Read to Jacob Read, December 29, 1795, South Caroliniana Library, University of South Carolina.

254 *More than those factors:* William R. Casto, *The Supreme Court in the Early Republic* (Columbia: University of South Carolina Press, 1995), 95.

254 *"Mr. Rutledge has lost ground":* William Read to Jacob Read, December 29, 1795.

254 *"rapid accumulation of the capital":* James Wilson to Pieter van Beckel,

March 17, 1785, in James Wilson Papers, Historical Society of Pennsylvania.

254   *Wilson planned to build:* Robert McCloskey, "Introduction," in Robert Green McCloskey, ed., *Works of James Wilson* (Cambridge: Harvard University Press, 1967), 43.

254   *Forced to travel to New Jersey:* Trotta, "James Wilson," 22.

254   *"hitherto waited patiently":* Butler to William Slade, May 26, 1798, in James Wilson Papers, Historical Society of Pennsylvania.

255   *"young A——d":* Robert Allen Rutland, *George Mason, Reluctant Statesman* (Williamsburg: Colonial Williamsburg, 1961), 103.

255   *"it is no small satisfaction":* Farrand, vol. III, 129 (Madison to Washington, October 17, 1787).

255   *"one of the few men":* Mason to Jefferson, January 10, 1791, in Rutland, *Papers of George Mason.*

255   *You know I believe:* Mason to John Mason, March 13, 1789, in ibid.

256   *Pride on the one hand:* Washington to James Craik, September 8, 1789, quoted in Henriques.

256   *Mason, still a homebody:* Mason to Beverley Randolph, March 27, 1790, in Rutland, *Papers of George Mason.*

256   *"[A]t my time of life":* Mason to John Mason, July 5, 1792, in ibid.

256   *"my neighbor":* Washington to Hamilton, July 29, 1792, in Rowland, vol. II, 361.

256   *By the time of his death:* Reardon, 310–14, 331–34, 363.

257   *Together, Jefferson and Madison:* Leibiger, *Founding Friendship*, 197–225.

257   *"never again even mentioned":* Ibid., 220.

257   *Within two years of his death:* Wiencek, 353–58.

CHAPTER 21. MAKING AMENDS

PAGE

259   *"the plan now to be formed":* Farrand, vol. I, 202–3 (June 11, 1787).

259   *in three states:* Connecticut, South Carolina, and Georgia.

259   *North Carolina and Rhode Island:* Tadahisa Kuroda, *The Origins of the Twelfth Amendment* (Westport, Conn.: Greenwood Press, 1994), 28–38.

260   *If a few electors:* Hamilton to Wilson, January 25, 1789, in Harold C. Syrett, ed., *Papers of Alexander Hamilton* (New York: Columbia University Press, 1961), vol. 5, 247–49.

260   *Hamilton's maneuver:* Amar, 337.

260   *After thirty-five ballots:* Chernow, 636.

261   *Beginning with the 1804 election:* Also, in the event that an election were referred to the House of Representatives because no candidate had a

majority vote, only the top three (not the top five) candidates would be sent to the House.

262 *John Adams would have won:* Garry Wills, *Negro President: Jefferson and the Slave Power* (New York: Houghton Mifflin Co., 2003), 2–3.

262 *Nineteen of the first thirty-four:* Leonard Richards, *The Slave Power* (Baton Rouge: Louisiana State University Press, 2000), 9, 62.

262 *House seats created:* Ibid., 80–82.

262 *When southern states adopted:* Amar, 95–98.

262 *Some single out:* Rossiter; Collier and Collier.

263 *Those states could not have stood:* Gary B. Nash, *Race and Revolution* (Lanham, Md.: Rowman & Littlefield Publishers, 2001; originally 1990), 27–28; Amar, 95–97.

263 *"the sins of this guilty land":* Jules Abels, *Man on Fire: John Brown and the Cause of Liberty* (New York: Macmillan Co., 1971), 365 (reproducing Brown's statement).

264 *Lincoln himself:* Goodwin, *Team of Rivals,* 296.

264 *Only two states have ratified:* David C. Huckabee, "Ratification of Amendments to the U.S. Constitution," Congressional Research Service (September 30, 1997).

APPENDIX 1: THE ELECTOR SYSTEM

PAGE

265 *Some analyses conclude:* Kuroda, 174; Lawrence D. Longley and Neal R. Peirce, *The Electoral College Primer* (New Haven: Yale University Press, 1996), 143.

266 *On eight occasions:* Longley and Peirce, 23, 110–11. Because John Kennedy had such a substantial lead in the electoral college, the fourteen unpledged electors from Alabama and Mississippi were unable to strike any advantageous bargain for their anti-integration interests.

266 *"assembly of wise men":* Ibid., 98.

FURTHER READING

Those with an appetite for further exploration of the Philadelphia Convention, and that period of American life, might consider the following further works:

America in the 1780s: Several Europeans visited America during this period and left pungent observations: J. P. Brissot de Warville, *New Travels in the United States of America, 1788* (Cambridge: Belknap Press, 1964, originally 1792); Marquis de Chastellux, *Travels in North America in the Years 1780–1781–1782* (New York: Augustus M. Kelley, 1970 ed.); Johann D. Schoepf, *Travels in the Confederation* [1783–84], translated and edited by Alfred J. Morrison (New York: Bergman Publishers, 1968). An excellent description of the political situation before the Convention appears in Merrill Jensen's *The Articles of Confederation* (Madison: University of Wisconsin Press, 1966). For Shays' Rebellion, I recommend Leonard L. Richards's *Shays' Rebellion* (Philadelphia: University of Pennsylvania Press, 2002).

The Convention: For forty years, the classic treatment of the Convention has been Catherine Drinker Bowen's *Miracle at Philadelphia* (Boston: Little, Brown, 1966). Other useful treatments appear in Richard Morris's *Witnesses at the Creation* (New York: Holt, Rinehart & Winston, 1985), and Clinton Rossiter's *1787: The Grand Convention* (New York: Macmillan Company, 1966). The serious reader about the Constitution should look at Akhil Reed Amar's *America's Constitution* (New York: Random House, 2005).

Slavery: The Convention's handling of the slavery issue is addressed well in Paul Finkelman's *Slavery and the Founders* (Armonk: M. E. Sharpe, Inc., 2001), and Donald Robinson's *Slavery in the Structure of American Politics* (New York: Harcourt Brace Jovanovich, 1971).

George Washington's special struggle with the issue is covered in Fritz Hirschfeld's *George Washington and Slavery* (Columbia: University of Missouri Press, 1997).

Individual Framers: For Washington, I would suggest two works by James Thomas Flexner, *Washington: The Indispensable Man* (Boston: Little, Brown, 1974) and *George Washington and the New Nation, 1783–1793* (Boston: Little, Brown, 1970). Among the flood of recent works on Franklin, an excellent and complete treatment is Walter Isaacson's *Benjamin Franklin: An American Life* (New York: Simon & Schuster, 2003). For those lacking the stamina for Irving Brant's multi-volume biography of Madison, Ralph Ketcham produced an able (albeit still thick) single volume, *James Madison: A Biography* (Charlottesville: University Press of Virginia, 1990), while Stuart Leibiger's *Founding Friendship* (Charlottesville: University Press of Virginia, 1999) explores the relationship between Madison and Washington. Alexander Hamilton gave an unsatisfying performance at the Convention, but has been blessed with a magisterial biography by Ron Chernow, *Alexander Hamilton* (New York: Penguin Press, 2004).

For the irrepressible Luther Martin, a full life is portrayed in *Luther Martin of Maryland* (Baltimore: Johns Hopkins Press, 1970), by Paul Clarkson and Samuel Jett. For Gouverneur Morris, try Richard Brookhiser's *Gentleman Revolutionary* (New York: Free Press, 2003), while the surviving materials on John Rutledge are so scanty that he must share a volume with his brother, in James Haw's *John & Edward Rutledge of South Carolina* (Athens: University of Georgia Press, 1997). On James Wilson, there is only Page Smith's *James Wilson, Founding Father, 1742–1798* (Chapel Hill: University of North Carolina Press, 1956).

ACKNOWLEDGMENTS

Many of the source materials for the Convention are readily available in either bound or online format. As explained in the beginning of the Notes, these include the proceedings of the Convention itself and much of the correspondence of the delegates. Nevertheless, many archivists, librarians, and scholars have been generous with their time and expertise in helping me answer the more exotic questions that arose throughout this project.

The resources of the Library of Congress and the skills of its staff are unrivaled. Wonderful assistance was extended in the Main Reading Room, the Manuscript Room, the Rare Books Room, the Newspaper Room, the Prints and Photographs Department, and even the infernal Microfilm room (with its dreaded fiche readers). I would thank particularly Thomas Mann for getting me started on the Library's collections, and James Hutson, Chief of the Manuscripts Division and a scholar of the Convention, for reassuring me that John Rutledge really left behind very few written records.

Important help came from Karen Stevens, Coxey Toogood, Karie Diethorn, and James Mueller of Independence National Historic Park, and from the research staffs at the Historical Society of Pennsylvania, the Massachusetts Historical Society, the South Carolina Historical Society, and the South Caroliniana Library of the University of South Carolina. My pursuit of the Ipswich Miracle was materially aided by Stephen Hall and Darren Brown of the Beverly Historical Society, and by Arthur Crosbie and Edna Barney of the Hamilton Historical Society. For Shays' Rebellion, Richard Colton of the National Park Service at the Springfield Armory shared his fascinating studies, while important materials were brought to my attention by Elise Bernier-Feeley of the

Forbes Library in Northampton and Michele Plourde-Barker and Maggi Humbertson of the Connecticut Valley Historical Museum. Also generous with their time and collections were Phil Lapsansky of the Library Company of Philadelphia, Barbara McMillan of the Mount Vernon Library, and Ellen Clark, librarian for the Society of the Cincinnati in Washington. For secondary sources, the Martin Luther King Jr. Memorial Library of the District of Columbia is a treasured resource.

I have received useful advice from several scholars, including Henry Wiencek of the Virginia Foundation for the Humanities, Prof. James Haw of Indiana University/Purdue University at Fort Wayne, and Emeritus Prof. Peter Henriques of George Mason University. Perceptive readings of early drafts were contributed by writing colleagues, including Paul Vamvas, Catherine Flanagan, Wayland Stallard, Susan Clark, Phil Harvey, Ken Ackerman, Lawrence Ellsworth, Patricia Pearson, Frank Joseph, Katherine Lorr, Bert Brandenburg, Solveig Eggerz, Clyde Linsley, Leslie Rollins, Robert Gibson, and Matthew Stewart (the other writer in the family). I am grateful for the guidance and friendship of my agent, Robert Lescher, and have benefited from the uncommon sense and insight of Alice Mayhew at Simon & Schuster and the patient assistance of Serena Jones. By dedicating the book to my wife, Nancy, I can only hint at her importance to this volume.

INDEX

Page numbers in *italics* refer to illustrations.

ILLUSTRATION CREDITS

Architect of the Capitol: 235.

License granted courtesy of The Rt Hon The Earl of Derby 2006:143.

Emmet Collection, Miriam and Ira D. Wallach Division of Art, Prints and
Photographs, The New York Public Library, Astor, Lenox and Tilden
Foundations: 90, 120, 145.

From the collection of Gilcrease Museum, Tulsa, Oklahoma: 28.

HarperCollins College Division, map reproduced from *The Rise of
the West, 1754–1830* by Francis S. Philbrick, 1965: 128.

Courtesy Independence National Historical Park: 48, 76, 97, 212.

Library of Congress: 14, 32, 36, 62, 93, 193, 196, 200, 242, 249.

Michael D. McCumber: 6.

National Portrait Gallery, Smithsonian Institution: 60, 108, 170, 181, 221.

National Portrait Gallery, Smithsonian Institution; gift of the Morris and
Gwendolyn Cafritz Foundation: 111.

Ohio Historical Society: 138.

Courtesy of The Pennsylvania Academy of the Fine Arts, Phialdelphia.
Bequest of Mrs. Sarah Harrison (The Joseph Harrison, Jr.,
Collection): 3.

Special Collections and University Archives, Rutgers University
Libraries: 209.

David O. Stewart: 160.

About the Author

David O. Stewart clerked for Supreme Court Justice Lewis Powell in 1979–80 and for appellate judges J. Skelly Wright in 1978–79 and David Bazelon (1978). He has practiced law in Washington, D.C., for more than twenty-five years, often handling constitutional law cases, and is currently with Ropes & Gray, LLP.